Customer Experience Excellence

Customer Experience Excellence

The Six Pillars of Growth

David Conway and Tim Knight

KoganPage

First published in Great Britain and the United States in 2021 by Kogan Page Limited

2nd Floor, 45 Gee Street	1518 Walnut Street, Suite 1100	4737/23 Ansari Road
London EC1V 3RS	Philadelphia PA 19102	Daryaganj
United Kingdom	USA	New Delhi 110002
		India

www.koganpage.com

© David Conway and Tim Knight 2021

The right of David Conway and Tim Knight to be identified as the authors of this work has been asserted by them in accordance with the Copyright, Designs and Patents Act 1988.

ISBNs

Hardback   9781398601055
Paperback 9781398600997
Ebook   9781398601048

British Library Cataloguing-in-Publication Data

A CIP record for this book is available from the British Library.

Library of Congress Control Number

2021941124

Typeset by Integra Software Services Pondicherry
Printed and bound in India by Replika Press Pvt Ltd
Kogan Page books are printed on paper from sustainable forests.

CONTENTS

FOREWORD

Every day, each of us awakes with an objective, a mission, a raison d'être and a purpose. Each of us wants to accomplish something. Small. Large. Whimsical. Relevant. Lasting. Passing. Rudimentary. Life changing. Memorable. Equally on our journey, we are a customer, a consumer or business oriented, an employee, a citizen, a colleague and – always – we are human.

We also know how those who treat us well make us feel. We know what a good experience feels like and we want to engage with those who make an experience worthwhile. This applies to all who partake in the experience. Those who deliver it. Those who receive it.

Most of us can recall and recount a story of an outstanding experience and a dreadful experience. It is through our tone, volume and emotion that we make it clear where we will spend our precious time, resources and energy in the future and where we will not. In our digital world this perspective is amplified.

Senior executives, management and employees around the world profess to want to deliver a great experience to attract and retain customers in order to propel growth. Every morning, thousands of employees at companies around the world go to work with the goal of serving customers. Most have the desire to do a great job, connect emotionally and create great experiences for their customers. For the fortunate few this is an energizing, human and life-enhancing remit. For many, though, it is just another day of frustration as they grapple with outdated processes, disconnected systems and broken cultures.

Every month, business leaders worldwide study their accounts and forecasts, looking for evidence of high growth and profit. However, many are frustrated when their carefully wrought strategies, tactics, investments and passion fail to deliver. Many tend to look towards technology to help them change the trajectory, yet they continue to struggle to transform and serve the market in a manner that delivers profitable and meaningful customer experiences.

This need not be so. The path to excellence is evolving, but there are key milestones and guides that can help us on the journey. While each company's journey is its own, there are lessons from former leaders that can help. It is a path that any willing organization can study and adopt. This book is about that approach.

My colleagues David and Tim co-founded the Customer Experience Excellence Centre (CEEC) out of the UK in 2010, seeking to quantify and codify what it takes to be a leader in delivering great customer experiences and generating strong outcomes for the business, for customers, for employees and for shareholders. When we started working together, I was immediately struck by the simplicity and relevance of the Six Pillars. These Six Pillars helped articulate how to navigate the ever-changing experiential requirements of the marketplace.

Working together, we chose to extend the work worldwide. Initially this involved reports in countries such as Australia, the USA and the UK. More recently, we have expanded to 34 markets, examining over 3,500 brands. The work tells us who leads, how they do it and how their principles can be applied to the business challenges each of us is struggling with.

Using this and other source material, the authors have captured their learning into a single volume. It's about a better, more human and more connected way to grow businesses.

As such, it is not just a beacon of hope for companies striving to achieve excellence, but a guide to help your business move forward. It outlines a sequential process through which better customer, employee and marketplace engagement is the outcome. The lessons are based on the culmination of millions of customer data points, financial analysis and hundreds of interviews with business leaders.

I believe this material should be essential reading for anyone who wants to engage with the marketplace, be they customers, employees, students, shareholders, regulators or suppliers. Have a read, walk in each of these individuals' shoes and contemplate the guideposts to consider.

The good news is that you can benefit from the knowledge of leaders who preceded you. The bad news is that there is no silver bullet. Despite the promises of customer gurus and technologists, no single factor guarantees success. Indeed, the pathway is multifaceted and requires organizations to multitask in a cohesive and integrated way. It requires an appreciation of ever-changing market demand – from consumers, employees and stakeholders. It also requires the hard work of understanding that execution needs to be done in a way that is informed, managed, connected and aligned, where each element is mutually self-reinforcing. It demands a new type of leadership.

It may seem a tall order but in every country there is an elite set of companies that have demonstrated the science and art of excellence. At the heart of this is a human, emotional connection, enabling better experiences for customers, colleagues and, consequently, shareholders.

In uncertain and volatile times, I'd argue that these lessons on business and human excellence have never been more important.

Julio Hernandez
Global Customer COE Lead
US Customer Advisory Practice Lead
KPMG in the US

ACKNOWLEDGEMENTS

This book would not be possible without the kind support of KPMG, whose published research on customer excellence and the Six Pillars has been referenced throughout. In particular we would like to thank Dan Thomas and David Rowlands from the UK partnership, and also Julio Hernandez, who leads the Customer Centre of Excellence globally for KPMG, for their encouragement and support.

We would also like to thank the amazing people of KPMG who have embedded the Six Pillars in their consulting and digital transformation work worldwide. They have helped innumerable organizations to put customer best practice at the heart of sustainable business. It has been the privilege of our careers to work alongside each of you.

We're grateful of KPMG's permission to reproduce its Six Pillar concepts within this work and to reference other published thought leadership on the future of enterprise (`Connected Enterprise') and the changing consumer (`Me, My Life and My Wallet'). For Connected Enterprise, we are especially indebted to Miriam Hernandez-Kakol, Julio Hernandez, Duncan Avis and Adrian Clamp. For Me, My Life and My Wallet, Coleen Drummond, Eliza Radford, Jennifer Linardos, Urvashi Roe, Julio Hernandez and Willy Kruh provided further inspirational content. Thanks also to Georgina Severs, who has been a constant source of encouragement and great ideas.

We would like to recognize the contribution of Chris Pitt, CEO of first direct, and David Duffy, CEO of Virgin Money, who were generous with their time and their wisdom and without whom the book would have been considerably the poorer.

We'll be forever grateful to Jo Tait, who has contributed enormously to the articulation and the expression of our ideas and has brought rigour to our thinking.

At Kogan Page, Stephen Dunnell has provided great insight and recommendations on how the book could be improved and refined.

This book has been the labour of love over many weekends and evenings, alongside our day jobs. Thanks to our families for giving us the space and understanding to make this possible.

Finally, there is one person who has taken the Six Pillars from a good idea to a global think tank, now supporting business leaders in 34 countries. Tamsin Jenkins, who leads this, has been the mainstay of its work for over a decade and, without her, it would have remained merely a good idea. Thank you, Tamsin.

PREFACE

For the past 12 years, we have researched customer and employee excellence around the world. We have examined the world's best businesses and those that have transformed most rapidly.

From the outset, we were curious about what defines the connection between brands and the humans they serve. What does a mutually rewarding emotional connection look like? How do leaders create this at scale? And what are the human and economic rewards of success?

Initially, we had five objectives in mind:

- We wanted to define what a great experience looks like from the perspective of the customer and the colleague. We sought to understand at a fundamental, psychological level why a particular type of emotional connection influences future commercial behaviour or productivity.

- Crucially, we wanted to identify the exemplars: the leading organizations across the globe that consistently deliver outstanding experiences. We used quantitative analysis and league tables to track these and the rising stars, the organizations that were making significant progress despite technological, market or regulatory constraints.

- We wanted to codify how leaders created consistency and scale. Most organizations can deliver a great experience on occasion but rarely do so consistently, interaction after interaction. This requires something special. By forensically examining the capabilities and leadership paradigms of exemplars, we set out to uncover the keys to scaling excellence.

- We sought to define the rewards of achieving this. Meaningful, human connection with customers and employees is arguably an end in itself: a higher purpose for business leaders. However, we also aimed to establish the economic payback, through the lens of both revenue growth and reduced costs.

- Finally, we sought to codify this secret sauce in a way that would enable aspiring companies to embed best practice across their organizations. To short-cut to success, sequence their plans better and unlock excellence.

Working with KPMG, these objectives inspired one of the world's largest ongoing research programmes on customer excellence. Over the past 12 years, this research has spanned 34 markets across four continents, encompassing more than 4 million consumer evaluations of their experiences with 3,500 brands. The research findings have been made publicly available across the globe and are in use in over 100 countries, from Brazil to Russia, where they shape and define the strategies of the world's leading companies.

At the heart of the research has been the discovery of a universal set of emotional qualities that define excellence in employee and customer experience. These are the Six Pillars of Experience: integrity, resolution, expectations, time and effort, personalization and empathy. Each of the Six Pillars leads into a behavioural framework, a set of competencies and design principles, which can be applied to any digital and human interaction.

They are universal, defining human connections that reward us emotionally and financially. They 'explain' common headline metrics, like Net Promoter Score (NPS), and predict business outcomes, such as loyalty, acquisition, lifetime value and cost to serve.

In writing this book we have drawn on the CEEC's published findings, other works and – most importantly – our experiences embedding best practice in some of the world's leading brands. The combined result is intended to be valuable to anyone whose job it is to serve humans – from customer practitioners and digital leaders to CEOs and beyond.

Is this book for you?

Do you need to move the dial on growth? Billions are being invested globally in customer experience. Yet, with a few notable exceptions, customers have yet to feel a difference. What we don't perceive does not cause us to behave differently or to spend more. Equally, employees increasingly report a gulf between their own experience and the espoused aspirations of their leaders.

Many executive teams struggle to address this. The lack of a consistent, scientific approach to managing customer and employee experiences is frustrating many. Most want to know why their latest investments in digital transformation are failing to move the dial or deliver promised benefits. As well as growth, every CEO is under growing pressure to create clear, visionary purpose and inclusive culture. However, most preside over disconnected approaches to customers and employees.

The rewards for getting this right are enormous. Creating experience is the key to fulfilling purpose: the only way strategy is made real is by what human beings see and hear as a result. Creating excellence in human experience is a chance to do good, delighting others at scale. Economically, the organizations that do this outperform the market. In an analysis conducted in 2016 we observed that organizations which are highly effective at customer experience achieve higher revenues and twice the margin of their lesser competitors (www.nunwood.com/media/1294/making-memories-2016-uk-customer-experience-excellence-analysis.pdf).

So, whether you are a CEO, HR director, CMO, customer director or practitioner, this book has been written for you. If you are running Finance, or IT, or Operations, you will find principles here that can make your teams more customer-centric and your business better. It is for anyone whose job it is to create great organizational results by leading other humans. It is the distillation of over a decade of research and hundreds of conversations with business leaders around the world. It seeks to answer the universal questions:

- We've struggled to adapt our operating model or structure to deliver customer centricity – how do we manage the internal change?

- We have implemented Net Promoter Score and invested in the latest customer relationship management technology – why is the dial not moving?

- We've laid out a lot of sensible principles for colleagues and customers – why is the organization ignoring them?

- We've targeted growth – but all we are seeing are more change requests and more costs.

- We've prioritized the customer – but how do we balance what sounds sensible in the long term with immediate regulatory or shareholder pressures?

- We've defined our purpose and culture – but we're struggling to make it real for our customers and colleagues. How do we rewrite the 'unwritten rules' of our business?

- We've got a lot of different frameworks and theories – we are overburdened with insights and consultants. How can we connect these ideas to real business impact?

The reason for many of these universal questions is that customer and employee experience is not part of a mature management discipline, or a well-trodden path. Technology and social expectation have been colossal forces for change over the last decade, rewriting what every business needs to do to succeed. Most businesses have struggled to keep up.

Consequently, organizations around the world are populated with millions of people who, unfortunately, are having to make it up as they go along, supported by dozens of consultants offering single point solutions that do not endure into the long term. The available literature is strong on *what* organizations need to do but, unhelpfully, is much sparser on *how*.

That is the gap this book seeks to fill. Our research demonstrates there is a clear pathway to success. A pathway that leaders and CX practitioners can follow, secure in the knowledge that this path has been forged by leaders in their field. Following it will provide not just improved customer and colleague experiences but a better way of doing business.

Introduction

Brooke Narum works in a bank. But this is no ordinary bank. For Brooke, no two days are the same. She has a customer who has just lost his wife in a car accident. The customer had known his wife since the third grade and the pair married in 1981. They have two sons.

Following the fatal accident, Brooke calls the customer to walk him through everything, from the medical bills to funeral costs. Her help, in his time of need, makes a powerful impact. After the call the customer, a retired Marine Corps major, says he felt the 'fog of war' more than ever at that time. It was Brooke's empathy and expertise that helped him through. 'She has been almost like a family member looking out for me in my ignorance on procedures and things to do,' he says.

Brooke's role is to solve customer problems, no matter how they arise or how complex they appear. She works for a bank where the senior executives are rewarded not on sales or internal performance measures but on whether customers believe the bank has made a positive difference to their lives.

This bank's closeness to its customers and the understanding of their problems result in continuous market-leading innovation. The bank is a world leader for digital, not because it fixates on technology but because it obsesses about humanity. It was the first bank to enable photographic cheque deposits because many of its customers couldn't get to a branch. The bank pioneered paperless insurance claims, launching an app that not only enabled the customer to record all the important elements of an accident but also rapidly delivered a replacement car. The bank offers a car purchase app that pre-clears the customer for a loan and insurance and conducts all pre-purchase checks. Vitally, it provides a special discount, so the purchaser doesn't have the hassle of negotiating. This enables the customer to see a car and confidently drive it away from the sales lot in under an hour.

This is one of the world's most customer-centric organizations. It is based in Texas, has 11 million customers, 22,500 staff and is highly profitable. It also has one of the lowest expense ratios of any bank, anywhere. Proof, if it is needed, that lowest cost and highest customer satisfaction are very happy bedfellows.

This organization is USAA. It primarily serves members of the US military and their families and it has built its reputation through 'weaponizing' empathy. On joining USAA every new employee must experience life as one of the bank's customers, undergoing military training, eating military meals, going to military events. Understanding the customer is a core competence at every level of the organization.

The Marine Corps major, writing to the USAA customer relations team to praise the help he received from Brooke, put it as follows: 'I am so thoroughly impressed and blessed that my wife utilized USAA that I am switching my current bank that I have had since 1978... I could not be more honored or grateful for your USAA professionalism and family-value-attitude staff.' Empathy pays (The American Legion, 2021).

On the other side of the Atlantic, 4,000 miles away in Leeds, England, an employee at a different bank faces a difficult situation. She is talking to a young customer who indicates during the call that he is feeling very down; in fact, he is life-threateningly depressed. The bank's employee notices that the customer lives with his mother. She doesn't hesitate. She engages the help of a colleague while she keeps the customer talking. The colleague contacts the mother, vets local taxi firms, facilitates payment and asks for a driver who will be empathetic and caring, to ensure the young person is collected and safely returned home to his mother. A little later the employee rings the mother to check all is OK.

She mentions the incident to her team leader, who immediately turns the agent into a hero, the story is transmitted all over the office, it is lauded as doing the right thing for a customer, no matter that maybe one or two small rules may have been broken. What is important is the behaviour, showing that you care. Doing the right thing for customers can never be wrong.

This bank is first direct, also one of the world's most customer-centric companies. Its mantra: 'Pioneering amazing service.' Its focus is on having 'amazing conversations' with its customers. The staff make an enormous effort to deeply understand their customers and know exactly what their customers want from them, and they have learned how to deliver this consistently (Gordon, 2020).

Thousands of miles away in Taiwan, Lexus salesperson Hui-Chen Lin receives a call from a customer demanding a very stretching delivery date too soon for all details to be settled. However, Lin uses every mechanism at the company's disposal to complete the necessary requirements to deliver the customer's car on the preferred day.

Before the delivery date, she stops at the customer's company to deliver some documents. She discovers that the customer's wife is due to start chemotherapy treatment the following day. Lin then decides to create a surprise for the customer and his wife.

On the delivery date, Lin invites a taiko performance team to the couple's home to play an encouraging song to wish the customer's wife good luck. In addition, she writes them a couplet, a poem that stands for having a healthy life. The customer's wife is so surprised and moved that she weeps, declaring it the best present she has ever received (Lexus, 2016). Lin's behaviour is guided by 'omotenashi', the Japanese tradition of hospitality that anticipates and fulfils people's needs, where the customer is treated as if they were a guest in your home.

In western France, an insurance company has created an entire function with no other brief than to solve customer problems. Called the 'Organisation Vie Pratique' it is a virtual A to Z of one-off or regular personal services for its customers, helping with everything from childminding to assistance for vulnerable persons and from educational support to meals on wheels. The company views solving customer problems as central to its ethos, aspiring to make customers' lives simpler, to be at their side ready to assist with life projects. The company is MAIF and it sells a philosophy of collaboration, not products (ESS et Société, 2006).

In Sweden, a young entrepreneur envisages a new type of pharmacy, one that is exclusively online and brings better, more accurate service to its customers as well as completely changing the economic model for distribution of pharmaceuticals. Apotea is Sweden's largest online pharmacy. It has built its reputation on innovation and sustainability. The CEO's philosophy is to make online shopping as convenient and appealing as possible. That includes everything from product information to payment solutions and delivery. The company is focused on sustainability – its offices generate more power than they consume; each aspect of the business is analysed through the sustainability lens. It is now the number one brand for customer experience in Sweden (KPMG, 2020a).

We live in radically changing times. While many companies merely observe customers grappling with uncertainty, those that create excellence see this as an opportunity: an opportunity to excel, an opportunity to become more instrumental in their customers' lives and an opportunity to differentiate. Their confidence stems from a deep knowledge of their customers and their circumstances. These companies are so close to their customers, know them so deeply and so intimately, that they can stay relevant while everything around them changes.

Many struggling executive teams talk of a glass ceiling for their complex, legacy business. Without the digital tooling and airy cultures of a Silicon Valley unicorn, progress is often felt to be too hard and failure should be excused. It is worth noting that both MAIF and USAA have existed for over 120 years, and first direct, while a relative youngster by comparison, still has decades of heritage. Staying relevant to customers and creating emotional connections is not merely the preserve of the younger companies but a constant project, an ongoing process of reinvention.

These examples of great experiences do not arise by accident, or in isolation. These leading companies share common characteristics – they are completely in tune with their customers, they have created an environment where the exceptional happens every day, where colleagues unite around a central organizing principle, an enduring sense of purpose, where new stories of excellence naturally arise and there is a reason for their existence beyond making money for shareholders. The world would miss something special if they ceased to exist.

These businesses have, over time, skilfully and intentionally crafted their approach to the customer. They have seen this as more than a front-office preserve – the domain of marketers and digital gurus – but rather as a 'golden thread' that runs through every part of their enterprise, connecting every function and capability.

Across our global research with KPMG, we have analysed and worked alongside some leading businesses – the rare 5 per cent – that consistently deliver excellence and outperform the market. We have reached the firm conclusion that there is no material factor giving these organizations an advantage. They span multiple sectors, geographies and sizes. The one thing they have in common is that they have built their global leadership positions by following a process.

It is a process that we systematically define and explain in this book. It is a process rooted in understanding human nature: the organizations that excel are those that recognize we are emotional animals and cater for this in everything they do. Crucially, it is a process that any company can follow. Any business, department, ministry or social enterprise that is committed to excellence can deploy this process to deliver excellence. Doing so demands leadership and management expertise, but few special skills beyond the commitment not to waiver or compromise when traditional business norms suggest an easier way forward.

The book is structured around this process, divided into three parts.

Part 1: The changing world of customers and employees

Great businesses understand the humans they serve. In Part 1 we explore the macro trends that are shaping the commercial world. The trends that mean that organizations need to reconsider the appropriateness of their business models, the extent of their real knowledge about the customer, the role of their employees, their social purpose and the agility of their organization design to respond to future change.

Crises have a habit of accelerating macro trends and bringing the future forward. Through the difficulties of COVID-19, humanity is emerging permanently changed. The new customer and our changed workforces demand a different kind of engagement. This in turn has driven a need for new experiences – experiences that are increasingly purposeful and empathetic, yet digital, socially distanced and more convenient.

Chapter 1: Understanding excellence

This chapter draws on our research, what we know about successful companies and the extraordinary changes that are leading successful companies to rethink their strategies, structures and processes. Using case studies and examples from leading brands, we begin to identify the look and feel of a successful company. Excellent brands create consistent, emotional connections in the service of a higher purpose. They must be deeply focused on the needs and experiences of their specific customer groups, while transparently delivering more value to the planet than they take.

Chapter 2: Understanding the new customer

In the new context, we see that COVID-19 has led to accelerating macro trends and in this chapter we identify how consumer behaviour has changed and how this affects the path to purchase. We introduce the concept of the '5 Mys', a mechanism for understanding the influences on customer behaviour, and we set these firmly in the context of life events and changing circumstances. We recognize the need to incorporate increased concern for the environment and ethical values, the move towards an integrity economy.

Chapter 3: Understanding the new employee

At the heart of the experience sits an employee, either directly at a touchpoint or as a developer and architect of a digital experience. At many brands, however, the internal experience is at odds with what each employee is being asked to repeatedly serve up externally. There is a great disconnect that undermines authenticity and frustrates success. In response, leaders are adopting a servant-like approach, where their role is to empower, enable and engage employees in doing great things for each other, as well as for the customer. The best CEOs are now custodians of the customer and employee experiences, focusing on long-term human connections rather than short-term financial results.

Chapter 4: The new enterprise

This chapter looks at how firms need to organize for success. Traditional, Victorian business models are being replaced by organization designs that put customer needs or journeys at the centre. Firms that organize around the customer make it easier for their employees to understand human needs and exhibit their own humanity. Freed from the constraints of many traditional enterprises, they achieve better, more innovative results a lot more easily.

Chapter 5: Putting it all together

We look at a number of successful companies and provide an extended case study of first direct, a UK bank that leads the world when it comes to customer experience. We examine the company's approach to customers, employees and organization design. We unpick how and why it has become so successful and how companies might learn and replicate what first direct has done. For many companies, systems and technologies represent seemingly insurmountable obstacles to change, but this need not be so.

Part 2: The Six Pillars of Experience: a framework for excellence

Through global research, we see that all failing organizations are different, but all outstanding businesses are excellent in a universal way. Distilled from millions of customer interviews, the Six Pillars are the defining characteristics of world-leading companies.

Chapter 6: Introducing the Six Pillars of Experience

The roots of the Six Pillars are in human psychology and neuroscience. We examine how they play out in every interaction, human or digital.

- Integrity: *Being trustworthy and engendering trust.*
- Resolution: *Turning a poor experience into a great one.*
- Expectations: *Managing, meeting and exceeding customer expectations.*
- Time and effort: *Minimizing customer effort and creating frictionless processes.*
- Personalization: *Paying attention to people and their circumstances to drive emotional connection.*
- Empathy: *Achieving an understanding of the customer's circumstances to drive deep rapport* (KPMG, 2020b).

Companies that master the Six Pillars achieve market-leading advocacy, loyalty and commercial returns.

Chapter 7: Applying the Six Pillars

The Six Pillars provide a systematic approach to embedding excellence that spans strategy formulation to experience design, to transformation and ongoing measurement. We discuss how this is done in traditional customer functions, across the enterprise and both digitally and physically. Following the Six Pillars system is like weaving a golden thread that connects all aspects of the company around customers and employees, embedding consistent best practice in human connection at every stage. To be effective, customer centricity must be 'CFO credible'. Where it is not linked to growth, every boardroom will revert to the traditional business of managing costs and controlling risks. This is a failure of discipline that the Six Pillars can help us to navigate by eliminating the false dichotomy between low costs and experience excellence.

Chapter 8: The Six Pillars and memorable customer experiences

Organizations around the world state their desire to create experiences that will live on in their customers' memory and inspire them to advocate, stay loyal and increase their spend. We draw on the science of memory to identify what constitutes a memorable experience, in particular the psychological architecture of an experience that will lead to commercially beneficial behaviours.

Part 3: The 90-day plan: achieving a quantum leap

For those aspiring to deliver excellence like the world leaders, this final section offers a way forward, step by step. This relies on changing the mind and heart of the organization, starting at the top. It looks at the sequence of activities needed to generate a self-reinforcing set of results, where the whole is considerably greater than the sum of its parts. We examine common pitfalls: why many companies hit seemingly insurmountable barriers in emulating leading companies. We then identify the causal factors and provide insights as to how these barriers might be systematically overcome.

Whether you are embarking on widespread digital transformation or attempting to create a more customer-centric culture, by comparing your programme against the checklist for best practice you can identify gaps and opportunities.

Chapter 9: Preparing for change

Change starts with the senior team and the challenges faced by their teams in the face of the new customer. Over the last decade of social and digital progress, a lack of customer closeness/separation from customers has developed into a debilitating disease for many previously successful businesses. We look at how to rapidly cure this.

Chapter 10: The first 30 days

Many companies view the world inside out. They filter all inputs through their own administrative conveniences, biases, unwritten rules and limiting lenses. Consequently, they fail to take advantage of opportunities, or worse still they find themselves becoming increasingly less relevant to their customers and less engaged with their staff.

The single most important catalyst of any successful transformation is immersing the senior team in the new customer and the challenges their teams face. This is more than the traditional 'voice of the customer', but rather a form of 'customer surround sound'. It is likely that many years have elapsed since individual members of the senior team worked with customers on a regular basis. In normal times, this is a significant competitive disadvantage. Over the last decade of social and digital progress, this lack of customer closeness has developed into a debilitating disease for many once successful businesses. We look at how to cure this at speed.

Chapter 11: The second 30 days

This chapter focuses on the internal route map, the pathway to a better future. It addresses which capabilities to build first and how to manage the portfolio of change. We examine a change approach that transforms the organization through different states rather than simply progressing projects. It goes beyond critical path and analysis and interdependency; it defines what the organization will be able to do as an entity at a point in time.

For those not ready to fully revise their whole organization structure, we examine the need for a Centre of Customer Excellence; this recognizes that customer journeys are here to stay and will require a consistent methodology for definition and centralized version control of journey improvements.

Chapter 12: The final 30 days and beyond

This chapter is about creating momentum for change, building the capability road map. To lock in a new trajectory, we recommend that small but far-reaching symbolic changes are made first to prepare the ground for more fundamental change to come. These are signals of intent that embody a new paradigm for the business. They are a chance to signal to employees across the whole enterprise how things will be different. We summarize the power of these small changes, which are often more successful than attempting massive change in one go. While recognizing that keeping abreast of potential new customer use cases is not a trivial task, we highlight practical ways to solve customer problems, improve customer journeys and make life simpler and more rewarding for employees.

Constantly creating unity on the new vision for the organization – through whatever means necessary – is the last and vital step in creating a launchpad for excellence.

References

ESS et Société (2006) La Maif lance OVP, sa nouvelle offre de services à la personne. www.ess-et-societe.net/La-Maif-lance-OVP-sa-nouvelle

Gordon, J. (2020) CEO first direct [Interview], 8 July.

KPMG (2020a) Sweden. https://home.kpmg/xx/en/home/insights/2020/09/sweden.html

KPMG (2020b) Customer experience in the new reality. https://assets.kpmg/content/dam/kpmg/xx/pdf/2020/07/customer-experience-in-the-new-reality.pdf

Lexus (2016) How do Lexus dealers demonstrate omotenashi? https://blog.lexus.co.uk/lexus-dealers-demonstrate-omotenashi/

The American Legion (2021) USAA member stories that 'tug at your heart'. http://dev.legion.org/usaa/customer/93145/usaa-member-stories-tug-your-heart

PART 1

The changing world of customers and employees

01

Understanding excellence

For any organization to be excellent, it must start by understanding its customers. Globally, this has become harder in recent years. A decade of pandemics, digital transformation, political changes and social progress has affected most of humanity, in both subtle and profound ways. Behaviourally, we are interacting with a narrower set of brands, with changed purchasing frequencies and more digitally than ever. Psychologically, the change is more fundamental and interesting, with new attitudes and beliefs redefining how we make decisions, what we value and where we invest our time. A 'new customer' has emerged.

The new customer describes each of us: as consumers, social animals, citizens and employees. We are each fraught with complexity and contradiction: slow to trust, but craving integrity and purpose. More digital than ever, but fundamentally motivated to seek authentic human connection, which now transcends previous consumer–brand relationships. Cynical, wise and knowing, yet seeking wonder and escapism more than ever before.

Businesses can become excellent only when they master the new customer. While every part of the business is important, it is only through the customer that the enterprise breathes, grows and thrives. A business will endure a failure in the finance team, can battle through shaky HR processes, absent executives or faltering digital rollouts. But without customers, it is naught. Without meeting its customers' needs, every business would cease to exist. However, the pace of change in the last decade has meant that most businesses are not ready to understand or meet these needs, with most leaders still struggling to rewire their enterprises to meet yesterday's challenges.

The genesis of these changes is not hard to identify. In the first half of 2020 alone, a generation of forced evolution occurred in a handful of months of national lockdowns, home working and business adaptation.

Satya Nadella, the Microsoft CEO, observed, 'We have seen two years' worth of digital transformation in two months' (Spataro, 2020).

Our behaviour has had to change. We have had to work differently, to consume differently. However, there has been a corresponding global psychological shift in values, beliefs and needs. Existing trends have been accelerated and new ones are emerging all the time. Customers feel more vulnerable, less secure and more pressured than at any point in recent living memory. Values have evolved, with renewed demands that business leaders are champions of social purpose, employee experience, diversity and political change, as well as custodians of shareholder value.

Unsurprisingly, the basis for many customer decisions has shifted. These are the fundamentals that every business is built upon. To compete and grow, every enterprise has been fine-tuned over many years based on assumptions about customers that no longer hold true. CEOs and customer leaders have never faced a challenge of this nature (KPMG, 2020).

Against this backdrop of change, customer insight has become more important than ever. The voice of the customer – the systematic collection of customer sentiment, behaviour and other data – has become a critical management capability. Such data provides an early warning or foresight system that, if used correctly, can positively impact every business decision and enable leaders to maintain agility in times of change.

But is it working? Seemingly not. According to the UK Market Research Society, only 1 in 10 customer-impacting decisions is based on customer insight (MRS, 2016). This implies that the remaining 90 per cent of decisions are based on guesswork or intuition born of experience. *Harvard Business Review* reaches similar conclusions, suggesting only 11 per cent of marketing decisions (arguably the ones where customers are most central) are made using insights (Hinshaw, 2016). But what happens when that experience or guesswork is no longer relevant or correct? The answer is a stark one: a slow death for previously successful businesses.

Prior to COVID-19, customer experience (CX) was identified as one of the last competitive battlegrounds. Now the challenge is greater – not only for competitive differentiation but to innovate, adapt or perish.

A human or digital revolution?

To compete tomorrow, business leaders must adapt to the new, changing customer more quickly than ever before. But surely customer centricity is nothing new? Is this not a familiar challenge?

It is true that commentators and pundits have written avidly for years about 'the age of the customer'. Between 2010 and 2020, an entire industry was birthed of customer consultants and CX experts, offering expert advice on how best to transform, optimize or evolve. Most CEOs have written 'being customer centric' into their strategy and insisted on reporting on progress, proudly tucking NPS or CSAT (customer satisfaction) measures alongside traditional accounting reports.

Unfortunately, it is not working. If we look at the data from the KPMG Customer Experience Excellence Centre and the level of improvement from 2010 to 2020, we see that from the customer's perspective this has yielded only minor improvements globally.

Similarly, 'digital transformation' has been the biggest spend item for most organizations as they systematically swap out legacy systems and wiring – a $6.8 trillion industry by 2023 (Business Wire, 2020). However, making vast investments in technology does not necessarily result in excellence. For many organizations, digital first was the mantra as they replicated existing processes online. Often these processes existed because of history rather than from a fundamental assessment of how customers might have their problems solved. The result is that only a few companies have really delivered excellent experiences through digital. What is important is that, online or offline, it is how the investments deliver the organization's purpose and make life easier for customers that determines success.

Now, consider that this languid progress has been achieved pre-pandemic, before COVID re wrote so many rules. If we look to the future, everything suggests that all previous commentary on 'the age of the customer' or 'digital transformation' will become just a footnote to the change to come. We are not facing an orderly transition to a new age of the customer but a revolution.

So, if the starting point for understanding the new customer is not through the lens of digital transformation, and previous models are not working, where should leaders start on their journey to excellence? Reviewing the insights from our global research shows that the customer leaders – and those that transform the most rapidly – have a single, defining characteristic: absolute clarity of purpose. This is more than simply vision, or principles, so much more than the profit motive. To identify that purpose, then to embed it in every experience, for customers and employees – that will transform your business. Against the current backdrop of customer revolution, excellence begins with a coherent and good purpose.

A change in values

Excellence is rooted in noble purpose. Since 2010 we have tracked the enduring power of purpose: brands that stand for more than profit outperform the market. Customers experience this as integrity, which forms the foundation for everything else the business does. Organizations increasingly manage this via environmental, social and governance (ESG) initiatives, but purpose and integrity are often much broader, forming the basis for fast-growth enterprises and strong internal cultures.

Post COVID-19, public health and safety, the state of the labour market, good governance and societal imbalances will be near-term priorities for businesses and governments. In the new reality, the move towards high-integrity business has truly come of age. For many businesses, the starting point for responding to the new reality needs to be purpose (KPMG, 2020).

In the 2020 KPMG CEO outlook report, 79 per cent of CEOs said that following the pandemic they needed to revisit their purpose and reassess how their businesses related to the environment and to society in general (KPMG, 2020).

Research into the new customer shows that we are entering an 'integrity economy', one where the ethics of an organization are as important as its products and services. As Mary Portas describes it, people are moving from 'buying from to buying into' (Cassidy, 2019). With 64 per cent of the UK population now more concerned about the provenance of the companies they deal with (KPMG, 2020), the responsibilities an organization has towards its communities and its social and environmental impact can no longer be left to the corporate social responsibility (CSR) department. These issues need to be front and centre as part of the company's brand, delivered through communications but fundamentally made real every day through the experiences it delivers (KPMG, 2020).

Through COVID-19, and for the foreseeable future, the triple bottom line of people, profit and planet has become more important than ever. For our leaders it has long been the way they see the world. Successful leaders realize that the relationship between the three is symbiotic – a focus on people and planet can reduce costs and engage more customers in the brand. As former CEO of Interface, Ray Anderson, said in 2003, sustainability is 'a better way to bigger profits'. He also wrote, 'Done right, sustainability doesn't cost. It pays' (Anderson, 2003).

IKEA, for example, set out to be 100 per cent powered by renewable energy by 2020 and now generates more renewable energy than it uses. The retailer has invested in 70,000 solar panels for its stores, selling the extra energy and generating a new revenue stream (RE 100, 2018).

M&S Food, through its Plan A programme (M&S, 2020), constantly reminds its customers, often subliminally through in-store posters, of what it is doing every day to deliver on its responsibilities towards the environment, supplier and customer welfare.

For first direct, it is 'pioneering amazing service' (first direct, 2020).

For Lush, it is 'making a difference to the world through the choices we make as a brand' (Lush, 2021). Lush is a brand where CSR is at the heart of all that it does: every facet of its business is seeking to make the world a better, and often a more responsible, place.

For Monzo, it is being 'focused on solving problems, rather than selling financial products. We want to make the world a better place and change people's lives' (Monzo, 2020).

For Ritz-Carlton, purpose and customer obsession are inextricably linked. Every day every team across the globe shares stories of great things that have been done for customers the previous day. The day starts with what great looks like and Ritz-Carlton's purpose, 'unique, memorable, and personable customer service experiences', is infused through every activity (Ritz-Carlton, 2021).

Southwest Airlines uses the power of storytelling to communicate its purpose and make sure each one of its 46,000 employees pursues its vision of being the most loved, most travelled airline each and every day. Southwest is doing so by rallying employees around a common purpose: 'We exist to connect people to what's important in their lives through friendly, reliable, and low-cost air travel' (Southwest, 2021a).

Corporate communications are filled with real examples and compelling storytelling to help employees visualize what each step of the purpose looks and feels like. Every week CEO Gary Kelly gives a 'shout-out' – public praise – to employees who have gone above and beyond to show great customer service. Each month the *Southwest Spirit* magazine (Southwest, 2021b) features the story of an employee who has gone above and beyond. Southwest highlights positive behaviours through a variety of recognition programmes and awards. For customers of purpose-driven organizations, if the organization disappeared tomorrow, then the world would miss something meaningful. Purpose is the organization's 'why'; it sits alongside the 'what' – the mission – and the 'where' – the vision. It answers the question, 'Why do we exist beyond what we make, do or sell?'

CASE STUDY
Virgin Money: interview with CEO David Duffy

UK bank Virgin Money is a 'challenger' bank, focused on disrupting the status quo in UK banking. With approximately 6,500 employees, 6 million customers and £75 billion in assets it is the UK's sixth largest bank.

It is a bank that strongly believes in its purpose, 'to make you happier about money'. Whether with respect to a student, family or homeless person, its purpose is what drives it, to ensure people feel comfortable with their money and secure in the knowledge it is in safe hands with people who really care about their customers. It is a purpose that was derived by employees and 'infuses all of our behaviours, we are purpose driven'.

The commitment to its purpose is total. Every decision made by the leadership team must outline how what it proposes will advance the purpose of Virgin Money. Data in banking is ubiquitous and Virgin Money is no exception; however, 'that data carries deep responsibility and we are increasingly aligning data to our purpose so we can see how we are doing, whilst ensuring we deal with data in the most ethical way possible'.

To emphasize the bank's concern for the customer experience, a member of the leadership team has the role of Chief Customer Experience Officer, a role that carries the voice of the customer and ensures that all decisions have to consider the impact on customer experience before they are progressed. This person is responsible for making sure the end customer experience is brilliant and works to ensure the purpose, products, brand and technology are all aligned. It is, of course, a collegiate and constructive role, but nonetheless it sends a powerful message. 'There will always be teams that from time to time feel that their way is the right one, there are pushes and pulls in every organization, that is a factor of organizational life. The responsibility of this role is to ensure this always works in favour of the customer and that we have the right processes to deliver the best outcomes for customers.'

To ensure organizational focus on the things that matter the most, targets are set that drive remuneration. These targets span the mutually self-reinforcing metrics of customer, colleague, financial and ESG. These drive the long-term incentive programmes and are central to how the bank is managed.

Purpose goes beyond brand positioning and is reflective of the values, culture and ethos of the organization. It is the fundamental source of authenticity and the platform that brings the brand alive throughout the customer experience. Purpose is the great connector and it is important because it has an integrating, aligning and cohesive effect across all customer touchpoints. Today, business and societal impact must go hand in hand. Consumers are too informed, too connected and too sceptical in this information age to fall for a brand that claims to be pursuing a profound 'purpose' when what it's really after is a stronger P&L. As human beings we are inspired by purpose, we have a desire for connection and meaning, it is the satisfaction we achieve over and above our employment. It creates advocates of both employees and customers. As a first step, businesses need to be clear on the relevance of their purpose to the new customer.

Without purpose, the customer experience can become hollow and inauthentic. At the heart of purpose lies a controlling idea, a north star – an idea that resonates deeply with employees and customers alike. It shapes the experience both internally for employees and externally for customers. The leading companies are world-class exponents of connecting people and purpose.

Purpose-led firms are:

- led from the top – it is the CEO who sets the purpose agenda, articulating ideas that go far beyond the business impact. For organizations such as Lush, Amazon and Specsavers, it is the founder who wraps business around a purpose. For organizations such as first direct, where the purpose was established in 1989, it is the role of each incoming CEO to make it relevant for the current age;

- open and transparent – businesses need to be open about how their purpose connects to their business, while at the same time creating a positive impact on society. A sound storytelling approach is essential, one that clearly and simply paints a picture to explain why shared value creation is beneficial to everyone involved;

- participatory – today's consumers know that actions speak louder than words and they want their actions to make a difference. That's why successful brands provide them with opportunities to engage, to co-create. It is no accident that many of the top companies in recent rankings foster customer engagement where participation and involvement are a way of life (KPMG, 2020).

Defining purpose

Simply writing down a compelling purpose is not enough. It needs guidelines or principles that amplify how it should be implemented. It must be

TABLE 1.1 Customer purpose and simple rules

USAA	**Customer purpose:** To contribute positively to members' lives. **The simple rules:** • Understand the customer at a deep and profound level. • Treat the customer as you would want to be treated yourself. **Experience:** Extraordinary levels of empathy and emotional connection.

Disney Parks	**Customer purpose:**
	To create happiness for others.
	The simple rules:
	• Make every experience magical:
	  o I project a positive image and energy.
	  o I am courteous and respectful to all guests.
	  o I stay in character and play the part.
	  o I go above and beyond.
	• Treat the customer as you would want to be treated yourself.
	
	Experience:
	A magical, captivating 'wow' experience that delivers a 70% return rate.
	SOURCE: Ciotti, 2021.

Amazon	**Customer purpose:** Customer first. **The simple rules:** • Put the customer in control at all times. • Become the world's most customer-centric company. • Excite and inspire the customer. **Experience:** Amazon has defined the online shopping experience for its customers.
Publix	**Customer purpose:** Making shopping a pleasure. **The simple rules:** • Never let making a profit stand in the way of doing the right thing. • Make the food the star. • Deliver outstanding customer service and competitive pricing. **Experience:** Customers love the experience of shopping at Publix

(continued)

TABLE 1.1 (continued)

Wegmans	**Customer purpose:** Ensure customers are truly put first. **The simple rules:** • Happy, knowledgeable and superbly trained employees. • Treat customers like guests. • Enable customers to take time, relax and enjoy the experience. • Care about the wellbeing of every person. • High standards are a way of life. **Experience:** Empowered, passionate staff working in a theme park of food, creating an almost unbreakable bond with its customers. A destination in its own right. Listed as one of the best employers in the US in Fortune's '100 best companies to work for' (WHAM, 2021).

Zappos	**Customer purpose:**
	Uncommon service.
	The simple rules:
	• Create a customer culture based on:
	  o Deliver wow through service
	  o Embrace and drive change
	  o Create fun and a little weirdness
	  o Be adventurous, creative and open-minded
	  o Pursue growth and learning
	  o Build open and honest relationships
	  o Build a positive team and family spirit
	  o Do more with less
	  o Be passionate and determined.
	
	Experience:
	Continually having your expectations exceeded.

SOURCE Reproduced with permission from KPMG Nunwood: https://thecxcompany.com/wp-content/uploads/2017/06/US-2016-CX-Report.pdf

connected to every part of the enterprise, not merely a functional construct of marketers or customer service teams. If your finance team or business services function does not believe the purpose, then it is not real. It is these simple rules, or design principles, that ensure a consistent experience across all touchpoints.

Think of migrating birds: cohesive, integrated, they have a single purpose, to fly to warmer climes. However, the way they exercise control is based on a few simple rules: keep an optimum distance from the next flight partner; match their speed and velocity; anticipate changes in direction arising from elsewhere. The power of a few simple rules to drive cohesion has long been known, but our global leaders use it to their distinct advantage – see Table 1.1.

CASE STUDY
Disney Parks

When Walt Disney began to define the experience in his theme parks, his central purpose was the creation of happiness and appropriately the simple rules reflected the characters from Snow White (Kober, 2016). They are as relevant today for any business as they were in the 1950s:

- Be Happy ... make eye contact and smile!
- Be like Sneezy ... greet and welcome each and every guest. Spread the spirit of hospitality.
- Don't be Bashful ... seek out guest contact.
- Be like Doc ... provide immediate service recovery.
- Don't be Grumpy ... always display appropriate body language at all times.
- Be like Sleepy ... create dreams and preserve the magical guest experience.
- Don't be Dopey ... thank each and every guest!

CASE STUDY
Delivering purpose through simple rules: Mozilla

Mozilla is the San Francisco-based not-for-profit organization behind Firefox, the fourth most popular web browser, and it's a mission-driven advocate of equality of access and transparency on the internet. Firefox's 300 million monthly users choose it over Chrome, Safari and Edge at least partly because it helps protect their personal data and puts limits on how their activities are tracked online (*The Times*, 2019).

CEO Jascha Kaykas-Wolff joined in 2015 and immediately set about being clear on the organization's purpose, stating that Mozilla's responsibility is to ensure that the internet is open and accessible to all, but lofty statements are only as good as the organization's ability to deliver on them. Kaykas-Wolff discovered the systems development method 'agile' in place in some of the technical areas of the business and set about using agile at scale as the mechanism for codifying the purpose into day-to-day activity by applying some of its simple rules.

He noticed that there was a fundamental problem in the business – it was an organization that was very good at creating silos based on functional expertise. This inhibited progress and introduced barriers between functions. He therefore focused on breaking out of the silos. This called for a new approach based on collaboration. It involved learning how to apply the lean and agile project management processes used in other parts of the business to his marketing, product and central teams. Building cross-functional teams, teams that looked ostensibly like mini businesses, was the way to break down the artificial barriers caused by silos. This enabled previously isolated disciplines to be brought together, not only fostering greater mutual understanding and insight but also producing better results (*The Times*, 2019).

The approach has also boosted the pace of productivity in the C-suite. Adopting the philosophy of agile, Kaykas-Wolff and his fellow business leaders moved to agile-inspired 'stand-up' meetings three times a week – these are seven-minute management meetings where each executive talks about what's most important that day. Tactical meetings are held once a week: they consider vital customer insights and then determine the mix of resources required to develop new and better products and features – fast.

This was demonstrated by the announcement that, as of 2020, Firefox would move to a new monthly update cycle – twice as fast as before and something that would not have been possible previously. It has also inspired a range of new products based on providing better online protection to users – developed collaboratively rather than in the old silos. Products include private network technology to improve security when using 'coffee shop' public internet access, and free-to-use Firefox Monitor, which will alert users if their data is involved in a hack (*The Times*, 2019).

Mozilla has become a purpose-driven organization that now drives organizational decision making, not profit or shareholder value, using the simple rules of agile to speed the delivery of that purpose for the benefit of its customers (*The Times*, 2019).

In the 'integrity economy', where purpose writ large will determine the soul of every organization, this is much wider than a single facet of purpose – brand, social, ESG, moral or customer experience – but rather the fundamental requirement to stand for more than profit. As we will see in Part 2, this commitment to integrity forms the foundation that each and every experience must be built upon.

KEY TAKEAWAYS

1 The world has changed dramatically in a short space of time, macro trends already in evidence have been accelerated by the pandemic and new ones have emerged.

2 In this new world, excellence is rooted in customer mastery and purpose.

3 The underlying values of customers are increasingly focused on how a company conducts itself, how it relates to the environment and the noble purpose it pursues.

4 Increasingly customers are attracted to companies that share their values, their view of the world and the value that is brought to local economies.

5 Companies need to be clear on what they are, what they stand for and what the world would miss if they didn't exist. If the answer is nothing, then it is time for coherent thought about who they are serving, the enterprise they need to build and the contribution they can make to the greater good.

References

Anderson, R. C. (2003) A better way, try it. www.raycandersonfoundation.org/assets/pdfs/rayslife/08-13-03-A-Better-Way.pdf (archived at https://perma.cc/7YQC-HCEY)

Business Wire (2020) IDC reveals 2021 worldwide digital transformation predictions; 65% of global GDP digitalized by 2022, driving over $6.8 trillion of direct DX investments from 2020 to 2023. www.businesswire.com/news/home/20201029005028/en/IDC-Reveals-2021-Worldwide-Digital-Transformation-Predictions-65-of-Global-GDP-Digitalized-by-2022-Driving-Over-6.8-Trillion-of-Direct-DX-Investments-from-2020-to-2023 (archived at https://perma.cc/S2DA-H3YH)

Cassidy, F. (2019) Mary Portas: Retailing is entering a brand new era. www.raconteur.net/retail/mary-portas-retail/ (archived at https://perma.cc/RA59-QDGX)

Ciotti, G. (2021) How Disney creates magical experiences (and a 70% return rate). www.helpscout.com/blog/disney-customer-experience/ (archived at https://perma.cc/M6PW-BFJQ)

first direct (2020) first direct in the community. www1.firstdirect.com/uncovered/in-the-community/ (archived at https://perma.cc/7MRB-8V9B)

Hinshaw, M. (2016) The real value in voice of the customer: the customer experience. https://blog.adobe.com/en/publish/2016/03/20/the-real-value-in-voice-of-the-customer-the-customer-experience.html#gs.u7yqtp (archived at https://perma.cc/PG8T-9CLN)

Kober, J. J. (2016) Disney's four keys to a great guest experience. http://disneyatwork.com/disneys-four-keys-to-a-great-guest-experience/ (archived at https://perma.cc/Z5K7-WASA)

KPMG (2020) Responding to consumer trends in the new reality. https://home. kpmg/xx/en/home/insights/2020/06/consumers-and-the-new-reality.html (archived at https://perma.cc/N5VH-XMWS)

Lush (2021) Our values. www.lushusa.com/stories/article_our-values-lush.html (archived at https://perma.cc/6JFR-BGEG)

M&S (2020) Sustainability. https://corporate.marksandspencer.com/sustainability (archived at https://perma.cc/H72D-4F38)

MRS (2016) Towards an insight driven organisation. www.mrs.org.uk/pdf/ insightdriven.pdf (archived at https://perma.cc/69FB-2VLK)

Monzo (2020) The Monzo transparency dashboard. https://monzo.com/ transparency/ (archived at https://perma.cc/X9F5-5GV9)

RE 100 (2018) Ikea Group has committed to producing as much renewable energy as it consumes by 2020. www.there100.org/our-work/news/ikea-group-has-committed-producing-much-renewable-energy-it-consumes-2020 (archived at https://perma.cc/VYZ6-2T49)

Ritz-Carlton (2021) Gold Standards. www.ritzcarlton.com/en/about/gold-standards#:~:text=The%20Employee%20Promise-,The%20Credo,%2C%20 relaxed%2C%20yet%20refined%20ambience (archived at https://perma.cc/ S6R3-VB33)

Southwest (2021a) About Southwest. www.southwest.com/html/about-southwest/ index.html (archived at https://perma.cc/BV9Y-2CH3)

Southwest (2021b) The Magazine. www.swamedia.com/magazine (archived at https://perma.cc/H9G4-7KH9)

Spataro, J. (2020) 2 years of digital transformation in 2 months. www.microsoft. com/en-us/microsoft-365/blog/2020/04/30/2-years-digital-transformation-2-months/ (archived at https://perma.cc/KV7V-M8QC)

The Times (2019) How a not-for-profit firm took on the planet's most powerful tech giants. www.thetimes.co.uk/static/how-a-not-for-profit-firm-took-on-the-planets-most-powerful-tech-giants/ (archived at https://perma.cc/U3CX-2ES7)

WHAM (2021) Wegmans named no. 4 on Fortune list of 100 Best Companies to Work For. https://13wham.com/news/local/wegmans-named-no-4-on-fortune-list-of-100-best-companies-to-work-for#:~:text=4%20on%20Fortune%20 list%20of%20100%20Best%20Companies%20to%20Work%20For,-by%20 WHAM%20Staff&text=(WHAM)%20%2D%20Wegmans%20Food%20 Markets,Companies%20to%20Work%20For%20list. (archived at https:// perma.cc/2Y4W-M9B5)

02

Understanding the new customer

A clear identity is essential. But the individual customer will always be complex and multifaceted. We are each a cluster of rational and emotional needs, beliefs and motivations. Before any organization can start to design the offer – the experiences – that will meet these needs (our focus in Part 2 of this book), it needs to be clear on *who it is serving*.

This is the traditional preserve of market segmentation, a discipline more relevant and sophisticated today than at any point in previous decades. In times of slow progress or limited change, it might be that a chief marketing officer or customer service team would update their models every few years. For most organizations, many models of the customer would exist across research teams, digital personas and advertising functions. Overlaid on this were multiple streams of data, of insight. Much like the blind man and the elephant, the customer was described through many lenses, with many languages. In simpler times this may have been frustrating and confusing, but not fatal.

Facing into the customer revolution ahead, the absence of a coherent and universal view on who the organization is serving is a critical failure of leadership. To react to the change and opportunity ahead, everyone needs to be clear on who the customer is and have the shared vocabulary to discuss them accurately.

Many approaches exist for doing this. Some are more suited to tactical automation and decisioning – optimizing marketing technology to make offers or configuring a customer relationship management (CRM) database to micro-personalize service interactions. The best of these update in real time, drawing in multiple signals to assign customers to groups and machine learning to recommend the most suitable actions. Other models are more strategic, focusing on consumer motivations, needs and economic drivers.

Our recommendation is to start here before diving into technology – the organization needs to be coherent on where it sees value and what customers expect.

There are several good models to choose from, each with its own factors and determinants. For the purpose of this discussion, we will look at research conducted around the world by KPMG. This has identified five consistent factors that allow us to understand the new customer, their motivations and behaviour – the criteria by which the customer is increasingly making purchase decisions. Described as the '5 Mys', they provide a useful framework for creating consistent understanding across the enterprise (KPMG, 2017a).

In each of these the customer has changed in profound ways. To compete in the new reality, a good grasp of these factors will be the starting point for any competitive advantage.

---

1 **My motivation:** Trust, authenticity and social values are the critical but intangible motivators of the choices today's consumers make.

2 **My attention:** The fight for consumer attention has never been more intense, exacerbated by unprecedented volumes of content at our fingertips.

3 **My connections:** Today's technology connects humans to information and each other 24/7, driving shifts in our social interactions and behaviour.

4 **My watch:** The companies that understand the constraints of time and anticipate how that changes across life events are best placed to engage customers in the moments of greatest impact and to meet their needs head on.

5 **My wallet:** How consumers adjust their share of the wallet across life stages and pivotal life events is changing, creating a ripple effect of change across not just one but all categories to which they allocate their money (KPMG, 2017a).

My motivation: characteristics that drive my behaviours and expectations

Purchase triggers are shaped by conscious and subconscious life and personal goals that guide and prioritize purchase decisions. Theodore Levitt observed that we don't buy quarter-inch drills but quarter-inch holes (Levitt, 1969); Charles Revson, the founder of Revlon, once memorably remarked that in the factory we make cosmetics, in the store we sell hope (Revlon, 2021).

The customer who rushes to a DIY store for materials to fix a burst pipe has a different set of motivations, priorities and expectations than the same customer returning two weeks later to buy garden furniture. It is our circumstances and the triggers to purchase that determine the experiences we need.

Against this backdrop the traditional forms of 'strategic' segmentation are no longer insightful enough. The three most frequently used types of segmentation are demographics, geographics and psychographics. Traditionally, marketing practitioners group people into segments with distinctive similarities – age group, gender, location, lifestyle, occupation, etc. But demographics are no longer a reliable indicator of a customer's purchase behaviour. Prince Charles and Ozzy Osbourne are at a similar age and life stage but are unlikely to exhibit similar purchase behaviour (Ward, 2016).

More recently, technology has enabled behavioural targeting, which allows us to understand a user's intent: 'tactical' segmentation. But firms are moving from selling products to providing holistic solutions to complex life problems across physical, emotional, conscious and subconscious dimensions. This means they need to get to grips with the multiplicity of customer contexts. For most customers, it is their journey, across multiple channels, touchpoints and media, that determines their future behaviour – something fiendishly hard to establish even with the most sophisticated digital platforms. So new ways to understand customers and their motivations are needed.

The start point for the new approach is the customer's personal circumstances and the intent that arises as a consequence. By understanding these, experiences can be crafted to lock onto their highly personal needs and priorities and thus feel unique and special.

Let's consider, for example, a company that wanted to move smokers to lower-risk products. It started by understanding motivations, the reasons why smokers wanted to quit. The reasons were various: to smell better, to get fit, to protect family, to set a good example, to save money and to improve life expectancy. The company discovered there were several distinct reasons why people choose to give up. The majority of smokers, regardless of age, gender, geography or financial circumstances, fell into one of these. Once it had identified the primary reason, it was then able to design experiences that continually reinforced the reason for stopping and illustrated the progress the smoker was making towards their goal.

A lot of companies have become fixated on 'know me', recognizing the customer at a specific moment in time. This is often because of a regulatory requirement to do so (such as demonstrating compliance) or a commercial goal to meet (such as 'converting' a click-through). But few have made progress on 'understand me', i.e. relating to what is going on in the customer's life more broadly and providing a framework to enable employees to offer appropriate help.

USAA, the American bank, has consistently topped the KPMG Top 100 Index in the US. The bank prides itself on making a positive difference to its customers' lives (indeed, its senior executives are rewarded on the basis of this criterion). It is the world's most advanced company when it comes to understanding its customers' circumstances, motivations and triggers. Employees start with a circumstance segmentation based on a fusion of life stage and context. They look at the triggers, life events and the customer's end goal. A customer can enter the bank's communication strategy at one of several points, based on their circumstances, and they are then engaged and guided along the pathways followed by similar customers moving through that life stage.

Communications are initiated based on a customer's proximity to a life event. Predictive technology is used to determine when a customer is about to enter a life event and appropriate communications are triggered. There are millions of potential combinations of different types of contacts that USAA can make, so potentially the combination could be unique in every case. In this instance the contact strategy is orchestrated by technology and business rules but is rooted in circumstances and psychological outcomes (Mocker et al, 2015).

The father of disruptive innovation, Clayton Christensen, in his book with Michael Raynor, *The Innovator's Solution* (Christensen and Raynor, 2003), states that 60 per cent of all new product development efforts are terminated before they reach the market. Of the 40 per cent that do see the light of day, 40 per cent fail to become profitable and are withdrawn from the market. The authors believe that this high failure rate is a function of companies using attribute-based segmentation, where product attributes and customer attributes are compared and marketers seek to find a relationship between the two.

The authors suggest a circumstance-based segmentation strategy: the critical unit of analysis is the circumstance and not the customer. They provide a case study that proves their point. It involves a fast-food restaurant that sells milkshakes. Seeking to improve sales and profits, the company attempted an attribute-based segmentation, profiling customers who are most likely to buy a milkshake. Despite pursuing this, the company's performance stubbornly refused to change.

Researchers then used a circumstance-based approach, based on an ethnographic study of purchasers of milkshakes. They found to their surprise that the majority of milkshakes were purchased in the morning as a takeaway. When the researchers interviewed the morning customers, they discovered that purchasers were buying milkshakes to see them through their journey to work. Compared with other breakfast products such as bagels and doughnuts, it seemed that milkshake was the best product for the job: it took time to consume, wasn't messy and didn't get the motorist's hands sticky or interfere with their driving. Milkshakes purchased later in the day were mainly bought by parents to appease their children after a long day of saying 'no'. Where drivers in the morning had appreciated the thickness of the milkshake, children in the afternoon often didn't finish the shake because they wanted to drink more quickly.

After completing the circumstance-based research, the restaurant had a clear picture of how it could improve its milkshake sales and profit. Milkshakes purchased in the morning should take longer to consume and require little effort to purchase; they could be made more interesting by adding fruit and new flavours. Milkshakes purchased in the afternoon should take less time to consume and should appeal to a younger audience. This *circumstance* suggests strategies such as thinning the milkshakes and serving them in smaller, entertaining cups. Circumstance-based market segmentation offers a powerful, strategic way to determine whether a company is providing products that its customers will want (Christensen and Raynor, 2003).

CASE STUDY
Know your customer: QVC

QVC is a television-centred home shopping organization with annual revenue of $9 billion that incorporates a high-level brand promise into its name (Quality, Value and Convenience). A brand promise that it delivers against every day. As a consequence, the company has become one of the biggest players in the UK beauty and womenswear market. QVC shoppers are constantly looking for good value and they find it at QVC. It has some of the most loyal customers in the world – its customer retention rates are unparalleled in the retail industry, averaging 90 per cent.

QVC has focused intensely on both employee engagement and the delivery of an outstanding customer experience. It has, steadily and inexorably, moved up the KPMG index every year, becoming number one in 2017.

At the heart of QVC's success is its mastery of the art and science of what consumer psychologists call 'para-social relationships'. A para-social relationship is the one-sided sense of connectedness that people can feel with a celebrity or fictional character. The phrase was coined by Donald Horton and Richard Wohl in 1956 (Horton and Wohl, 1956). They describe it as intimacy at a distance. Or, as one participant in our study described the QVC presenters, 'my imaginary friends'.

QVC understands the psychology of its chosen customer. This requires a very tight description of the target customer and QVC describes its customer very carefully. She (86 per cent of customers are female) is someone for whom shopping is a defining characteristic. She views shopping not just as therapy (as in retail therapy) but as an essential part of her approach to the world. It is how she relaxes, how she seeks entertainment and how she determines her sense of self-worth. QVC enables her to see and interact with others who share these values. It is a unique and deep connection.

Every day, QVC's television presenters provide the face of empathy to their audience. Their style of presenting means they are easy to relate to, the friendly style has the feel of a discussion between friends – an essential part of the shopping experience. Presenters are carefully chosen and then trained (for up to six months) in how to appeal and communicate with such a person. QVC describes the approach as an 'over the fence conversation'. These are friends explaining to friends why a particular product would be uniquely suitable for them. No hard sell, a focus on the product quality, but, primarily, a focus on how the product will leave the customer feeling.

Presenters start each programme by setting expectations. 'We have a great show for you today.' 'In this show we have a one-time offer you will not see again.' Contact centre staff are encouraged to listen to customers and build emotionally connective relationships with them. Having great people who really care about the customer is a critical ingredient, ensuring they are skilled and empowered to offer the best service. Indeed, it is fair to say that empathy is the platform on which QVC has built its success.

The product is framed by how it will make you look or feel. Jewellery, for example, is described in terms of how you will feel as you wear it: flirty, confident, stylish, an individual, beautiful, depending on the event. Perfume, particularly intangible, is offered in the light of how you would feel giving it as a gift. It is all about expectations. The creation of a sense of anticipation. Where the wanting is as important as the having (KPMG, 2017b).

My attention: ways I direct my attention and focus

It is said that Generation Z has an attention span of 8 seconds and that the attention span of millennials is 12 seconds. For older demographics it is a little more, but it is reducing – we are all time poor and face multiple competing demands on our mental processing time. This means that every marketing moment needs to count (Patel, 2017).

Hoping to gain the customer's attention only when they are in the market to make a purchase, faced with myriad options and limited by their attention span, is no longer a viable option. The leading companies in the KPMG index and those that have risen the fastest in recent times are those that have learned to harness technology to nurture customer relationships between sales. So, they remain psychologically present in their customers' lives, particularly in the moments that really matter.

CASE STUDY

Joe Girard

Joe Girard was the first super-salesman (Girard, 2021). From 1963 to 1978 he set new standards of achievement when he averaged more than 100 car sales a month and broke the record in the *Guinness World Records* book for 1,425 individual car sales in a single year. He didn't offer a discount, a superior car or any incentives. He simply approached sales differently from his competitors. He didn't sell a product, he wasn't focused on transactional sales; he sold a deep personal relationship, based on trust.

He kept himself psychologically present in his customers' lives, constantly keeping in touch. With the average car replacement cycle of four years, ongoing continual interaction was, for him, the key to a relationship, so much more than just getting in contact when he knew the customer was in the market. He employed two secretaries to manage his customer communications. He wrote a personal note to his customers every month. He became almost a member of their families. He saw the customer as a gateway to a network. His guiding principle was to always let customers know how important and special they are and let them know you don't take their business for granted. Crucially, he managed the life cycle of car ownership from end to end. He believed that the real selling begins after the sale. Consequently, most of his business came from referrals. He was a Master of Advocacy before it became fashionable.

Today, of course, technology can replace the two secretaries and generate personalized interactions, timed to coincide with events in a customer's life to make communications interesting and relevant and to generate opportunities to build a relationship.

Many times, the moments that matter in customers' lives are not selling occasions but relationship-building occasions. For financial companies that top our index, such as USAA, Navy Federal, Edward Jones and Charles Schwab, where considerable periods can elapse between purchases, or for high-frequency, high-touch companies such as HEB, Publix and Wegmans, the recipe is the same: being there for their customers physically and psychologically, between purchases, and all mediated through digital technology.

Our brains come pre-equipped with an attention filter. This allows us to navigate much of our lives on autopilot. It also shifts us to a more considered position when something salient or relevant occurs; this is why we can suddenly hear our name mentioned across a crowded and noisy room.

Consumers will be attracted to things that have relevance to their life goals, life problems and desire for emotional satisfaction. A quiet night in, the arrival of a baby: the events vary in relevance by industry, but these events drive overt needs and the analysis of these surfaces unmet customer needs. So leading companies like Netflix, QVC, Hilton and first direct are architecting experiences around them.

An event is something of importance that occurs in a customer's life and provides a trigger for customers to undertake a journey to achieve an objective. An event gives rise to problems a customer will need to solve in a given circumstance. Some events are predictable, many are not. The event influences the customer's mindset and what they are looking for in terms of psychological and physical satisfactions. As mentioned above, a customer who rushes to a DIY store to fix a burst pipe has a very different mindset from the same person who returns a week later to browse garden furniture.

Most industries have evolved an understanding of the relevance of events, but few companies take advantage of them to architect experiences. Those that do are exceptional performers in the KPMG index. The leading organizations observe how customers are trying to accomplish these jobs from end to end, identify how they define successful completion and then note the barriers and obstacles that get in their way.

Finally, they analyse how these customers are being served with the current array of products and services at their disposal. Are they being underserved? Are the existing products inadequate? If so, then there are opportunities for innovation (KPMG, 2017c).

The industry descriptions of events vary, but there is a common thread – they are all aspects of life, as shown in Tables 2.1 and 2.2.

We have known for a long time that events in people's lives are highly indicative of future behaviour. Increasingly, organizations are focusing on events, moments in a customer's life that create a series of tasks, a 'to do list', or, as Clayton Christensen describes it, 'jobs to be done'

TABLE 2.1   Customer event examples by industry

Industry	Events
Retail	Purchasing occasions
Financial services	Life events (first home, new baby, retirement)
Healthcare	Episodes (incidences of illness)
Insurance	Moments of anxiety (e.g. burglary, car accident)
Asset managers	Critical life decision points (where their customer needs to reconsider how and what they invest in)
Utilities	Seasons, address change (e.g. preparing for winter, moving to a new home)
Telecoms, high-tech	Individual application use occasions

TABLE 2.2   Customer event examples by company

Company	Events
QVC	Mums' 'me time', night out with the girls, birthdays
M&S Food	Evening meal, dine-in meal for two, meal of the day
first direct	Life events, birthdays, anniversary of joining first direct
Premier Inn	Business trip, family weekend away
Lush	Bath time, me time
Netflix	Setting up watching profiles, night in with the lads, family time
Emirates	Business trip, life experience, family adventure
Publix (US)	Evening meal of the day (the ingredients are all placed together and you watch a staff member prepare the meal)

(Christensen et al, 2016). Often, these jobs are to alleviate a problematic situation. Solving these problems is the key to innovation. Great organizations focus on where existing products and services are inadequate, or where the customer needs are underserved, and identify where a new approach creates value for the customer (KPMG, 2017c).

USAA applies a 'jobs to be done' approach to the experiences it creates for customers. Take, for example, its car-buying service, outlined in Table 2.3.

The company's process for dealing with bereavement also follows a 'jobs to be done' format. The death of a family member presents emotional challenges, naturally, but also a range of tasks that need to be completed: 'jobs to be done'. USAA has looked at all these tasks and made conscious decisions as to the jobs it will take on for the customer and those jobs where it

TABLE 2.3   Event and jobs to be done: car purchase

Event	'Jobs to be done'
Buying a car	Decide on car
	Decide when to buy
	Find dealer, negotiate discount
	Fund purchase
	Apply grants or government discounts
	Extend warranty
	Tax
	Insure (reduce premiums when on active service)
	Share on social media

TABLE 2.4   Event and jobs to be done: bereavement

Event	'Jobs to be done'
Bereavement	Notify registrar of births, deaths and marriages
	Stop direct mail
	Stop cold calling
	Inform government
	Notify banks, utilities
	Claim on life insurance
	Pensions and benefits
	Will executorship
	Estate management

will signpost a solution. Underpinning the entire approach is an event guide that provides a systematic route map for the customer to help them manage through the entirety of the event.

The bereavement process is run by a 'Survivor Relationship Team', highly trained and emotionally intelligent individuals who can provide counselling and support during this difficult period (USAA, 2021). Table 2.4 illustrates how USAA helps with the 'jobs to be done', where it draws the line around what the team will do and where they provide a signpost (KPMG, 2017c).

CASE STUDY
Hilton Hotels

Hilton Hotels, looking to launch a new app, examined in the minutest detail the checking-in experience of a business customer. This customer has specific needs arising from an overnight stay to attend a business event. What the company uncovered was a range of needs depending on the customer's circumstances. Focusing on the business customer, it identified the following needs:

- Untypical arrival and departure times yielding a desire to have access to the room outside of the 3 pm check-in, 11 am check-out.
- The need for frequent stayers to manage loyalty points and redemption.
- Often tired after a journey, an unwillingness to spend time in queues at reception.
- A series of additional 'jobs to be done', such as finding the room, organizing a late check-out, booking meals, navigating around the hotel.

The Hilton response was to create an app that completely bypassed the traditional hotel check-in process. The room could be booked online, the status of a room could be checked to see whether it was free before 3 pm or after 11 am, a favourite room could be booked, loyalty points could be accumulated and redeemed. The app provided navigation around the hotel and to the room and, finally, an electronic key to open the door (KPMG, 2017c).

My connections: how I connect to devices, information and each other

The connections that are important to business mainly occur at three levels: first, the psychological connection directly with a brand and its products and services; second, the associations we make *around* the brand; and third, the connections any individual has with their network of influencers.

The first and second are related to an organization's purpose. The third, however, has been amplified exponentially in the digital age. This requires organizations to rethink how they perceive the customer and the customer's value: their value as an influencer may well exceed their value as a consumer.

COVID-19 has had a significant impact on brand loyalty. Market research group Nielsen says that only 8 per cent of the world's consumers now self-identify as brand loyalists (Nielsen, 2019). More digital interactions mediated by search engines and paid-for ads, when coupled with an inherent desire for immediate satisfaction, are disrupting brand loyalty. Similarly, KPMG identifies that 87 per cent of consumers are influenced by others before making a major purchase (KPMG, 2020).

Customers are not only less convinced by brands, we are much more influenced by our social group. Social recognition, the envy of our friends that leads to improvements in self-esteem, have become quantifiably more important than simple product satisfaction. Loyalty to our social connections and a sense of belonging to a social group have become more important than brand loyalty. In short, other people's behaviour matters. Social proof is now a major factor in purchasing decisions.

Customers are no longer passive consumers but nodes within a dynamic network of relationships as they interact with brands, markets and each other. Firms need to understand how these networks reshape the customer's path to purchase and open up new ways to create value with customers.

Instead of thinking of customers as a single set of rows in a CRM or moment-in-time interactions to be managed, we should think of them as a connected network. There is considerable value in understanding the nodes in that network. New groupings of customers, with values-based belief systems and common interests, are redefining how marketing communications should be targeted. Social media platforms actively encourage groupings around a particular interest.

David Rogers of Columbia Business School describes a customer network as the set of all current and potential customers linked to the organization, and to each other, via a set of digital tools and interactions (Rogers, 2013). Customer networks matter because we are all linked through digital devices for communicating, interacting and recommending on an increasingly substantial scale. The formulation of these networks shapes and can even control purchase behaviour and, ultimately, financial performance. Organizations used to achieve success through a mass market model. They could communicate to, but not interact with, individual customers. That has changed with digital tools; now the key to success is to be found in a customer network model where businesses listen to, interact with and innovate based on their network of connected individual customers who participate dynamically and enthusiastically.

My watch: how I balance the constraints of time and finance

Economists have long talked about opportunity cost: the inherent time and money trade-offs we as individuals consider when we make different choices. How much time we have, or think we have, influences how we interact with other people, services and companies. And we're increasingly using technology to automate or accelerate tasks throughout our lives, whether with recurring grocery and household orders or the use of algorithms to curate and help guide us on what to purchase, watch or listen to next.

However, the frenetic pace of life, the exponential increase in choice, the growing sophistication of digital technology and our 'always on' lifestyles have led to a phenomenon called 'time poverty' in which we feel we have less time that is under our individual control. This can influence our behaviour in many ways, leading us to prioritize convenience (click and collect), speed (meal delivery) and ease (a preference for virtual contact over personal).

In addition, we thirst for information, but we want it fed to us like baby food: pureed to its most simple and easy to digest form. Dictated by our circumstances, urgency, immediacy and instant gratification all play a part in shaping our perceptions of time. We favour short periods of intense joy over long periods of moderate happiness.

For the emerging key customer groups, both Generation Z and millennials, a substantive change is taking place. These are macro segments who prefer to invest their time in experiences rather than accumulate money. For example, a major UK retailer is experimenting with a mass market concierge service where everything from interior design, cleaning and gardening to ongoing household maintenance and repair is available at the click of a button. We no longer have time for household chores, it appears.

It is important to understand what customers want to get out of the minutes they invest in specific interactions. Neuroscientist Daniel Kahneman in his book *Thinking, Fast and Slow* (Kahneman, 2011) notes that a 50-minute concert in which the first 48 minutes featured the finest singing with the last 2 minutes of poor singing will be recalled as a less pleasant experience than another concert which featured far less time of fine singing but featured one peak song rendered very well and a great finale. A phenomenon he codified as 'peak end theory'. We explore how organizations should respond to this in Part 2 of this book.

My wallet: how I adjust my share of wallet across life events

To achieve a level of intelligence beyond that offered by traditional demographic models, KPMG research suggests we focus on understanding the relationship between income, consumption, spend mix and accumulated wealth – and, importantly, how this relationship changes for different generations across life stages.

The forces that open and close our wallets are undergoing significant change. While some of the population may have prospered during the pandemic of 2020, the majority didn't. Previous economic shock waves (2008/9 and 2001/2) showed the emergence of a value-based segmentation model, dependent on a consumer's disposable income and their need to protect their families for the future. New segments have emerged which are likely to be with us for some years to come as the impact of the pandemic ravages economies. For many people, products are grouped into categories of necessity (essentials, treats, postponables, expendables) and moderated by their financial attitudes.

While potential earning power and disposable income have long been used in segmentation and in determining customer value, mass adoption of new technologies and the rise of the on-demand economy are transforming the trade-offs we're willing to make across different categories. Many organizations still ascribe to the dated belief that their primary competition is a rival company in the same industry, but, in reality, their true competitors are all the companies fighting for a share of the customer wallet.

The path to purchase

To make sense of the customer journey, it is important to think strategically and to consider the total context (regardless of any preferred framework). This context plays out over time – not the momentary interactions that call scripts, know-your-customer checks and marketing conversion metrics are

TABLE 2.5   Path to purchase optimization

Path to purchase (PTP) stage	New considerations	Delta moments: when the PTP is vulnerable to interception and change
Trigger – activates consumer goals, impelling action	My motivation: • Events that I am exposed to or planning for • My safety and protection • My conscious and subconscious life goals • My values and beliefs • Anticipated problems to solve • Anticipated rewards	1. When my safety and personal wellbeing is assured 2. Predictive analytics – when an event is likely to occur 3. Empathetic ethnography – detailed understanding of customer's life and their day-to-day and life problems 4. Brand values/customer values alignment – customers who will respond to a clear purpose and who share the firm's values
Awareness of possible options that will satisfy goals	My attention: • Salience – my type of product, company • Relevance – link to circumstances, events, wants, problems and needs • Timeliness	1. Communication of purpose 2. Corporate behaviour consistent with purpose 3. Communications timed to match life events
Consideration – decision mediators for assessing alternatives	My connections: • Information • Decision formation and concurrence with relevant social/interest group • Impact on self-esteem	1. Timely communications 2. Education not sales 3. Communications via influencers and targeting relevant social groups 4. The marketing of envy and social proof
Purchase – the dynamic balancing of inhibitors and selection	Time/wallet trade-off and inhibitors: • What can I afford? • Is my time worth more or less in the context of this purchase (do it myself or get someone else)?	1. Purchase point interception – reduce inhibitors 2. Value-based experience 3. Understand competitive forces for wallet share

(continued)

TABLE 2.5 (continued)

Path to purchase (PTP) stage	New considerations	Delta moments: when the PTP is vulnerable to interception and change
Immediate post-purchase reflection	Decision confirmation bias and purchase reinforcers: • Reaction of my social group • Delivered against expectations • Fulfilled my mental use case	1. Post-purchase reinforcement 2. Avoid cognitive dissonance 3. Exceed expectations

optimized for but engagement over hours, weeks or months. The *customer journeys* that describe these interactions are the critical unit of currency and will be explored later in this book as the management tools of successful leaders.

These same customer journeys are also the tapestry on which customer understanding should be woven. This means more than descriptive insights or wall charts. There needs to be a clear process for agreeing actions to be taken by the organization, or, more accurately, people in the organization.

One good example of this is the path to purchase journey – one of the most critical places to understand the customer for almost every enterprise. Like many journeys, it is important to recognize it will be interacting with customer habits that have formed over many years and may be tough to change. To help with this, global marketing research firm Nielsen (Nielsen, 2021) has pinpointed the concept of 'omega rules', the autopilot-like behaviours that so many of us display when making routine and repeated purchases. If you reflect on your most recent supermarket shop and your rapid choice of brands, you will doubtless be experiencing omega rules hard at work.

Alongside this, Neilsen has the concept of 'delta moments' – the specific, often imperceptible, moments in a customer's journey when their pre-programmed behaviour can be interrupted. This often requires new stimuli, which force them to consciously re-evaluate their unconscious intentions.

Combined with a framework of understanding the customer, these concepts of omega rules and delta moments clarify where the organization should act on its insights. Table 2.5 illustrates how the omega rules and delta moments play out along the path to purchase.

KEY TAKEAWAYS

1 The customer is changing: new values, new behaviours and new priorities are having a profound effect on purchasing behaviour. Firms need to be clear on how their customer has changed: their values, their concerns and the impact of life events. This requires new methods of segmentation more focused on circumstance and context than on demographics.

2 The global pandemic has reset how customers perceive firms should engage with the wider social, economic and environmental context. Customers are gravitating towards firms that prize values before profit. We are seeing the emergence of the 'integrity economy'.

3 Customers no longer operate singularly when it comes to purchasing; they are a node in a network. Customer understanding should include their networks, who they influence and who influences them.

4 The path to purchase has to start before the purchase trigger (understanding motivations). It continues long after the purchase is made (being psychologically present in the customer's life).

5 Customers are also employees. It should come as no surprise that the employee experience needs to change so that authentic interactions with customers can emerge. In the next chapter we draw out how the employee experience needs to evolve to keep up with the new customer.

References

Christensen, C., Hall, T., Dillon, K. and Duncan, D. (2016) Know your customers' 'jobs to be done'. *Harvard Business Review*, September.

Christensen, C. M. and Raynor, M. E. (2003) *The Innovator's Solution: Creating and Sustaining Successful Growth.* 18th edn. Boston, MA: Harvard Business School Press.

Girard, J. (2021) The history of Joe Girard. www.joegirard.com/biography/

Horton, D. and Wohl, R. R. (1956) Mass communication and para-social interaction. www.tandfonline.com/doi/abs/10.1080/00332747.1956.11023049?journalCode=upsy20 (archived at https://perma.cc/G2EP-XYHV)

Kahneman, D. (2011) *Thinking, Fast and Slow.* New York: Farrar, Straus and Giroux.

KPMG (2017a) Me, my life, my wallet – first edition. https://advisory.kpmg.us/articles/2017/me-life-wallet.html (archived at https://perma.cc/A4XB-PSR2)

KPMG (2017b) The connected experience imperative. https://assets.kpmg/content/dam/kpmg/br/pdf/2017/11/the-connected-experience-imperative-uk-2017.pdf (archived at https://perma.cc/SQU9-H6BC)

KPMG (2017c) UK customer experience excellence analysis 2017. www.nunwood.com/excellence-centre/publications/uk-cee-analysis/2017-uk-cee-analysis/qvc/ (archived at https://perma.cc/Z9P2-UB44)

KPMG (2020) Responding to consumer trends in the new reality. https://home.kpmg/xx/en/home/insights/2020/06/consumers-and-the-new-reality.html (archived at https://perma.cc/ZWV4-T7M5)

Levitt, T. (1969) *The Marketing Mode: Pathways to Corporate Growth.* New York: McGraw-Hill Book Company.

Mocker, M., Ross, J. W. and Hopkins, C. (2015) How USAA architected its business for life event integration. https://core.ac.uk/download/pdf/35286962.pdf (archived at https://perma.cc/R9FW-3T88)

Nielsen (2019) Consumer disloyalty is the new normal. www.nielsen.com/eu/en/press-releases/2019/consumer-disloyalty-is-the-new-normal/ (archived at https://perma.cc/XAU2-T5FE)

Nielsen (2021) Shopper fundamentals. www.nielsen.com/au/en/landing-pages/shopper-category-fundamentals/ (archived at https://perma.cc/8DUF-565U)

Patel, D. (2017) 5 differences between marketing to millennials vs. Gen Z. www.forbes.com/sites/deeppatel/2017/11/27/5-d%E2%80%8Bifferences-%E2%80%8Bbetween-%E2%80%8Bmarketing-%E2%80%8Bto%E2%80%8B-m%E2%80%8Billennials-v%E2%80%8Bs%E2%80%8B-%E2%80%8Bgen-z/?sh=2f602f762c9f (archived at https://perma.cc/6BXQ-M4NH)

Revlon (2021) Our company, our founders. www.revloninc.com/our-company/our-founders#:~:text=Charles%20Haskell%20Revson%20was%20born,the%20store%20we%20sell%20hope.%E2%80%9D (archived at https://perma.cc/4J9X-ED4A)

Rogers, D. (2013) The network is your customer. www.slideshare.net/DavidRogersBiz/2013-1105-customer-networks (archived at https://perma.cc/C7S9-Y6GT)

USAA (2021) Loss of a loved one. www.usaa.com/my/survivorship?akredirect=true (archived at https://perma.cc/DJ7Y-LRAA)

Ward, M. (2016) What do Prince Charles and Ozzy Osbourne have in common? www.bbc.co.uk/news/technology-37307829 (archived at https://perma.cc/FEL7-J6AZ)

03

Understanding the new employee

The leading brands in the world not only perform well for customers but are typically also outstanding places to work. This is one of the main attributes of organizational excellence: not just solid commercials and deep relationships with customers, but happy, motivated colleagues. These organizations recognize there is an inextricable connection between the experience the employee has day to day and the resulting experience they deliver for customers. While there are outliers, the greatest predictor of customer excellence is employee experience excellence. Job one, then, in improving the customer experience is to start with the employee.

Employee engagement is widely held to make commercial sense. A Gallup study of 23,910 businesses (Ott, 2007) compared the results from those in the top 25 per cent of employee engagement with those in the bottom 25 per cent. Those with engagement scores in the bottom quartile averaged 31–51 per cent higher employee turnover, 51 per cent more inventory shrinkage and 62 per cent more accidents. Those with engagement scores in the top quartile averaged 12 per cent higher customer advocacy, 18 per cent higher productivity and 12 per cent higher profitability (KPMG, 2019).

The same study looked at the earnings per share growth of 89 organizations: those with engagement scores in the top 25 per cent enjoyed growth 2.6 times that of organizations with below-average engagement scores (KPMG, 2019).

There are two influential studies that link employee experience and customer experience. The first is the famous service profit chain (first coined in 1994). The 2008 *Harvard Business Review* article 'Putting the service-profit chain to work' (Heskett et al, 2008) updates the classic model and describes the relationship between profitability, customer loyalty and employee satisfaction, loyalty and productivity. Loyalty arises from customer satisfaction.

Satisfaction is largely influenced by the value of services provided to customers. Value is created by satisfied, loyal and productive employees. Employee satisfaction, in turn, results primarily from high-quality support services and policies that enable employees to deliver results to customers.

It is a seemingly simple connection often paraphrased as 'happy employees lead to happy customers which create happy shareholders'. However, its beguiling simplicity requires a deep understanding of the causal link between customer satisfaction and employee satisfaction in the individual firm.

CASE STUDY
Virgin Money: interview with CEO David Duffy

Happy employees lead to happy customers. It has always been so. It is our role as leaders to ensure we create happy employees and give them the tools they need to be successful. Our culture, represented by day-to-day behaviours, is shaped by the values, critical determinants that guide the employee and the customer experience. These are: heartfelt service (being warm and authentic), insatiable curiosity (keeping on learning), smart disruption (innovative and willing to shake up things that matter), red hot relevance (bold and progressive), straight up (straightforward, build trust) and delightfully surprising (looking for the little things that make a big difference).

This is more than just shaping how we work; we want our employees to live their best lives, to be the best they can be. We are adapting our processes and ways of working to enable this.

The second, a study by David Ulrich, a Professor of Business at the Ross School of Business at Michigan, into the link between employee engagement and business performance, sought to identify a causative effect and quantify the impact each variable has on the other. He conducted research that demonstrates that, for every 10 per cent increase in employee engagement levels, a company's customer service levels go up by 5 per cent and profits by 2 per cent (O'Donovan, 2007).

As well as creating the right environment, the highest-ranked organizations in our research understand a simple truth: employee experiences and customer experiences can be built on the same principles. Curiously, most organizations have organization designs that place responsibility for customer strategy and people strategy in completely different places, with different functions and different vocabularies. While the humans are the same animals, it is the exception rather than the rule that they are treated as equals. At best, this results in a confusion of language, vision and purpose, most often visible through clumsy links between internal values and people strategy to their customer goals. At worst, the organization is cynically seen as practising Orwellian doublespeak: writing ambitious cheques for customers that its failing culture is unable to cash.

Employees are the principal lever for delivering and continuously improving the customer experience. In our global research, it is the brands that master this human truth that outperform – not those with the biggest investment budgets or the most impressive digital agenda. The challenge for companies is ensuring the experiences employees have align with the experiences they want their customers to have: in other words, to design employee experiences with the customer experience outcomes in mind.

Just like the customer, employees are changing radically, too. They are, after all, the same humans, just seen through another lens. The same changes in behaviour, beliefs and values are driving a workforce revolution. The leaders in our research are successfully grappling with this, reconciling advancements in technology, multigenerational workforces and global economics.

Organizations are facing a radically changing context for their workforce and the workplace. Life events are no longer tied to life stage, millennials can be carers as well as boomers, those over 75 are getting married and remarried. The redefinition of life stages affects not just customers but employees, too. COVID-19 has dramatically accelerated working from home, requiring new leadership styles, greater employee trust and new mechanisms for collaborative working. These shifts are changing the rules for almost every organization and impact the way they think about culture and the overall management of change. As such, the roles of managers and leaders are evolving rapidly.

The nature of employees is changing – they are more digital, more global, more diverse, more media savvy and, as such, more connected than ever before. More fundamentally, millennials and members of Gen Z have a quite different view of the role of work in their lives than their forebears (KPMG, 2019). They come into the workplace expecting greater life–work balance and their employer to make a meaningful, distinct difference to the world.

So, what new challenges does today's CEO need to understand and face to create an outstanding employee experience?

- There is an increasingly diverse mix of demographics in the workforce, from millennials and baby boomers to Generation Z. Differences in mindset and values drivers means a segmented approach is needed, as with customers.

- Employees expect their employer to take an active interest in their health. This goes beyond traditional 'do no harm' safety management. It also clearly transcends the physical, with mental health in the face of continuous change becoming an area of corporate concern.

- Purpose is, again, the lifeblood of successful business. Every rule we have discussed previously applies, yet for employees, purpose must have bulletproof authenticity. Expect colleagues to sniff out incoherency and hypocrisy in moments.

- Technology is both connecting and isolating. After decades of wanting more time at home, many employees now yearn for the workplace. Remote working loses a sense of community, spontaneity and meaning that physical colocation creates.

- Employee journeys are the currency of change. Removal of pain points, frustrations and frictions is just as important here as it is for customers. The goal is to create an emotional connection at scale rather than simply administering 'human resources'.

- Silos are no longer an acceptable way of working. Being able to connect cross-functionally is a key skill. T-shaped people, those who have a depth in one skill but a wide experience of how to apply it, are much in demand.

- The expectation of workplace technology is that it is the same standard as consumer technology: beautiful, useful and valuable. Great technology won't make the employee experience, but its absence will certainly prohibit high performance.

- Leadership is evidently key and is discussed below. For leaders, the pressure has never been higher – to be human, accessible, empathetic and authentic, in every forum, while embodying the organization's purpose.

Aligning the employee experience and the customer experience

In a *Harvard Business Review* article, Denise Lee Yohn notes that the most common, and perhaps the greatest, barrier to customer centricity is the lack of a customer-centric (or human-centric) organizational culture (Yohn, 2018a). At most companies, the culture is resolutely product-focused and sales-driven: an unintended and much-neglected consequence of the need to work together to make money. More often than not, customer centricity is followed in name only, leading to the great disconnect between external aspiration and internal reality.

To successfully implement a customer-centric strategy and operating model, a company must have a culture that aligns the internal culture with the external customer. It must have leaders who deliberately cultivate the necessary mindset and values in the employees.

The defining characteristic of each of the leading companies is organizational alignment behind a strong sense of shared customer purpose. At the heart of alignment for the leading organizations is the link between the employee experience and the customer experience. This organizational 'spine' is how every business translates human connection into commercial value. It starts with culture and ends in commerce.

In our work with KPMG, we have referred to this as 'the human equity continuum', shown in Figure 3.1.

As we've discussed, in many organizations responsibility for each of these areas falls in different departments. Culture formally sits with HR or is increasingly centralized in a transformation team. Informally, it is owned by every leader and every unwritten rule within the enterprise. The formal rules for the colleague experience are often set by HR but implemented and subverted in different ways across the organization. Similarly, employee behaviour in the customer-facing parts of the business is driven by rules set by local management. At best, this is like having five engines all pulling in different directions, with leaders shouting at each other in different languages. Each of these links on the 'equity continuum' is an engine of growth, so the result is not only dysfunctionality but also sub-par business performance.

FIGURE 3.1   Human equity continuum

| Company culture | Employee experiences | Employee behaviour | Customer experiences | Customer behaviour | Business outcomes |

Top companies, though, have bridged the gap between great strategy and rigorous execution by focusing on alignment of these engines of value. They have focused on bridging the gaps between the organizational drivers of their business to ensure that all five engines are pulling in the same direction. Similarly, a few have also put in place common principles and ways of talking about human interaction – whether a customer or an employee. (In Part 2 we will examine the Six Pillars, which help every leader understand what these common principles should be.)

At the root of all value is culture: the invisible shaping hand of organizational change or inertia. It has the power to accelerate or subvert change initiatives. In our experience, most companies attempting organizational change find it repeatedly disrupted by cultural constraints. Some brands are famous for it, with a corporate graveyard of CEOs who have tried and failed to tackle the unwritten rules at the heart of the enterprise. The reality is that for many companies, their culture, their organizational mental model of how the world works and how they should participate in it, has been left behind. At best, it is an outdated view of what is needed to compete effectively. At worst, it is full of 'anti-human' ways of working that make for miserable employees and dissatisfied customers. One of the most powerful and brave questions an executive team can ask is: 'Does our culture support or inhibit our strategy?'

From culture comes employee experience. For most businesses, this is not a well-defined or documented concept. This does not stop it existing, however: the employee experience is governed by the mental model the organization holds about the role of employees. Are they to be controlled and managed, or empowered and enabled? Most organizations are still managed and structured in a way Adam Smith, the 18th-century economist famous for his pin factory, would instantly recognize. Silos, functional, departmental, a structure based on the colocation of expertise, not the customer. Leadership models and organizational designs that owe their principles to our great-great-grandparents rather than truly reflecting today's challenges.

It is no surprise that this experience leads to employee behaviour which begets the customer experience and shapes how customers will behave in the future. Employee behaviours are a function of their experience and the culture and are shaped by myriad unwritten rules, the origin of which is often lost in the mists of time but casts a long shadow over how people work together today.

Looking at the world's worst performers in the league tables, there is no shortage of organizations that have spent heavily on the trappings of customer centricity: sophisticated digital platforms, journey mapping and NPS programmes. Most frequently, it is employee behaviour and culture that hold them back: the unwritten rules that constrain the dream of excellence.

A similar constraint is language. Even for businesses that have positive cultures and good colleague experiences, often the way in which they describe the world internally is disconnected from their external strategy with customers. Whether values, vision statements, capability frameworks or beliefs, it is often the case that the internal principles of the business have been built in relative isolation from the external ones. Simply putting them on the same page, with a fresh coat of paint, does little to create an intellectually coherent vision for colleagues or customers.

CASE STUDY
'W' Hotels

'W' Hotels arose from the Starwood Hotels and Resorts innovation laboratory 'Starlab' in 1998. The lab focused on future hotel formats, and, in response to the emergence of a financially well-off younger population, W Hotels was born, a unique lifestyle hotel aimed at a younger, more fashion-conscious traveller. The 'W' stands for 'wow', the experience that is captured in the brand promise 'Whatever whenever'. Every dimension of the guest experience has been designed to appeal to this target customer group.

At the heart of the experience lies the physical surroundings, the staff culture and the brand promise, which combine to create a multisensory experience.

Staff are carefully recruited. When the Boston hotel opened there were 7,000 applicants, leading the local newspaper to remark that it was easier to get into Harvard than get a job at 'W'. Staff are motivated and incentivized to make every experience memorable. They are seen as an almost theatrical troupe there to inspire, to entertain and to transport their customers to a better place. Language and definitions shape cultures. 'W' has developed its own language (especially any words beginning with 'w'– 'whimsical', for example, which shapes the physical experience of the hotel). So staff are called 'talents', uniforms are 'wardrobe' and housekeepers are 'stylists'. Areas of the hotel are also redefined – lobbies are 'living rooms', swimming pools the 'wet' and pool bars the 'wet deck'.

Staff behaviours are rooted in the brand values:

- Flirty: playful without being childish, teasing in a witty and clever way, having fun with guests.
- Insider: in tune with the times, linking guests to events and happenings that play to their sense of self and provide a sense of belonging and being welcomed into the circle of those in the know.
- Escape: where you go to recharge and regain your sense of self and to reconnect with what interests you.

In addition, staff (talents) are selected for their mindset: energetic and vital. Interviewees are expected to be able to recount the times they have wowed guests and explain how they can do that for 'W'. New employees are treated as celebrities, exposed to the paparazzi and shown the experience first-hand that they will be expected to deliver to guests. As 'W' puts it, it is all about feelings and knowing what the feeling is like so they can evoke it in others.

There is a focus on brand moments of truth, the details that make a good experience a great experience. Staff are trained in delivering the 'W' seven secrets of customer service. This starts with listening – active eavesdropping is a key competence, listening to what customers want and need and identifying problems early so they can be resolved. This includes smiling, using the guest's name and going above and beyond whenever an opportunity presents itself. Every detail is examined for brand consistency and ruthlessly executed.

What is interesting is how 'W' has focused on customers who share the organization's values and see themselves reflected in what the chain stands for. This centres on music, design, fashion and being current, delivering what is new on a continual basis.

With industry-leading occupancy rates and market-leading revenue per room, 'W' is both an experience and a commercial success (KPMG, 2017).

The challenge of customer-centric culture

FIGURE 3.2   Human equity continuum

| Company culture | Employee experiences | Employee behaviour | Customer experiences | Customer behaviour | Business outcomes |

In Figure 3.2 we see that the model starts with culture. Leadership and culture are naturally and inextricably linked. A culture of service internally, unsurprisingly, gives rise to a culture of service externally. Conversely, a culture of austerity, or mistrust, gives rise to the same kind of customer experience.

Our leading companies know this. For many of these exemplars, the culture is set by the founder and can live on for as long as that leader is in charge. However, subsequent leader behaviours, both conscious and unconscious, will shape and morph the culture, often in unexpected ways. The best companies in our index are aware of the culture of their business and can sense when nudges or nurturing are required.

Most businesses are not so fortunate. Many are the product of decades of mergers and acquisitions, with all the cultural adhocracy that accompanies this legacy. Unfortunately, most customer experience efforts significantly underestimate the difficulty of changing culture. Because leaders fail to understand what really drives the way people work in their organizations, few companies are successful when it comes to changing culture. There are a number of reasons for this:

- A lack of 'line of sight' from culture to customer experience to rewards. Lots of anecdotally interesting observations, but no intellectual discipline or leadership commitment to linking up the 'engines of growth'. As a result, no business case for change.

- No defined customer goals, vision or articulate account of the organization's purpose, either externally or internally. If a senior executive cannot describe what it should look, sound and feel like to be a customer, then there is no target for the 'to be' culture.

- A lack of real understanding or model of what the culture actually is. Institutionalized leaders and middle managers are desensitized to their environment, with no formal understanding of the 'unwritten cultural rules' that run their business for them.

- A failure to understand the drivers and shapers of culture at sufficient levels of detail so that the invisible norms that reinforce and cement the existing ways of doing things remain potent and resistant to change.

- Leaders lack the long-term incentive or the political support to tackle long-term, hard culture change. As one banking executive recently quipped to us when discussing timescales for customer-centric transformation, 'We will all have different jobs by the time that project is complete.' Focusing on short-term costs or managing risk is a safer, more well-rewarded path in most enterprises.

- Leaders lack the cognitive diversity or emotional capability to take on the 'internal servant' role. As we have discussed above, until very recently executives (predominantly men) have been encouraged to perform well on the unemotive, analytical business disciplines first and foremost.

The organization creates a vision for the desired customer experience that is fundamentally at odds with the character and culture of the organization. As a result, its initiatives fail to produce a noticeable shift in the customers' actual experience.

- Several cultures exist across isolated functions, most commonly a customer-centric 'front office' (of sales/service/marketing), which clashes with a process-centric 'back office' (HR/finance/IT). The disconnect between the two undermines culture and impairs results.
- The right leadership is in place but cultural change lacks a compelling vision or north star. As such, it is reduced to a series of incremental attempts to 'do better' rather than a bold rallying cry for a differentiated employer brand.

These are tough problems to resolve. When the number one company in our US index, USAA, decided it needed to organize around the customer, it had to disempower the teams that previously held sway over organizational thinking, namely the product teams. New cross-functional teams were created that were the custodians of the customer and the experiences needed to maintain the customer relationship. It was the role of these teams to understand the customer and to specify to the product team what products were required. Previously the product team had called the shots and took a very product-centric view of the customer. Now they were more of a factory function, working to specifications that were driven by those closest to the customer (Mocker et al, 2015).

When a UK bank sought to 'restore humanity to banking' it had to tackle the function that had removed it, namely over-zealous compliance teams which had unwittingly turned customer-touching staff into robots through detailed behavioural prescriptions designed to ensure compliance but not to build an emotional connection to the customer. The bank solved this particular dilemma by getting the CMO to chair the compliance committee meetings to ensure the customer was in the room at all times and that the customer impact of the decisions being taken was fully understood.

Elsewhere, top firms from around the world, such as Wegmans in the US, Ocado in the UK and MAIF in France, start with the target customer experience and work backwards. They identify the employee behaviours required, then determine what the employee experience needs to be for those behaviours to naturally emerge, manipulating their cultural levers accordingly. This idea of line of sight is at the heart of human value – the essential link from culture to business results.

Employee experience

In Figure 3.3 we can see that culture shapes the employee experience. We define the colleague experience as 'the employee's rational and emotional reactions to how well their organizational working environment affects their ability to accomplish their goals and satisfy needs important to them'.

As with customers, the company must start by understanding what's important to its employees, what motivates them and what role work plays in their lives. As we've explored above, this means leaders having a natural closeness not only to the new, changed employee who has emerged from the pandemics but also to the different segments that make up their workforce. Recently, companies have paid far more attention to influencing one aspect of the employees' experience – their level of engagement in their work – than to understanding, defining, designing and delivering a holistic and intentional employee experience (Capek, 2011).

High engagement is necessary, but it is not, by itself, sufficient to ensure employees deliver the experience you intend customers to have (Capek, 2011). Typically, the employee experience is the default outcome of multiple different initiatives implemented over time. It is an amalgam of rules and practicality. It is rarely defined, monitored and kept relevant to the changing employee, market or external environment.

FIGURE 3.3 Human equity continuum

Company culture · Employee experiences · Employee behaviour · Customer experiences · Customer behaviour · Business outcomes

Leading companies, however, are embracing the concept of the 'workplace as an experience', where every aspect of work is carefully designed, arranged and controlled to energize and inspire employees to deliver the prescribed customer experience. Why? Because innovation, creativity, passion, commitment and the desire to do great things for the customer start and finish with the employee (KPMG, 2019).

The pressure on employees to perform is considerable. At the nexus of employee and customer interaction lies emotional labour. Modern customer experiences require the frontline employee to act in a way that is not always consistent with how they feel internally. The complexity of delivering a personalized, emotionally connective customer experience while dealing with customers with different needs, wants and personalities requires high degrees of empathy, emotional intelligence and resilience.

The level of emotional intelligence individuals possess can vary widely. That is why leading companies are very focused on the type of person they recruit, their values, motivations and natural ability to care. They support their people with wellbeing and mental support programmes, recognizing that emotional labour brings stresses all of its own (KPMG, 2019). Starbucks, for instance, is among many companies that recognize this increasing mental wear and tear on their employees and provide mental support and wellbeing services free of charge for them.

However, delivering 'emotional labour' and performing well is made many times harder if the internal experience is at odds with the mask each employee is asked to wear in front of customers. To overcome this, organizations are looking at their people through the same lens as they do their customers and applying the same marketing and sales-oriented strategies to improve attraction, motivation and retention. It spans propositions, experiences, journeys and personal growth and manifests itself in a customer-obsessed culture.

They are seeking to create the same deep emotional and experiential connection between individuals and their workplace as they do with customers. It begins with selection, recruitment and onboarding strategies and continues throughout their employment life cycle within the organization, for the ultimate benefit of all stakeholders, especially their customers.

As with customers, good practice in employee experience starts with understanding, but needs to be projected onto a clear tapestry. This is where the concepts of the employee lifecycle and the journeys each of us undertake become particularly useful.

CASE STUDY
Starbucks: segmentation

The leading coffee chain took a customer 'action segmentation' approach to understand what attracted, motivated and retained employees. Based on the results, it found three clusters: 'skiers', who work mainly to support other passions; 'artists', who desire a community-oriented and socially responsible employer; and 'careerists', who want long-term career advancement within the company (Adams, 2021). The clusters helped managers better tailor programmes to multiple sets of employee needs, as well as enabling the company to understand what needs span groups, such as schedule flexibility or tuition assistance (KPMG, 2019).

The employee life cycle and employee journeys

Designing and delivering the intended customer experience cannot be accomplished without understanding the end-to-end employee experience life cycle. This spans attracting and onboarding the right employees to developing their potential, communicating with and managing their efforts, and making efforts to retain them.

Firms looking to establish an emotional connection with their employees need to consider both their working and non-working lives and find a mechanism that links the two. In the same way that life events impact consumer purchasing habits and priorities, so too do they with employees' work needs and requirements. In fact, life events, and how they are managed, become critical moments that matter across the employee life cycle (KPMG, 2019).

In Part 2 we look in detail at what kind of engagement we need to create, understood through the lens of the Six Pillars of Experience. At each stage in the life cycle, as with customers, a different type of emotional connection needs to be emphasized. By using a common language, a singular set of principles, we will see how the worlds of employee and customer can be bridged, helping to align all the 'engines of growth' with common goals and language.

For now, let's take a look at the requirements of managing the employee life cycle and how some of the world's leading firms are responding.

1   **A focus on local empowerment.** Firms are recognizing that great customer service demands employee discretion, enabling those closest to customer problems to make sensible decisions. Consequently, they are having to

become much clearer on what empowerment means for their workforce. This is leading to frameworks that describe what employees can and can't do, greater personal control over how employees perform their role and greater accountability for the outcomes. This in turn requires employees to exercise judgement and to ensure they have the necessary knowledge and experience to make the right judgement. Ritz-Carlton has long been the exemplar of employee empowerment, enabling its employees to spend up to $2,000 to put things right for a customer (Toporek, 2012). Singapore Airlines empowers its frontline crew to make decisions on customer service delivery and take corrective action when customer service recovery is required.

2 **A focus on enablement.** This means ensuring employees have access to the right tools and techniques to move their part of the business forward, using clear methodologies and techniques that enable them to make improvements to processes, services and experiences at point of need. There is continuous feedback from customers as to the relative success of the actions employees take at a local level. Voice-of-the-customer systems are being integrated with voice-of-the-employee processes to bring a 360-degree perspective on customer and employee problems. Apple Store is constantly monitoring customer feedback in the context of the employee experience and the degree to which employees feel enabled to resolve customer issues themselves.

3 **A move from hierarchies to cross-functional teams or networks of employees.** The traditional hierarchy cannot manage the pace of change required to survive. Cross-functional teams have historically been a means of overcoming the limitations of traditional silo structures. General Stanley McChrystal describes the organization of tomorrow as a team of teams (McChrystal, 2015). For firms like Kiwi Bank, USAA and Netflix, cross-functional teams have become the new steady state, by which the day to day is managed. (We'll explore this as one of the principles for the future enterprise in more detail in the next chapter.)

4 **The development of learning cultures.** For most companies, career development is the responsibility of the employee; however, predicting a career path in this new multifunctional, rapidly evolving team-based world is less easy for employees and firms are having to think through how employees grow outside of silos and specialisms. Moving between teams requires an environment where team members can develop the necessary skills quickly and easily. Micro learning packages, ready access to the

latest knowledge and education are being facilitated by technology and advanced learning systems. This is an area that the hospitality industry excels at. Firms such as Taj Hotels, Hilton and Marriott are focused on continuous learning and development, creating an environment where employees learn from each other.

5 **Talent acquisition becomes more scientific.** As machines replace people for certain jobs, the intellectual requirement on employees to deal with the more complex issues means it is no longer about throwing low-cost resources at customer service. It requires employees who share the values of the firm and its customers, have the desire to deliver outstanding customer service internally and externally, and care about the firm and what it does. first direct recruits new employees from the caring professions (KPMG, 2016). Zappos famously relocated from San Francisco to Las Vegas to get access to a large pool of hospitality-trained staff (Hsieh, 2010). Emirates Airlines recruits over 140 different nationalities, yet each recruit needs to be able to convey the Emirates experience (Seal, 2014).

6 **New skills are required.** The skills that distinguish employees at world-leading companies are changing dramatically. No longer 'button pushers', employees need vital cognitive skills such as complex problem solving, critical thinking, systems thinking, creativity and emotional intelligence. These are the skills that are powering firms such as Emirates Airlines to break traditional service boundaries and set new standards in customer service. Emirates employees need to be able to deal with problem solving when faced with flight disruptions, complaining customers, agents who have technical issues or difficulties in reissuing tickets, making manual calculations, quoting fares, monitoring attendance and sickness for the team members, giving coaching as appropriate and providing feedback on their performance (Emirates, 2018).

7 **Professionalism of employee experience design and employee journeys.** Across the life cycle, leaders need to support multiple employee journeys. Some are those also in service to customers, such as onboarding, bereavement or debt management, which require special skills and support for the employee. Others are discrete to the colleague themselves, such as induction or parental leave. In either instance, the best firms approach employees with the same professionalism and rigour that they would adopt when designing customer experiences. This means dedicated teams, a compatible operating model and a way of working that encourages cross-functional collaboration. For instance, Apple Store has defined key

employee missions and designed self-service systems that mirror its approach to customers. Conversely, many in the worst firms inadvertently treat employees merely as resources to be administered, fraught with risks and mistrust, an inconvenient necessity in the pursuit of profit.

8 **Reward, recognition and performance management.** This has moved on within many top firms, from being centred on position and title to rewarding for skills development and performance. We have seen this grow in importance for all employee segments, though it is critical for millennials and members of Gen Z joining the workforce. Ongoing mentoring and coaching, the provision of regular feedback and an organization environment that enables people to be the best will only grow in importance. They will be critical enablers in recruiting, motivating and retaining the new generation of the workforce.

CASE STUDY
first direct

Call centre employees at first direct's Leeds campus have access to a concierge and ironing service. It exists to solve employee problems. first direct describes it as 'looking after the people that look after our customers'. 'Whether you need a parcel sending, your favourite shoes repairing, a prescription picking up or your dry cleaning sorting out, our concierge will be more than happy to help at no extra cost.'

If an agent requires an urgent delivery of nappies, or someone to child sit because they will be late home, the concierge service takes the problem off their hands and leaves them free to concentrate on giving great service to the customer.

CASE STUDY
Octopus

Notably, Octopus Energy was named the 'Best company to work for' in the 2020 UK Employee Experience Awards. It is clear that the organization cares for, and invests in, its employees as much as it does its customers.

An interesting example of this is the recruitment of its Digital Operations (DigiOps) team, a customer-facing remote team working out of hours across all digital platforms, which consists entirely of professional women working from home, the majority of whom are returning to the workforce after having children (KPMG, 2019). This is a group with specific lifestyle needs and requires a new level of flexibility in how those needs might be met. The example is set at the highest level by the CEO, who leaves the office at 3 pm twice a week to do the school run (Clark, 2020).

Director of Operations Jon Paull explains that the Octopus 'model also gives teams a high level of autonomy for serving their customers. As a result, people on the same team are more inclined to work together to resolve complex issues instead of handing problems over the wall to someone else. There is a focus on improving processes. Rather than having standardized processes and procedures, which people often hide behind, and which lead to poor customer outcomes, teams are given the autonomy and scope to challenge and decide how they do things. This keeps the work interesting while allowing the business to innovate and move at pace' (Clark, 2020).

CASE STUDY
Google

Google is consistently ranked as the best company in the world to work for. It strives to treat both its customers and its employees well. It makes the connection between the employee experience and the target customer experience they are seeking to create every day.

Google employees have an enormous amount of freedom and are empowered not just to find the best way to solve problems but to be the best they can be. Google's philosophy is that with the right tools you can attract the best talent and develop happier and more productive employees. Consequently, enablement is critical. The role of managers is to be resources, not bosses.

There is a flat hierarchy, with only such structure as is absolutely necessary. For many years founders Larry Page and Sergei Brin headed a Q&A every Friday. They wanted people to stand up and say if they thought something was wrong.

Team working and collaboration are a way of life. The working environment is designed so that teams can easily combine and work together in the right atmosphere. It is also designed so that people can 'bump into each other' and make their own connections.

Google realizes that in such an environment finding the right career path is not as straightforward as climbing the hierarchy. Google has an 'optimize your career' programme to help people understand how to progress. At the centre of its approach is its hiring process, choosing the right people well, then giving those people the freedom to express themselves. These are people excited and energized by Google's purpose, making information available to everyone.

Finally, the Google culture is very important. Across 70 global locations there are 'culture clubs', teams of local volunteers who strive to ensure Google's culture remains true to itself regardless of the geographic location (Alton, 2021).

Employee behaviours

Figure 3.4 shows the relationship between employee behaviour and customer experience. Creating the right culture and employee experience will establish an environment that naturally gives rise to the right behaviours. It is the foundation of everything that follows. However, there are other steps that business leaders may take to define and propagate excellence. Yet again, this is not about isolated examples of heroism or outstanding service but engineering it into millions of human-to-human interactions, consistently and at scale.

When it comes to exemplary employee behaviour to customers, we should look at the travel and hospitality sectors. They lead the way in managing the process of customer interaction. A process focused on by Jan Carlzon when as CEO of Scandinavian airline company SAS he described every employee–customer interaction as a 'moment of truth' (Hyken, 2016).

FIGURE 3.4   Human equity continuum

| Company culture | Employee experiences | Employee behaviour | Customer experiences | Customer behaviour | Business outcomes |

From Ritz-Carlton to Marriott, from Southwest Airlines to Virgin Atlantic, this industry is a hotbed of excellence. One such exemplar, Singapore Airlines, tops our indices in 5 out of 30 countries. It is how its employees behave that makes the difference versus other airlines.

CASE STUDY
John Lewis theatre training

The John Lewis Partnership (JLP) regularly appears among the leading companies in our UK index. It is a business owned by its employees and it is this collective ownership that inspires its thousands of staff to regularly go above and beyond for its customers. However, great service is not enough on its own; every moment has to be memorable, every interaction needs to count. Unusually, JLP has worked with the National Theatre Company with over 500 of its staff – known as partners – trained by actors in an attempt to help improve their customer service skills. The training sessions cover voice and body language skills, which will help staff when they interact with consumers in store.

This activity recognizes the power of communication and that actors are outstanding communicators, and that is an important element in delivering personal service, where it is not just what you say but how you say it. Body language, visual expression and voice are as important as the words themselves. Ultimately it is about giving staff the confidence to be their authentic selves and to be able to project their ambition for great service (National Theatre, 2018).

CASE STUDY
Delta Airlines

Concert violinist Giora Schmidt arrived late for a Delta Airlines flight to find all of the overhead bins were full and his violin, an Italian antique, could not go in the hold. The Delta flight attendant came up with a novel solution. She asked passengers to create space in an overhead locker and in return Giora would play a concert. Space was found and Giora, to the delight of the passengers, performed Bach's Partita No. 3.

Delta Airlines, commenting to the media, said that this is what happens when you meet a flight attendant whose approach to customer service is based on decency, thoughtfulness and surprise (Scott Clark, 2019).

Recruiting for behaviours

Employee behaviour is a combination of nurture and nature. On the one hand, behaviours are a product of culture, unwritten rules and each colleague's long-term experience with the organization. However, the starting point is the kinds of human being that the brand attracts and retains. How this can be done ranges from the purposeful to the haphazard, with varying levels of emphasis on competency or hard skills versus character or innate behaviours.

The unparalleled success of customer-centric firms such as Southwest Airlines, Zappos and first direct has at its heart the quality and passion of their people. Consequently, those looking to learn from the best have focused on how these companies approach recruitment and how cultural fit and personal values outweigh skills and competencies.

Southwest Airlines was the first company to articulate its recruitment approach as 'hire for attitude, train for skills'. In the UK, first direct describes it similarly: 'We hire for the smile and train for skills' (Taylor, 2011).

The travel and hospitality industry again sets the standard for customer experience, where firms are very clear on the type of person they want to recruit. Leading customer experience airlines such as Air New Zealand, Singapore Airlines and Emirates all have a clear personality blueprint that they recruit against. They want people who have a desire to deliver great service, who approach the world empathetically and have a naturally customer-friendly disposition.

For most companies it is sufficient to test for capability and hard skills, supplemented by an intuitive feeling from the recruiter as to whether the individual will 'fit in'. The leading companies start from the other end of the spectrum, asking whether the individual shares the values of the company, its purpose and ideals. This needs to be more than trivial lip service, but if done well it is a powerful way of ensuring new colleagues add to the culture and experience of the brand.

Ideally, of course, every business wants high levels of skills and competency coupled with appropriate values and cultural fit. However, when faced with medium competency and high cultural fit, the exemplars often choose cultural fit. They recognize that it is much easier to learn specific job duties than to learn how to work well with a team and behave within an organization.

This requires firms to be highly targeted in their recruitment approach, designing the appropriate journeys very intentionally to deliver not only the right experience to their new colleagues but the right long-term culture for the business. In doing this, for many exemplars the defining personality characteristic is empathy. Excellent companies, such as USAA and QVC, have built their customer experience around this. They recognize that the ability to intuit how another is feeling and the emotional intelligence to respond to an individual's psychological needs, as well as their physical or transactional ones, is essential. Empathy is one of the Six Pillars, and, as we will see in Part 2, the hardest to 'train in' if it is absent from the offset.

The employee assessment

So how do the world's best brands recruit for excellence? Each of the firms that perform excellently in our indices globally has a similar recruitment process. This starts with a clear template of what a 'good' employee looks like across multiple dimensions and covers the following aspects.

Cultural fit

How will the individual fit in with how things get done in the firm, the management style and philosophy? Do they subscribe to the vision for the company and want to be part of it? If there is a desire to move towards a different culture, how will the individual fit with the future cultural template and how can they contribute to the cultural transition?

Researchers from Stanford Graduate School of Business and Haas School of Business, University of California, Berkeley have found that, counterintuitively, employees with the best chances of long-term success may have low initial cultural fit but high enculturability – that capacity to change and be flexible. Employees who can evolve with the company's culture and who are comfortable with change are better performers in the long run, presumably in part because they bring more value to the company (Lyons, 2017).

The researchers suggest three enculturability questions to ask potential candidates during the hiring process:

1   To what extent do candidates seek out diverse cultural environments?

2   How rapidly do they adjust to these new environments?

3   How do they balance adapting to the new culture while staying true to themselves?

Cultural fit is critical to recruitment success because it is essential to long-term employee engagement, productivity and retention. Cultural fit or enculturability isn't always immediately obvious and firms are increasingly using psychometric and personality tests to ensure a detailed understanding of the individual to assess their likely success in the organization.

Values

The intangible factors that drive behaviours, the personality of the individual and how they will behave, will be defined by their values. To determine how the individual's values will fit, it is important the organization is clear and consistent on its values and purpose. We have discussed this previously, plus the risk that the organization is a cluster of different values, frameworks and lists of aspirations. To successfully recruit the best, most aligned employees, leaders first need an intellectually coherent framework that describes purpose, internal values and external values, ideally in one place.

Armed with this, the business can recruit accordingly. Understanding an individual's values requires more than just an interview. Increasingly, values-based assessment for both the organization and potential recruits provides predictive analytics which help determine the likelihood that a candidate will fit the role, the team and the organization.

Diversity

Similar values or ideals should not be taken as shorthand for similar people. The organizations that perform the best are the most diverse – the literature here is overwhelming. McKinsey (Hunt et al, 2018) summarizes this neatly: 'We found that companies in the top quartile for gender diversity on their executive teams were 15% more likely to experience above-average profitability than companies in the fourth quartile. Almost exactly three years later, this number rose to 21% and continued to be statistically significant. For ethnic/cultural diversity, the 2014 finding was a 35% likelihood of outperformance.'

When designing recruitment and onboarding processes, it is therefore important that diversity and inclusion are critical design principles. There are multiple dimensions to consider, from gender, age and ethnicity to background and cognitive profile. Again, it is important that leaders consider a personalized approach to employee experience, ensuring their value proposition delivers the right experience for multiple different colleague types.

Competency

This is the ability of the individual to discharge their skills effectively in the workplace. Usually companies test for this by asking situational questions: 'Describe a time when you ... .' Increasingly firms have become adept at separating competence from intelligence. The focus is on interpersonal and communication skills so that the knowledge can be imparted and used effectively within a team. Role plays and assessment centres are now widely used to measure competency. first direct, when recruiting telephone advisers, uses role plays extensively to assess candidates.

Skills

Compared with cultural fit, skill set is easier to define and identify, so consequently firms tend to focus on it in recruitment. Evidence of skills is provided by work experience and qualifications. Many organizations supplement interviews with aptitude, numerical and verbal reasoning tests to get a more rounded view of the individual.

CASE STUDY

Zappos

Zappos, the online shoe and clothing retailer, has a somewhat unusual hiring process. Recruits are carefully selected to fit in socially, intellectually and emotionally. Cultural fit is paramount. It is how quickly recruits are able to assimilate the culture, act in concert with it and ensure that they are contributing to its development.

Potential recruits are assigned a team ambassador whose role is to get a feel for the applicant through a number of different attributes: how they write, how they treat others and, critically, how they behave. Applicants then get the chance to meet with employees in their area of expertise and get a feel for the role and the cultural context within which it sits.

If applicants are given interviews and are not locals, they get a free ride from the airport to the Las Vegas headquarters. In addition to being a convenience, it is a subtle part of the application process. During the ride, the van driver is paying attention to how the applicants carry themselves and treat them, regardless of whether their travel was pleasant or not. After a full day that includes a tour and multiple interviews, a recruiter checks in with the driver to get his or her take.

Former CEO Tony Hsieh said in an interview with *The Wall Street Journal* in 2013, 'It doesn't matter how well the day of interviews went, if our shuttle driver wasn't treated well, then we won't hire that person.'

Being hired is just the first step. After four weeks of training and a week on the job, all new hires are offered payment for their time and a $2,000 bonus if they decide the company is not right for them – around 2–3 per cent of them take the offer (*Wall Street Journal*, 2013).

Communication versus understanding

'If I tell you, you will forget; if I show you, you will remember; if I involve you, you will understand.'

Most businesses make the mistake of telling employees what they expect them to do, then being surprised when the unwritten rules of culture subvert their immaculately organized instructions. Communication is an essential tool in locking in the target experience and behaviours but is often misunderstood and poorly practised.

There is no doubting most organizations' commitment to communication; businesses are striving hard to ensure their people are kept informed. Every manager has a strong view on how communications should be conducted and more tools at their disposal than ever before. But the results of this positive intent have compounded rather than resolved the problem. Employees are subjected to an endless flood of one-way, downward communication. People are communicated *to* rather than *with*.

Communication is above all a two-way process. A process that should enable a genuine discourse between staff and management, which implicitly means that soliciting and acting upon feedback are critical to effective communication. As well as the utilization of feedback, it seems to us that the central immutable obstacle to effective communication is the failure to address the underlying human and psychological dimensions of how understanding is achieved and personal meaning created.

Human beings achieve understanding through discourse and discussion, by listening to and probing other perspectives, and it is through this process that we form the views and attitudes (personal meaning) that guide our behaviours. Our research suggests that the majority of companies have poor employee communications. For many, it is an unintended consequence of a confused vision, leadership remit and priorities, rather than simply a failure of competence. In the customer world, great communication is a prerequisite. If employees do not have the context, they cannot make sensible decisions and judgements when it comes to managing customer interactions. There are a number of facets to the problem:

1 Communication has no north star. There is a lack of external purpose, social vision or target customer experience to tie everything back to, consistently, and in a way that motivates everyone involved.

2 Communication is poorly executed. There is a strong but erroneous belief in many organizations that good managers communicate well anyway. Most do not. This tends to cascade down the hierarchy, with systematic failures among senior executives rippling down the whole enterprise.

3 Communication is not seen as a true process. Therefore the design and measurement rigour that would normally accompany a business process is not present. There are no reliable indicators of the level of understanding achieved or feedback on the actions or behaviours that arise as a result of the communication.

4 Communications are typically 'tell' and 'sell' in format and parent–child in tone. 'This is what we are doing and this is why it is important that you do what we say.'

5 Communication is misleading and perceived as dishonest or inauthentic. There is a tendency towards 'spin', putting an overly positive hue on the subject matter, which results in cynicism and mistrust.

6 Communication is a 'fire and forget' exercise. The electronic age of the intranet is leading to a transfer of responsibility from the communicator, who should be validating that the message has been received and satisfactorily understood, to the individual, who is increasingly expected to ensure that they are up to date with information made available electronically.

7 Communication is a torrent, a cognitive load too great for employees to consume. All of our research respondents complained of being deluged with information. Often it's the same message couched slightly differently delivered through multiple, increasingly high-tech media. The principle seems to be, 'Say it often enough and creatively enough and eventually the message will get through.' The inverse is normally true.

8 Communication is hierarchical and mediated through layers, rather than collaborative and focused on agile problem solving. As Tesla CEO Elon Musk put it, 'Instead of a problem getting solved quickly, where a person in one dept talks to a person in another dept and makes the right thing happen, people are forced to talk to their manager who talks to their manager who talks to the manager in the other dept who talks to someone on his team. This is incredibly dumb' (Bariso, 2021).

Language is the most wonderfully complex tool at business leaders' disposal and so often used with great eloquence when selling, persuading or pitching. Internally, for the reasons listed above, the approach is haphazard at most of the businesses that are failing to deliver excellence.

The strategic role of communications is to ensure shared mental models across the organization, to reinforce purpose and shared vision. It is there to guide everyone to what to achieve and how to collaborate. Employees need to know what management is thinking about, not just what they are doing or intend to do. They expect to share the issues they are considering, what they see as the opportunities and threats, to discuss the plans they are developing and the alternatives they have considered. They seek insights into the rationale that lies behind decisions, the decision-making criteria, customer expectations and how they plan to meet them. It is a high bar, but only then will employees be truly engaged with the business, only then can empowerment take place. Without context, empowerment is like giving the keys of a car to a five-year-old.

Once employees have total context, they feel trusted and engaged. Most importantly, they become a bigger part of the solution and can begin thinking creatively using their frontline knowledge and experience to offer practical solutions to important problems. They can question decisions that don't appear to make sense based on what they understand about the business and its processes. The use of such feedback removes blockages by collecting and acting upon people's input; it removes the irritations and frustrations of not being consulted.

The following case study from a UK-based financial institution is an excellent example of such a mechanism in action and shows how a communication mechanism can be engineered into the fabric of the organization and used as the engine room for change.

CASE STUDY
UK bank

The internal communication and briefing process operates on a monthly cycle. Dates for the briefings are scheduled in diaries months in advance as team meetings. Some 400 managers are involved each month in briefing their teams. Attending the briefings is not optional. The process operates as a cascade and overcomes the usual problems of hierarchical communication through the systematic collection and analysis of feedback. This creates a two-way dialogue that enables the clarification of communications as well as the ability to adapt and modify in response to real-time feedback.

Each month the process commences with the Executive Team creating the input to the process. They start by assessing what they wish to communicate from the discussions and decisions arising from that month's board meetings. They also consider the feedback from the previous month's briefing and anything to which they need to respond. In addition, the briefing encompasses business performance, changes in market conditions, the introduction of new initiatives and the progress of existing ones. The CEO starts the cycle by briefing the immediate senior managers, and so on.

The briefing is formatted to generate discussion. It enables each employee to iterate with the briefing and identify issues and opportunities. Managers are encouraged to have 'localized' the content prior to the briefing so it is meaningful for attendees. The briefings are *facilitated* in that, rather than presenting and answering questions, the team leaders prompt discussion around the input by asking:

- Is there anything here we don't understand?
- What does this mean for us?
- What will we have to do differently as a consequence?
- What opportunities or issues do we foresee?
- How does this change our current priorities?

Because it is part of a team meeting, the team can then plan and schedule their workload and priorities in the context of the business direction.

Team learning is also encouraged by asking what has gone well, or not gone so well, over the previous month: what issues or problems are we facing that we can resolve collectively or feed to teams elsewhere in the organization?

What differentiates this process from team briefing is the systematic collection of feedback. The outputs of the team dialogues are input into an electronic system by the facilitators and a real-time picture is created across the entire organization:

- Did the teams understand the briefing?
- Was it misinterpreted anywhere?
- Are there different levels of understanding created in different areas?
- Have we created any unforeseen problems?
- Where are the pinch points?
- What are the key issues that the business is currently grappling with?

The technology enables this picture to be created at the point of understanding, structuring and assembling the feedback so that it is intelligible and actionable. Separate departmental reports are produced showing the feedback generated elsewhere in the business that is relevant to them and their activities.

This enables the senior team to stay connected with the organization and respond directly to issues and concerns: 'Last month you said ... As a consequence we will ... ' They do not lose touch with the impact of their decisions by quickly moving on to the next priority without checking that the solutions and interventions they have put in place are doing their job effectively.

The understanding process is also used to involve and engage employees around specific issues (e.g. costs, compliance, process improvement, the rollout of major systems). Within seconds the organization can harness the collective thinking power of 5,000 people.

Employee involvement in problem solving

When colleagues are part of a strong culture, have positive experiences and are communicated with (rather than to), they become part of a powerful problem-solving system. For the world leaders in our research, this provides an enormous competitive advantage. They unlock a superhuman potential in their organization, a latency, which enables them to outperform the competition, time and time again. They become a problem-solving organization, each cell motivated to continuously improve performance with a common goal, for the customer and for each other.

One powerful way to lock this in is to automate certain processes of problem-solving communication. This is often called the voice of the employee (VoE) and is best deployed to address issues in both the customer and the employee experience. Traditionally, these systems focus only on the latter, asking, 'How can we make our employees more engaged?' Such approaches have somewhat limited value.

To be truly effective, the voice of the employee needs to go beyond the traditional, annual engagement survey. Creating ongoing conversations around employee experience is important, but it is crucial that this is more than occasional surveys or discrete pools of data. Rather, leaders should consider the range of cutting-edge systems and platforms – from internal social networks to specialist VoE technologies – that will provide the infra-structure to continuously monitor, discuss and manage the experience. These become doubly powerful if the principles that define the employee experi-ence are the same as those used externally with customers (a subject we discussed in Chapter 2).

However, in isolation, the voice of the employee is often a squandered opportunity. In any given organization, the majority of knowledge is implicit rather than explicit. This means the majority of solutions sit in someone's head already – they are just not accessible to management. For any given problem, there is an excellent chance that frontline colleagues know exactly what needs to be done to solve it. They are simply lacking the communica-tions, context or tools to make this possible.

The real power of VoE is to create a problem-solving organization. This means systematically engaging colleagues in a conversation about how things can be improved for customers. It means presenting common customer prob-lems and inviting colleagues to be part of the solution. There is a variety of approaches commonly used for doing this, from 'closed loop' systems through to systems thinking. The technology to support these is now mature and accessible to every business, regardless of size. However, rather than reducing this critical conversation to a process or dashboarding widget, the key is to foster collaboration and innovation around the customer.

One company that has mastered using systematic employee feedback to drive both local and strategic customer decision making is Zara (Budds, 2016). One of the secrets of Zara's success is that it trains and empowers store employees and managers to be particularly sensitive to customer needs and wants and how customers demonstrate them on the shop floor (KPMG, 2019).

Zara empowers its sales staff and store managers to be at the forefront of customer research – they listen intently and note down customer comments, ideas for cuts, fabrics or a new line, and keenly observe new styles that customers are wearing that have the potential to be converted into unique Zara styles; in comparison, traditional daily sales reports do not provide such a dynamic updated picture of the market. Zara designers can get the new products in store within one to two weeks. The Zara growth story is built on two basic rules: 'to give customers what they want' and 'get it to them faster than anyone else'. Employees are instrumental in achieving this.

For Zara, employees are central to the customer solution. They are involved, listened to and invited to contribute their experience, expertise and ideas. The company has put mechanisms in place to have an ongoing conversation with staff, to ensure both the employee and the customer voice are heard (KPMG, 2019).

CASE STUDY
Virgin Atlantic

Many of the Virgin-branded businesses also put employee listening and shared problem solving at the forefront of their business strategy. Virgin Atlantic is one of the strongest proponents, visibly showing how much it values listening to its employees to show that they are valued, listening to their opinions and soliciting their ideas, enabling healthy debates and continuous innovation (Branson, 2015). As a result, it keeps learning and employees feel important and engage with it. This is reflected in a range of outcome measures, from NPS and CX scores to reduced cost of sale and increased retention.

Listening is at the heart of engagement: everyone wants to be seen and heard. It's a minimum requirement of leadership, yet often overlooked for the immense value it can bring, creating a more agile, problem-solving business, on top of it simply being the right thing to do. We see that employees who feel listened to want to reciprocate, they want to do their best because they feel valued and important (KPMG, 2019).

Responsibility for the employee experience

Often, mainly to be provocative, we ask members of the C-suite, 'When was the last time your HR Director, Customer Director, Chief Marketing Officer and Chief Operations Officer got together to agree the customer experience and the employee experience that is needed to deliver it?'

It is surprising how often the answer is 'never'. In most instances, no three of the above group have ever been in such a meeting together. Similarly, there tends to be an awkward embarrassment that each of their domains are not only disconnected but administered using different principles, language and theories of human behaviour. There is a shuffling of feet and wringing of hands as this awkward truth is discretely brushed away as a reality of corporate life. However, this wholly unnecessary disconnect prevents so many enterprises from achieving their true potential.

If the employee experience is to be designed in a way that delivers a defined customer experience, then a new working covenant is required between these roles. Indeed, the whole enterprise needs to be connected up in a new and more customer-centric way. The employee experience and customer experience can provide this connectivity, creating a golden thread that extends from the front to the back office.

As we've discussed before, there is a value chain, a 'human equity continuum', that links up the world's most successful businesses. When each element of the chain is managed by a different silo within the organization, the net result is that no one manages the end-to-end. Each individual department pursues its own agenda, on its own terms, using its own language, data, technology and models. If it all connects up, it is accidental rather than co-ordinated. It is analogous to having separate engines pulling in different directions. However, for organizations that are able to make the engines work in unison, there is a dramatic impact on employee, customer and commercial performance (KPMG, 2019).

Some organizations already recognize that this 'connected experience' is the key to success. Businesses such as Pizza Hut and John Lewis & Partners have combined certain executive responsibilities to enable this. Others have formed customer committees and working groups.

Another leader, Airbnb, has evolved its HR department and created a dedicated team to 'drive the company's health and happiness' (Sapling, 2021). This new Employee Experience department brings workplace culture to the fore, alongside traditional functions like recruitment and talent. It covers a far wider range of activities and responsibilities than its HR predecessor. From food to internal communications via innovations in the workplace environment, Airbnb is aiming to enhance the global sense of community on which it is founded by extending that within its own premises (Sapling, 2021).

Adobe established a team called Customer and Employee Experience that 'combines our customer experience organization – the people who are on the front lines of helping our customers utilise our products – with our human resources'. It works on the basis that all people want the same fundamentals, whether they are a customer or an employee (Yohn, 2018b).

KEY TAKEAWAYS

1   These progressive businesses recognize that the key to success is not merely understanding their employees or customers but using experience to create connections. Doing so creates high-performance, agile businesses. This is one of the foundational traits of the kind of enterprise leaders need to build to thrive in tomorrow's market.

2   The link between employee experience and customer experience is a profound one and is rooted in organizational culture. Employees and customers are not separate groups – their experience and journeys are similar and overlapping.

3   Servant leadership puts the employee at the centre of the customer relationship and focuses on equipping, enabling and empowering employees to make the relationship a success.

4   Responsibility for the employee experience does not lie with HR exclusively; it needs to be a function of collective organizational thinking.

References

Adams, L. (2021) Create my employee experience. https://disruptivehr.com/create-my-employee-experience/#:~:text=Tailoring%20talent%20management%20at%20Starbucks&text=They%20found%20three%20clusters%3A%20E2%80%9Cskiers,want%20long%2Dterm%20career%20advancement (archived at https://perma.cc/44Q3-KRQU)

Alton, L. (2021) Employee perks and benefits: insights from how Google approaches HCM. www.adp.com/spark/articles/2018/12/employee-perks-and-benefits-insights-from-how-google-approaches-hcm.aspx (archived at https://perma.cc/C94P-5K8R)

Bariso, J. (2021) This email from Elon Musk to Tesla employees describes what great communication looks like. www.inc.com/justin-bariso/this-email-from-elon-musk-to-tesla-employees-descr.html (archived at https://perma.cc/2MAF-V37M)

Branson, R. (2015) Listen to your employees' ideas. www.virgin.com/branson-family/richard-branson-blog/listen-to-your-employees-ideas (archived at https://perma.cc/8KCJ-FYR6)

Budds, D. (2016) The secret behind Zara's warp speed fashion: its store managers. www.fastcompany.com/3066272/the-secret-behind-zaras-warp-speed-fashion-its-store-managers (archived at https://perma.cc/UP9P-ANXV)

Capek, F. W. (2011) Getting the employee experience right. https://customerinnovations.files.wordpress.com/2011/05/ci-getting-the-employee-experience-right-20111.pdf (archived at https://perma.cc/X5WX-ZUJ6)

Clark, N. (2020) Power & utilities, retail: interview with John Paull. www.bcg.com/en-gb/publications/2020/interview-with-octopus-energy-jon-paull-on-cutting-edge-customer-service (archived at https://perma.cc/YWG5-GMCD)

Emirates (2018) Emirates Group careers. https://ae.indeed.com/cmp/The-Emirates-Group/reviews?fcountry=ALL&fjobtitle=Team+Leader (archived at https://perma.cc/EC99-U44V)

Heskett, J., Jones, T., Loveman, G., Sasser, Jr, W. E. and Schlesinger, L. (2008) Putting the service-profit chain to work. https://hbr.org/2008/07/putting-the-service-profit-chain-to-work (archived at https://perma.cc/D247-3XLG)

Hsieh, T. (2010) How I did it: Zappos's CEO on going to extremes for customers. https://hbr.org/2010/07/how-i-did-it-zappos-ceo-on-going-to-extremes-for-customers#:~:text=In%20search%20of%20high%2Dcaliber,to%20Las%20Vegas%20in%202004 (archived at https://perma.cc/NMT6-UZQT)

Hunt, V., Prince, S., Dixon-Fyle, S. and Yee, L. (2018) Delivering through diversity. www.ucl.ac.uk/human-resources/sites/human-resources/files/mckinsey_-_delivering-through-diversity_full-report_0.pdf (archived at https://perma.cc/Q4RL-GC8Z)

Hyken, S. (2016) The new moment of truth in business. www.forbes.com/sites/shephyken/2016/04/09/new-moment-of-truth-in-business/?sh=2f06021238d9 (archived at https://perma.cc/GTG5-2RUW)

KPMG (2016) Interview with a CX leader. www.nunwood.com/excellence-centre/blog/2016/interview-with-a-cx-leader-tracy-garrad-chief-executive-first-direct/ (archived at https://perma.cc/VZ7X-LQHH)

KPMG (2017) Engineering a human touch into a digital future. https://assets.kpmg/content/dam/kpmg/uk/pdf/2017/05/US-customer-experience-excellence-analysis-report.pdf (archived at https://perma.cc/FS9P-TKYV)

KPMG (2019) Power to the people. https://assets.kpmg/content/dam/kpmg/uk/pdf/2019/06/power-to-the-people-2019-uk-customer-experience-excellence-analysis.pdf (archived at https://perma.cc/VAL4-ET38)

Kruse, K. (2015) How Chick-fil-A created a culture that lasts. www.forbes.com/sites/kevinkruse/2015/12/08/how-chick-fil-a-created-a-culture-that-lasts/?sh=724f7e633602 (archived at https://perma.cc/WLY2-7MP2)

Lyons, R. (2017) Lose those cultural fit tests: instead screen new hires for 'enculturability'. www.forbes.com/sites/richlyons/2017/06/07/lose-those-cultural-fit-tests-instead-screen-new-hires-for-enculturability/?sh=52ed474063a8 (archived at https://perma.cc/527S-UT7K)

McChrystal, G. (2015) *Team of Teams: New Rules of Engagement for a Complex World*. London: Portfolio Penguin.

Mocker, M., Ross, J. W. and Hopkins, C. (2015) How USAA architected its business for life event integration. https://core.ac.uk/download/pdf/35286962. pdf (archived at https://perma.cc/VL7D-Z4PU)

National Theatre (2018) Theatreworks: creating the ultimate John Lewis and Partners experience. www.nationaltheatre.org.uk/blog/theatreworks-creating-ultimate-john-lewis-and-partners-experience (archived at https://perma.cc/SG27-Z5SS)

O'Donovan, D. (2007) The impact of benefits on business performance

Ott, B. (2007) Investors, take note: engagement boosts earnings. https://news.gallup.com/businessjournal/27799/investors-take-note-engagement-boosts-earnings.aspx#2 (archived at https://perma.cc/QY9N-MWHZ)

Sapling (2021) Companies leading the future of employee experience. www.saplinghr.com/blog/companies-leading-employee-experience (archived at https://perma.cc/Z92M-REF8)

Scott Clark, J. (2019) Delta flyer earns overhead bin space with inflight violin concert. https://thepointsguy.co.uk/news/delta-flyer-earns-overhead-bin-space-with-inflight-violin-concert/ (archived at https://perma.cc/VN4K-QCYZ)

Seal, M. (2014) Emirates Airlines: among the best. www.cirpac.com/emirates-airlines-among-the-best/ (archived at https://perma.cc/8M2Y-4Y3K)

Taylor, B. (2011) Hire for attitude, train for skill. https://hbr.org/2011/02/hire-for-attitude-train-for-sk (archived at https://perma.cc/ESD9-R4RE)

Toporek, A. (2012) The Ritz-Carlton's famous $2,000 rule. https://customersthatstick.com/blog/customer-loyalty/the-ritz-carltons-famous-2000-rule/ (archived at https://perma.cc/R29Z-WFGP)

Wall Street Journal (2013) CEO Zappos. www.wsj.com/video/story-of-the-week-zappos-ceo-tony-hsieh/27FDAFB3-1A1B-484F-8870-BBD390165C49.html#!27FDAFB3-1A1B-484F-8870-BBD390165C49 (archived at https://perma.cc/HAC2-6VMQ)

Yohn, L. D. (2018a) 6 ways to build a customer-centric culture. https://hbr.org/2018/10/6-ways-to-build-a-customer-centric-culture (archived at https://perma.cc/FR3J-3AGM)

Yohn, L. D. (2018b) Fuse customer experience and employee experience to drive your growth. www.forbes.com/sites/deniselyohn/2018/03/06/fuse-customer-experience-and-employee-experience-to-drive-your-growth/?sh=65abde6742e9 (archived at https://perma.cc/R9T4-GBTA)

04

The new enterprise

The Canadian Prime Minister Justin Trudeau made the prescient observation at Davos 2018 that the pace of change has never been so fast, yet it would never be this slow again (World Economic Forum, 2018). We live in a world of rapidly increasing complexity, which demands that firms must speed up their response to external change through an internal structure that is both flexible and adaptive.

Those businesses that subsequently thrived through the pandemics of 2020 were not the largest, nor the most established, but the most adaptive to change. It was the consumer-packaged goods firms that implemented digital direct channels overnight. The restaurants that became meal-box start-ups to maintain liquidity. The supermarkets that scaled their operations and rewrote their category rule books. The banks that leapt to the defence of the medically and financially vulnerable. The fashion businesses that repurposed their production lines to support healthcare workers.

Interestingly, from our global research, it was predominantly those brands already leading the field for experience, those topping the national indexes, that adapted most readily. It was those that best understood their humans – their customers and employees – that were quickest to react. Those that had the clearest purpose that were most decisive in the face of adversity.

We have already discussed the foundations of these firms' successes in understanding the customer and employee. We've looked at the need to connect experiences in order to unlock human value, to create a continuum that runs through the whole business, linking culture to business results.

These principles need to be implemented in a new kind of enterprise. One that is customer centric and connected around experience; digital, but human. Such enterprises are fiendishly complex to transform, so this chapter looks at that wider challenge: how do we define the enterprise of the future? What kind of organization must leaders aspire to lead to make our principles possible? And what are the pitfalls en route?

Defining the problem

Management theorist Peter Drucker noted that the problems that companies had when facing market turbulence were not only structural but to do with mindset also. The biggest danger was to respond to the turbulence using yesterday's logic. He observed that what worked in previous years was no indicator of what would work on today's problems (McConnell, 2020). Yet for most executives, previous experience is all they have to go on. Data and insight, as we have seen, are seldom used in the face of gut instinct and experience. But if that experience is no longer relevant, what does that mean for firms in responding to the social, technological and economic challenges of the future?

Mindset is a function of the structure that we work within. The problem is that most large companies are traditionally organized and focus on hierarchical structures, just like those of a military or industrial past. These clearly determine who is responsible for which tasks and what powers they have. They teach people how to think about collaboration and what their focus should be. Unsurprisingly, they also hinder the very flexibility and speed required to respond to the new customer. They inhibit the best employee experiences.

We live in an age of connectivity. Our customers are connected and expect a seamless experience. But our companies are not. Few firms are positioned to take advantage of the vast advances in technology, their numerous 'digital transformations' frequently mirroring the human disfunction at the heart of their operations.

The reason? We have looked at purpose, leadership, culture and a lack of connection with employee experiences and culture. But all of these factors operate within the design of the enterprise as a whole. One of the greatest constraints facing most businesses is a basic organizational infrastructure that is disconnected, rigid and slow moving. This is followed in a close second by outdated capabilities, a lack of expertise of competency in the core requirements of a truly future-ready business.

This is reflected in survival rates. The average life of a Fortune 500 company was 60 years in the 1950s; today it is 16 years (Sheetz, 2017), with technology as the single most disruptive force, and in fact certain sectors are being hit with multiple disruptive forces simultaneously. Firms that aren't adaptable and responsive, it would appear, die young.

At the very heart of the disconnection issue is how firms are organized – it affects how they think, how they operate, and is the root cause of inconsistency in experience delivery.

Organizing for the journey

Looking at leading businesses in our global research, one of the greatest determinants of consistent excellence is the design of the organization itself. The doyen of the quality movement, W. Edwards Deming, noted that a bad system will overcome the efforts of even highly motivated people on every occasion (Deming Institute, 1939). Misaligned organization structures are a bad system.

Organization design for many companies is an organic outcome, accreted or evolved over time, not an input to transformation. How the business is set up is a function of history, of mergers and management changes, or restructures and turf wars. The default aggregation of numerous forums, steering groups and processes that have grown incrementally over time.

Across the world we have seen growing awareness among firms that the functional structure and cross-functional journeys are an inefficient combination. It drives duplication and inefficiencies that ultimately impact both the customer and the cost base. It is these same customer journeys – with the happy paths that allow customers and employees to perform at their best – that represent the most effective ways to deliver results.

We are more frequently seeing new organization structures being developed that eschew the traditional forms of organization design and instead are arranged around the customer. When it comes to high-quality experiences for both employees and customers, this increasingly requires the fusion of employee and customer journey around critical customer and employee needs.

New entrants are unencumbered by the tendency to hang onto design models from the past. Companies such as Spotify and ING have created organization design models that are well adapted for the challenges faced by present-day businesses, but traditional companies still wedded to the models of yesteryear find their responsiveness to market change dulled and ineffective.

Great design means that something is structured in such a way that it allows it to serve its purpose well. Form follows function and structure follows strategy. The question becomes what the optimum design for the organization is to discharge its purpose and its strategy. The effective organizations of today that will still be around tomorrow are those that are able to achieve escape velocity from the ways of the past. This requires more than casual restructuring where new designs are mounted on the power structures of the past; it demands dismantling historical power structures and establishing new ones. In short, to achieve escape velocity you need to disempower the parts of the organization that sustain the old ways and empower new areas that meet the customer needs of tomorrow.

As mentioned in Chapter 3, USAA had to disempower the organizational power structures of the past, which were largely the product areas, and empower the customer-touching teams of today, the member experience teams. However, the organization needs controls to prevent itself from harm, the type of harm that can be destructive. W. L. Gore described the need to empower employees up to the point where decisions were below the waterline and could sink the entire ship (Gore, 2021).

The design principle here is that as much autonomy as possible should be given to those closest to the customer (functions such as sales and account management, contact centre and retail environments) while the ability to control for below-the-waterline risks (functions like accounting, legal and HR) should be as centralized as possible. This design principle recognizes that inherent conflict, plans for it and creates a structure that attempts to harness it for the overall good of the organization. However, the reality is that most organizations are still functional hierarchies. Flattened hierarchies in some cases, but hierarchies nonetheless. Hierarchies are the antithesis of connection, of customer journeys. Hierarchies are designed to manage steady states, to keep the engines of growth separated, running smoothly just the way they are. A stable model designed for more stable times that ensures the same thing happens over and over again.

About a third of firms in our research have moved to matrix structures, with customer journey owners and journey steering groups set up as new, cross-functional models. A more progressive, connected model grafted onto a traditional design. For some, this has been done to provide a transition state, a catalyst for further change. For others, it has been political and cultural – further change would just be too much and too disruptive. The reality is that firms have found these halfway houses complex to manage and over time equally as inflexible as the hierarchy they are designed to improve (KPMG, 2017).

More radically, our research in the US revealed that about 30 per cent of the Fortune 500 have now moved to customer-centric operating models. For some this involved structuring around customer needs groups, for others around customer segments, but each of these transformations required a root-and-branch reappraisal as to how the organization structured itself to get closer to the customer. The consequence has been dramatic improvements in the ideas and innovations that cement customer relationships. These companies have learned how to transform good ideas into customer benefits faster than their competitors can (KPMG, 2017).

This has not been without its pain or done without financial impact. Indeed, many of these firms saw profits fall in the first year and sometimes the second year and then recover well above where they were previously tracking in future years (Lee et al, 2015).

Pitfalls and constraints

Before looking in more detail at the characteristics of these new, customer-centric models, it is useful to look at what gets in the way of change. If better models are so well defined, so well case studied, then what is it that prevents firms adopting them? What constrains the traditional, disconnected organization and prevents its evolution?

This is sadly a long list. Across our global research, it is notable that all excellent businesses are excellent in remarkably similar ways. We see the outcome of this excellence is Part 2 when we look at the Six Pillars. However, we also see that all failing organizations fail in slightly different ways. The disfunctions of not being customer centric lead to a wide set of constraints, pain points and performance shortfalls.

The problem facing most businesses in achieving excellence is that there are many more routes to failure than there are to success. What has worked in the past is not an indicator of future success. So, if previous experience is no longer relevant, how should leaders progress?

We all know the numbers: 70 per cent of corporate change programmes fail to meet their objectives (Percy, 2019). For the organization to be world class, leaders need to understand and mitigate the reasons for failure. Step one of any customer-oriented programme must be to identify and design out the potential obstacles in order to create a bulletproof change plan.

Failure point number 1: the customer isn't important enough

Earlier in this chapter we referred to an observation from the sagacious Peter Drucker. He also observed that 'the purpose of a business is to create and keep a customer' (Trout, 2017). So, if that is what a business, at its most fundamental, exists to do, how much time do the senior team devote to thinking about the customer? It is a question we often ask and we are usually horrified by the answer. It is invariably almost none.

Yet as we have seen, what drives success is understanding customers' problems and solving them innovatively. So why are the senior team not devoting time to the process of developing great experiences, understanding customers and driving innovation? These custodians of the firm's relationships with its customers are fully occupied dealing with finance, risk, operations, sales, legal issues and administering human resources. It is no good expecting your company to do great things for customers if you do not lead the way. The firm will mimic your behaviour, and people will only do what you inspect.

Only when the customer is important to the leadership and each member of the leadership team is aligned around a clear vision of the customer and the experience necessary to keep them will progress be made. It is critical to recognize and resolve true misalignment issues early and eradicate them. Often leadership team members have different objectives and fundamentally different views. Organizational misalignment starts at the top and is magnified through the firm. Clear visioning on the desired future, the route map to success and the priorities is essential.

Failure point number 2: the organization is not clear on what good looks like

The second common failure point relates to the fact that it is difficult to exceed customer expectations if you don't understand them. It is also difficult to ensure every experience exudes the brand if you don't have a clear vision of what the target experience needs to look like. Staff need to know what psychological and physical buttons to press – the exact nature of the emotional connection that defines great human relationships. Leading organizations have clear target experiences that they can train employees to deliver and measure how successful they are.

Many businesses have taken a reductive approach to customer emotion, boiling it down to customer satisfaction, net promoter or effort scores. They reduce the total spectrum of human feelings to a metric on a dashboard, then wonder why the firm is not engaging. For example, Home Depot in the US has a segmented approach which links a target experience to each of its target markets (Soni, 2015). These include do-it-yourself customers such as homeowners. These customers buy products and install them themselves using online or in-store resources. They often require 'how to' support. Do-it-for-me customers include those looking for third parties to provide installation services. Home Depot offers several installation services, including for flooring, cabinets, countertops, water heaters and sheds. The company also provides in-house consulting and installation services. Professional customers include contractors, builders, traders, interior designers and renovators (Soni, 2015). These are in effect small businesses and need to be treated accordingly. Home Depot staff are trained to spot which category a customer falls into and to deliver the appropriate experience.

Failure point number 3: failing to see the organization as an organic system

Few organizations are structured in a way whereby they can take a holistic view of the customer and match that against how the organization needs to operate across all dimensions to deliver an exceptional experience. Silos are the natural enemy of customer thinking and a key reason for the failure of customer journeys to make a meaningful difference. This means that all the component parts of the organization need to interlock, often in new and radical ways.

Imagine that all the different parts of your organization are like pieces of a jigsaw puzzle. Tip the box and the pieces fall out in front of you. All the different parts are present, but the picture is fractured, opaque and incoherent. For the true picture to emerge requires that all the pieces are interlocked in exactly the right order and sequence. As it is with our jigsaw puzzle, so it is with most businesses – the pieces of the corporate jigsaw are assembled in a haphazard, evolutionary way. Each department shapes its own piece of the puzzle, usually with the best of intentions, and makes its own connections to the other pieces. The resultant design makes sense to every piece individually but does not lead to a coherent picture overall.

Culture is often central to the problem. Few organizations stop and ask whether their culture will accelerate or inhibit the achievement of the strategy. Culture shapes how an organization thinks, acts and works. To paraphrase Socrates, the unexamined culture is not worth living in. The leading companies take enormous care over their culture, it is constantly under examination and is gently nurtured to be ever more effective. The culture determines the employees' experience, which in turn determines how they behave with the customer. Are employees focused on the customer, are they enabled, empowered and engaged? Leaders own the culture; it is a critical element of the roadmap.

Failure point number 4: starting in the wrong place

Most businesses have focused on customer journey mapping, a powerful technique. But this is like building the roof of a house before sinking the foundations – you are left with a nice roof, on the ground.

Often, when engaged to conduct journey mapping, we have to encourage our clients to swim upstream first and formulate their customer experience strategy. What is the purpose of the organization, which customers are they seeking to serve, what is the target experience they are seeking to deliver that brings alive their brand values and design principles that will ensure cohesion and integration of the brand experience across touchpoints? In many cases, the focus has been on product journeys, for example the mortgage journey (product) rather than making a home (customer journey). Defining a journey in product terms misses the point and stultifies innovation and opportunities to wow the customer through the thoughtful design of solutions to life problems.

Focusing on journeys is particularly difficult if the organization is incapable of making decisions rapidly and moving at pace. Jeff Bezos, CEO of Amazon, describes the need for companies to be able to perform 'high velocity decision making', being capable of reacting quickly and authoritatively to opportunities and threats alike (Larson, 2018).

In fact, few businesses examine how they take decisions; for many it is a ponderous, hierarchical and often lengthy affair. The result is that customer initiatives drag on and eventually run out of steam. Bezos describes Day 1 companies that have retained their day one start-up mentality and Day 2 companies that make high-quality decisions but make them slowly. By which time the opportunity has often passed (Forbes, 2016).

The increasing adoption of agile working requires decision making to be rapid. Creating an environment where decisions around the customer can be taken quickly and effortlessly is job 1. For some organizations this requires careful governance, for others it requires delegation and empowerment.

Failure point number 5: a lack of customer insight or foresight

As we mentioned earlier, MRS research found that, only 11 per cent of customer-impacting decisions taken at a senior level are backed by insight on the customer (MRS, 2016). That means that nearly 90 per cent of decisions are guesswork. No wonder firms can appear so out of touch with their customers. There are several reasons for this:

- **Poor insight – remote from customer:** It is only through the voice of the customer that organizations can successfully monitor execution quality and drive ongoing continuous journey improvement. Increasingly, as organizations design new journeys it is critical to understand how the changes are being received by customers. A continuous stream of customer feedback is the necessary driver of improvement. A failure to listen to the voice of the customer leads to inconsistencies and poor experiences.

- **Customer insight does not fuel decision making:** The voice of the customer needs to drive decision making and strategizing. Great organizations practise customer 'surround sound', where the voice of the customer not only feeds into the governance and decision-making structures of the enterprise but also consciously shapes how people around the business think and perceive the customer.

- **Fragmented view of the customer:** Customer surveys alone no longer provide sufficient detail to create accurate, evidence-based business cases for change. Increasingly it is how well the organization harnesses an insights ecosystem that governs the success of a voice-of-the-customer programme. All the information sources available about the customer – internal, external, big data and social media – are all inputs into the single view of the customer (KPMG, 2017).

Failure point number 6: a failure to innovate

The quality of ideas that a business generates is given scant, if any, attention. The processes of thinking about the customer are as important as the underlying business or transaction processes. The quality of the ideas a firm generates is a function of its closeness to the customer and the quality of its thinking and conversations, in corridors, by water coolers and in meetings.

Our brains prefer to work by means of connections, connecting ideas and concepts to form new ones. Unfortunately, modern organizational life has led to mechanical thinking, meaning that we are ruled by habits, automatic departmental associations and historic responses. Getting stuck in fixed patterns of thought leads us to make fewer and fewer connections and as a result firms are being left behind by start-ups and digital tech firms unencumbered by the past.

It is the quality of their customer ideas that has propelled organizations such as USAA, Amazon, first direct and QVC to the top of our tables. However, few businesses are structured in a way that facilitates integrated holistic thinking about the customer and their needs. In fact, in most organizations, good ideas around the customer rarely see the light of day. Firms simply reinvent what has worked in the past because internally it is safer to do so. But this safety is illusory as rising expectations mean what has worked in the past is no longer good enough (KPMG, 2017).

Failure point number 7: a failure to understand the rewards of success

Customer experience economics is not understood, the ROI of customer experience is not well understood. Firms are unable to determine the value that will be delivered commercially from improving the experience. Consequently, the CFO is not engaged or supportive of customer experience.

The removal of negative experiences is worth more than driving great experiences. Many companies use NPS. The methodology asks customers whether they would recommend the company to others. It divides responses on an 11-point questionnaire into three categories: Detractors (who score the experience 0–6), Passives (who the experience 7–8) and Promoters (score the experience 9–10). It is often the case that firms pursue great experiences believing that moving Passives, those who are neither negative nor positive, to Promoters will be more financially beneficial; however, numerous studies, including our own, have discovered that removing Detractors is more financially advantageous than creating promoters (Marsden et al, 2005).

Customer centricity is not linked to cost. The typical mistake many customer professionals make is only to attempt to link their investments to some future growth metric, be it retention, acquisition or lifetime value. Regardless of the accuracy of the model (and we have seen numerous very good ones), for most business leaders future growth is abstract while cost is certain. The best models start with the drivers of cost – whether the size of the (often bloated) change portfolio, cost to serve or failure demand. All of these can be positively and rapidly influenced by customer centricity, something we will examine in Part 3 of this book. By doing this, rewards can be made more tangible and immediate.

Failure point number 8: lack of joined-up, modern and digital capabilities

Aligning the business to the customer is perhaps the hardest yet most profound step that a transformational leader can take. However, alongside this the business needs to have the right capabilities – the essential skills of commerce in the modern world. These span the full spectrum of business disciplines, from supply chain and finance to talent and operations. Each of these capabilities has a significant digital component – the best businesses in our research have long since moved away from having separate digital departments, 'garages' or functions. Importantly, unlike the functions of old, absolute clarity on the target customer and employee experience acts as a golden thread joining up these capabilities.

The journey to organizational excellence

In overcoming these points of failure, we have observed that there are potentially as many as five steps that organizations migrate through on their way to customer-centric maturity. Steps 1–3 leave the original hierarchical structure in place, while step 4 refines it into a new way of working and step 5 completely restructures the organization around the customer. The reality is that it is very difficult to go straight to the endpoint. Most organizations move through one or more of the following phases.

1 Individual journey owner

Step one for many companies having defined the organization's journey is to put a single individual in matrix charge of the journey end to end while leaving the reporting structure of the business unchanged.

While this is a useful first step in getting journey recognition across the organization, it has often proved to be an immensely difficult role for the individual concerned. It requires the diplomatic skills of Kissinger, the influencing skills of Nelson Mandela and the judgement skills of Solomon. It is rare to find one individual with all these traits. Navigating the different departmental agendas, inter-hierarchical politics and personal motivations is a hugely difficult task. Unless the individual has line authority over the participating members, there are few if any examples of success.

One of our banking clients gave the example of how the journey owner of the current account process was unable to stop the mail department deciding to change its mail classification because it saved it £500,000 per annum. The result was that debit cards delivery now took 10 days rather than two. The consequential impact on the call centre was huge as customers who needed the card immediately chased it up or those who thought it had been lost or stolen chased delivery. The result was that the overall organizational cost was considerably more than £500,000.

2 Journeys within products

An easier step is to look at journeys through a product lens and allocate the end-to-end journey to a product leader. The benefits of this approach is that it enables journey management approaches to be developed and perfected, and as the organization becomes more confident with journeys it can reorientate the journey to be more customer focused.

The downside, however, is that the journey is then defined in product terms, not customer terms, for example as the mortgage journey rather than a customer home-making journey of which a mortgage is only a part. Companies adopting this approach discover product ownership restricts creativity and inhibits a jobs-to-be-done innovation approach, but it is a simpler first step.

3 KPI-driven journey implementation across silos

In this model the journeys are defined in detail, the interactions and contributions of different departments within these journeys are mapped, and clear lines of responsibility are identified. Individual key performance indicators (KPIs) and diagnostic metrics are designed for each stage of the journey and allocated to the department responsible for that stage of the journey.

Departments collectively have matrix responsibility for the quality of the journey overall, but it is the line of sight at a senior level between departments and their effectiveness in contributing to the journey overall that enables it to work. It is reliant for success in top-down decision making.

4 Journey management committee

Increasingly, journey management committees or steering groups are appearing. In this model the leaders of each department or process that participate in the customer journey form a committee whose overall responsibility is the end-to-end management of the journey. It means decisions in scenarios such as the mail room/debit card mentioned above are taken by the whole team and individual departmental agendas are seen in the context of the whole.

The key features of this approach are:

- It comprises the leaders of individual departments that impact the journey.
- They have collective responsibility for the success (NPS/CSAT/commercial) of the customer journey.
- They elect the chair from their group.
- They must resolve departmental conflicts among themselves to ensure the end-to-end integrity of the journey overall.
- They are collectively responsible for design and journey improvement.

One UK bank defined 30 major journeys, bisected by 10 cross-journey journeys (for example, fraud, bereavement, new product applications). These bisecting journeys are designed once and implemented multiple times across the major journeys.

The bank started with individual journey owners but quickly discovered this was unworkable and moved instead to journey management teams. These teams were established across all journeys, including the bisecting ones, so it became a new way of managing and reporting but in a more customer-oriented matrix.

5 Needs states and journeys

The ultimate customer-centric model is where the organization is structured around customer needs groups and journeys are specified from the customer's perspective as things they want to achieve in their lives. For example, USAA has defined and is organized around eight customer needs groups. These relate to life needs, such as life after work (rather than a pension) and day-to-day money management (rather than a current account, debit card, personal loan, homeowner loan, car loan, etc). These needs groups are staffed by cross-functional teams responsible for the customer journey that takes place within the needs groups. In the case of USAA, the customer interaction points such as the contact centre are organized around life events.

USAA has driven massive cost reduction (by removing inefficiency and duplication) and now has a world-leading management expenses to profit ratio. The company has also driven massive innovation (photo cheques, car purchase, insurance claims) because it is closer to the customer. Its technical architecture has been designed to support a life event and journey perspective (Mocker et al, 2015).

The connected organization

Of course, not everything is about the customer alone. While customer centricity is a key to long-term growth, there is still a sophisticated enterprise to manage and run. Technology still needs to perform, finance must be disciplined, processes need to be effective, risk must be managed, the supply chain must be organized and operations must perform.

KPMG research conducted with Forrester across several geographies shows that there are eight key capabilities that companies need to nurture if they are to connect their enterprise across key operational areas and ensure that they are set up for success (KPMG, 2021). These are:

1 **Insight driven.** It is no longer enough to have a passing understanding of customer needs. All organizations will require a deep understanding of a customer's life and be able to translate that understanding into decision making, prioritization and experience design. Organizations need to:

   o unify data and analytics capability to generate rapid insights;

   o orchestrate disparate data sources intelligently and securely in a self-service and automated manner;

   o leverage data platforms such as data lakes, machine learning and other analytical techniques;

   o drive proactive enterprise performance management.

2 **Innovative.** A deep understanding of the customer's life drives innovation. A problem-solving mindset is required which, when coupled with a strong sense of purpose, provides focus, and a test and learn mindset enables continual refinement. Organizations need to:

   o establish redefined business models, products and services;

   o create newly tailored customer-value propositions and routes to market;

   o underpin innovation by digital means with flexible pricing mechanisms and consumption-based models.

3 **Experience centric.** The experience must be intentional, not the default outcome of multiple internal processes. It is how the brand promise is delivered at each touchpoint. How the brand is made real for customers every time they interact so that a strong relationship is formed. Organizations need to:

   o iterate experiential designs quickly and adapt to market feedback;

   o gauge the true impact of experience designs and execution by informing with sophisticated customer- and market-sensing solutions;

   o action pragmatic design thinking approaches.

4 **Seamless.** With the shift from physical to digital, organizations will need frictionless end-to-end customer interactions, with safe, secure payment options. Organizations need to:

   o accelerate the shift to optimal delivery channels;

o enable the business to generate, convert and service demand under evolving conditions;

o harness emerging channels and integrate them with existing operations;

o lead with cyber security.

5 **Responsive.** COVID-19 has demonstrated the need for organizational flexibility and responsiveness as companies pivot to maintain service through supply chains. The last mile has come to the fore and it is the end-to-end delivery of the experience that drives advocacy and loyalty. Organizations need to:

o establish agile, resilient and responsive supply chains and operations;

o leverage advanced data and artificial intelligence (AI) tools providing real-time and predictive insights;

o enable seamless processes and effortless decision making across the end-to-end supply or value chain;

o incorporate micro supply chains and supplier diversification for protection and flexibility;

o be supplier centric with procurement to better integrate suppliers across tiered procurement efforts.

6 **Empowered.** Employees underpin great customer experiences. Leaders, employees and the working culture need to be aligned through a brand purpose and a set of values that both inspires and shapes behaviours. Employees need to be able to make the judgements and decisions that customers expect at point of interaction. Organizations need to:

o thrive (not just survive) with new workforce models, including working-from-anywhere environments;

o create collaboration platforms for virtual workspaces when face to face isn't practical or possible;

o support with a culture that values and recognizes contributions based on accomplishments and collaboration versus hours worked.

7 **Digitally enabled.** A technology architecture that is built around the customer and is responsive to their needs and preferences is critical. Indeed, it must be supported by an agile mindset so new technologies and new products and services can be implemented rapidly. Organizations need to:

o access the underlying architecture and digital infrastructure to run at pace in a hyper-connected world;

o adopt the agile way of working not just in IT but across the business to be responsive and experience centric;

o deploy a digitally native architecture grounded in modern infrastructure and applications;

o be supported by reimagined service delivery models backed up by an engineering mindset.

8 **Integrated alliances.** The ability to identify and leverage synergies with third parties and external ecosystems is increasingly important as it is not always feasible for a company to do everything itself. The move to platforms is driving wider partnerships to satisfy related and often interconnected customer needs. Organizations need to:

o establish a 'shock-proof' ecosystem of partners who understand and enable the power of collaboration and communications;

o jointly execute against a clear set of business outcomes broader than service-level agreements and cost but inclusive of risk mitigation, execution flexibility and trust (KPMG, 2017).

Managing a team of teams

Companies are moving from the strictures of a functional organization by forming cross-functional teams often centred around customer journeys, customer needs and organization-wide initiatives. These are network-based organizations where multiple teams work together harmoniously, where dynamic collaboration is a way of life and where functions only exist in microcosm as communities of interest. In effect, the organization becomes a team of teams.

We first encountered the phrase 'team of teams' in the early 1990s when a UK finance institution began to restructure itself around business processes. It found that cross-functional teams were an effective antidote to entrenched hierarchies. So, instead of a traditional structure in which people work in hierarchies based on a function or a formal business unit, it formed a network of teams that came together around specific objectives, most often process design and customer solution design. The composition of each project team shifted as needed over time.

Teams and team members worked together in fluid, constantly evolving ways. This model emphasized decentralized autonomy, a sense of partnership and being part of something bigger, an overriding purpose. The company discovered that significant behavioural and co-ordination changes were required to make this model work. It implemented a co-ordinating management process, which evolved a sophisticated system of requirement setting and tracking to enable co-ordination across teams and key individuals. But the key issue was behaviour. Individuals needed to leave their departmental or functional agenda at the door, be able to contribute in the right way and participate as a subject matter expert in their own right. Team-based training and behavioural assessments conducted by the team itself were essential in making the transition.

More recently, retired US Army General Stanley McChrystal published a book titled *Team of Teams: New Rules of Engagement for a Complex World* (McChrystal, 2015). McChrystal outlines his efforts to reorganize the fight against Al Qaeda in Iraq and describes how a decentralized model can be effective even in a traditionally hierarchical institution like the US military (Meehan III and Starkey Jonker, 2018).

This is a style of working that has long been utilized in professional services, where the deployment of cross-organizational and cross-functional teams is an essential part of serving clients' needs and where the management of constantly changing teams is a core competence. Employees at professional services firms are adept at moving easily between teams, adding value as they go.

For some leading firms, such as USAA and Navy Federal bank, teams blur the lines between inside the organization and outside the organization as customers join these teams to co-create, inform and educate on needs, desires and issues. This results in a much deeper understanding of the role the organization can play in the customer's life.

For start-ups without the hierarchical history, adopting a team of teams approach from the outset has given them high levels of flexibility and resilience. Businesses such as Spotify have developed network-based organizations that reflect the team of teams philosophy but have supercharged it with new technologies and techniques such as agile.

Agile approaches

The growth in agile has been a major factor in helping organizations become more flexible. It chunks up work in a way that enables the creation of a minimum viable product, which is then developed iteratively over time based on feedback and insight on how the nascent product is performing. The concept of sprints means teams can produce results very quickly, often in one or two weeks. During these short activity bursts, the team holds frequent, often daily, check-ins to share progress, solve problems and ensure alignment. Between sprints, team members meet to review and plan, to discuss progress to date and to set the goal for the next sprint (Aghina et al, 2018).

Key to success is empowerment and ownership. There is no doubt that agile without empowerment loses momentum and progress is delayed or even stopped in its tracks. Decision making has to be devolved and rapid; by the nature of how they work, agile teams cannot hang around for decisions to be made.

Following this structured approach to innovation saves time, reduces rework, creates opportunities for creative 'leapfrog' solutions, and increases the sense of ownership, accountability and accomplishment within the team (Aghina et al, 2018).

Agile at scale

These days you need everyone in your company to have a holistic understanding of the organization's work. The European Space Agency failed because different countries made different parts of the rockets. Independently these parts worked, but when the rockets were assembled, they blew up or wandered off course. NASA avoided this problem by bringing its contractors in-house and mandating that everyone should understand the entire project. It is this combination of context and agility that will characterize organizations of tomorrow.

Agile has revolutionized the technology world, enabling the migration from lengthy, time-consuming waterfall projects where all the requirements have to be known at the outset to a more iterative approach that delivers value sooner and ensures that the project can be refined in real time as new requirements become apparent. It brings a mindset that increasingly is pervading entire organizations, where all initiatives from HR to IT and from product to journey mapping work in an agile way.

Agile at scale is becoming essential for responding to the rapidly changing external environment, but it does not sit well in a hierarchical organization where steady state is the order of the day.

KEY TAKEAWAYS

1 Successful organizations need to be flexible and responsive to survive, let alone thrive – leadership teams need to believe in/embody the purpose.

2 Complexity is increasing rapidly – clinging to Victorian organization structures will lead to a slow death. Organizations will need to be much more flexible and responsive to survive.

3 Organizations are finding that predominantly using customer-focused cross-functional teams that are constantly being created, disbanded and refocused offers the most flexibility.

4 Organizational designs are moving steadily towards the customer, primarily driven by the complexity of managing customer journeys.

5 Agile as a concept requires the right levels of empowerment for success – structures above and below the line will need to be different. Most organizations will struggle to reap the benefits of agile if they continue to use the procedural norms of the past.

References

Aghina, W. et al (2018) The five trademarks of agile organizations. www.mckinsey.com/business-functions/organization/our-insights/the-five-trademarks-of-agile-organizations (archived at https://perma.cc/BK6U-8YSR)

Deming Institute (1939) A bad system will beat a good person every time. https://deming.org/a-bad-system-will-beat-a-good-person-every-time/#:~:text=Quote%20by%20W.,the%20notes%20of%20Mike%20Stoecklein (archived at https://perma.cc/Q8TH-RUGF)

Forbes (2016) What is Jeff Bezos's 'Day 1' philosophy? www.forbes.com/sites/quora/2017/04/21/what-is-jeff-bezos-day-1-philosophy/?sh=7f955ea01052 (archived at https://perma.cc/BQ7Y-S6GW)

Gore (2021) Our beliefs and principles. www.gore.com/about/our-beliefs-and-principles (archived at https://perma.cc/2TDM-4BEA)

KPMG (2017) The connected experience imperative. https://assets.kpmg/content/dam/kpmg/br/pdf/2017/11/the-connected-experience-imperative-uk-2017.pdf (archived at https://perma.cc/5W75-3HKE)

KPMG (2021) KPMG connected enterprise. https://home.kpmg/xx/en/home/services/advisory/management-consulting/kpmg-connected-enterprise.html (archived at https://perma.cc/C7S4-8CD3)

Larson, E. (2018) How Jeff Bezos uses faster, better decisions to keep Amazon innovating. www.forbes.com/sites/eriklarson/2018/09/24/how-jeff-bezos-uses-faster-better-decisions-to-keep-amazon-innovating/?sh=2013d7087a65 (archived at https://perma.cc/GA65-CDSR)

Lee, J.-Y., Sridhar, S. and Palmatier, R. W. (2015) Customer-centric org charts aren't right for every company. https://hbr.org/2015/06/customer-centric-org-charts-arent-right-for-every-company (archived at https://perma.cc/D8K5-ECCA)

Marsden, P., Samson, A. and Upton, N. (2005) Advocacy drives growth. https://digitalwellbeing.org/wp-content/uploads/2015/05/Marsden-2005-06-Advocacy-Drives-Growth-Brand-Strategy.pdf (archived at https://perma.cc/M7W3-KFK7)

McChrystal, G. (2015) *Team of Teams: New Rules of Engagement for a Complex World.* London: Portfolio Penguin.

McConnell, J. (2020) Leadership everywhere means reversed leadership. www.druckerforum.org/blog/leadership-everywhere-means-reversed-leadership-by-jane-mcconnell/ (archived at https://perma.cc/9BQW-4S35)

Meehan III, W. F. and Starkey Jonker, K. (2018) Team of teams: an emerging organizational model. www.forbes.com/sites/meehanjonker/2018/05/30/team-of-teams-an-emerging-organizational-model/?sh=171984ae6e79 (archived at https://perma.cc/6XYY-WDVB)

Mocker, M., Ross, J. W. and Hopkins, C. (2015) How USAA architected its business for life event integration. https://core.ac.uk/download/pdf/35286962.pdf (archived at https://perma.cc/VL7D-Z4PU)

MRS (2016) Towards an insight driven organisation. www.mrs.org.uk/pdf/insightdriven.pdf (archived at https://perma.cc/7JS8-Q5YT)

Percy, S. (2019) Why do change programs fail? www.forbes.com/sites/sallypercy/2019/03/13/why-do-change-programs-fail/?sh=5edb8d472e48 (archived at https://perma.cc/MV4P-XL2Q)

Sheetz, M. (2017) Technology killing off corporate America: average life span of companies under 20 years. www.cnbc.com/2017/08/24/technology-killing-off-corporations-average-lifespan-of-company-under-20-years.html (archived at https://perma.cc/4NDJ-D4RY)

Soni, P. (2015) Home Depot's target market and customer base. https://finance.yahoo.com/news/home-depot-target-market-customer-230603019.html?guccounter=2 (archived at https://perma.cc/LKG8-V6KD)

Trout, J. (2017) Marketing CX. www.forbes.com/consent/?toURL=https://www.forbes.com/2006/06/30/jack-trout-on-marketing-cx_jt_0703drucker.html (archived at https://perma.cc/DS58-4W8Q)

World Economic Forum (2018) Justin Trudeau's Davos address in full. www.weforum.org/agenda/2018/01/pm-keynote-remarks-for-world-economic-forum-2018/ (archived at https://perma.cc/X8P9-BNHE)

05

Putting it all together

Markets change, customers change and companies change. Keeping a company relevant to its customers is always a work in progress – there is no ultimate destination, it is a continuous journey, one in which companies that are not flexible and adaptive fall by the wayside. Rapid responsiveness is no longer aspirational, it is a fundamental aspect of survival.

The ongoing synchronization between company market and customer requires an ever-increasing level of responsiveness. Markets open and close in short order, opportunities are increasingly fleeting and highly competitive, and customers are delightfully fickle and trend conscious.

In the previous chapters we have identified the components of adaptiveness, servant leadership, new organization designs, cultures and behaviours that put the customer first, all centred around a competitively differentiating understanding of the customer. So which companies can we look to as the exemplars, which organizations have mastered the art of synchronization? The ongoing alignment of company and customer? The league tables we produce around the world help provide some answers. The companies that top these tables span all industry types and come in all shapes and sizes – there is no sectorial advantage, no safe haven for success; these companies have synchronization in their DNA and are constantly adapting to changing circumstances.

In the US we see companies that maintain their position at the top of the table year after year – banks such as USAA, Navy Federal, retailers such as Costco, Wegmans, Publix and H-E-B, airlines such as JetBlue and Southwest, fast-food companies like Chick-fil-A and In-N-Out Burger.

In Europe companies like ÖAMTC (roadside rescue) in Austria, Zalando (online retailer) in Belgium, Lush (cosmetics retailer) in Holland and Fielmann (eyecare) in Germany are constant members of our Hall of Fame.

In the Middle East, it is companies such as DEWA (the Dubai Electricity and Water Authority) in the UAE and Emirates Airlines; and, in Asia, Singapore Airlines tops the index in six countries. In Australia and New Zealand, it is banks such as TSB, Kiwibank, Bendigo and Commonwealth. Retailers such as First Choice, utility companies like Electric Kiwi and airlines such as Air New Zealand. In South America it is retailers such as Sodie Doces and Zaffari, banks such as Nubank and hotel groups such as Marriott and Hilton. Even airports make the Hall of Fame, with Changi Airport in Singapore proving that airports can be experience centres, much more than just a shopping mall with a runway attached.

These are all adaptive companies that have learned the art of responsiveness and staying relevant to their customers.

The master plan

Synchronization is no accident. It is carefully and methodically planned, designed and implemented. For the companies listed above it is a way of life, the constant evaluation of relevance. While there are different challenges in individual industry sectors, the approach is the same: be clear on purpose, focus on culture, align organizationally around customers, and continuously monitor and improve performance from a customer perspective. Each sector has its stars, companies that, in the minds of their customers, stand apart from the others. Certain sectors such as retail, airlines, hotels and financial services do deliver overall better experiences, but even in the less glamorous sectors of public services and utilities there are exemplars.

Utilities

One of our world leaders is DEWA, whose adoption of artificial intelligence and digital technologies has transformed every aspect of its business (DEWA, 2021). An enthusiastic participant in the 10× initiative, a government-sponsored programme to put Dubai 10 years ahead of other global cities, DEWA has set itself a very high benchmark, being 10× better than any other utility.

DEWA provides all its services through various smart channels. By November 2019, 94 per cent of its customers were using its smart services. DEWA provides all its services around the clock through several smart channels and platforms.

The company launched 'Rammas', a virtual employee that uses AI to respond in English and Arabic. It is available round the clock on DEWA's smart app, website, Facebook page, Amazon's Alexa, Google Home, robots and WhatsApp Business platform. Rammas can continuously learn and understand customers' needs based on their enquiries. Rammas analyses them, based on available data and information, to best respond to and streamline transactions.

The Smart Response Service for electricity and water notifications has several features, such as self-diagnosis of interruptions. This reduces the steps to deal with issues from 10 to only one step for customers if they can self-diagnose the issue. It finds the best solutions to deal with, follow up and resolve technical notifications in a simpler and easier way, using DEWA's smart app and website. This enhances customer experience and service efficiency.

The company's 'My Sustainable Living Programme' encourages customers to use electricity and water responsibly and to reduce their carbon footprint. The programme, the first of its kind in the Middle East, enables residential customers to compare their monthly electricity and water usage with the average usage of similar efficient homes and make informed decisions based on current data, with other highly efficient homes. This inspires a healthy competition among customers to reduce their consumption (Water Online, 2020). The 'green charger' initiative involved rolling out more than 200 charging stations for electronic vehicles to promote their usage and reduce carbon emissions.

In New Zealand, Electric Kiwi consistently achieves five stars on social media review sites and tops our global index of utility companies for customer experience. It has a culture based on integrity, which prevents conduct issues as employees always strive to do what is right for the customer, and through its digital prowess lowers costs and delivers an outstanding customer experience.

With a business built on smart technology it strives to offer electricity that is cheaper, smarter and easy to manage. Its goal is to avoid limited one-off discounts and joining specials and instead lower the price of power, overall. It has an honest, transparent and authentic approach to its pricing which rewards loyalty, not switching. It is also pretty smart at marketing. It offers a free hour of power every day. Customers can choose when to have the free hour, so they can take advantage and allocate the hour during their peak usage. A simple offer, but it puts the customer in charge of their power usage and gives them control (Electric Kiwi, 2021).

Electric Kiwi customers can manage their account entirely online through a personalized online account and are able to view their billing and power use information right down to the half-hour. Interactions are mediated primarily by live webchat, increasing productivity and reducing costs.

Similarly, in Australia, AGL (Australian Gas Light Company) has developed a reputation among its customers for easy access to support in a way that helps them build trust with the brand and feel empowered. It is a business guided by its purpose – 'Progress for life' – and its values, which guide everything it does, especially how it supports customers and the community through challenging times. From the bushfires and drought that ravaged large parts of Australia in 2020 to the COVID-19 pandemic, it recognizes that its role in the community goes beyond just the provision of energy.

AGL is three years into a digital transformation programme, which has three core components: foundational capability, such as IT systems; digital adoption; and 'signature moments' for customers around their experience with the company (Simple, 2021). Data-driven decisioning for the personalization of services has made a large difference in customer engagement. The customer experience is now mediated digitally. Through in-app messaging, customers can message the contact centre team directly instead of needing to call, while the native payments functionality means easy bill payment through a preferred payment method stored in the app.

Public services

The Australian New South Wales (NSW) healthcare organization, NSW Health, performs highly in the Australian country league table at number 7. It is a highly customer-orientated environment. The NSW government appointed Australia's first Minister for Customer Service. The ambitious goal? Match or exceed customer experiences in the private sector. It is focused on three areas of change: 1) focus resources on what's most important for customers and mission success; 2) elevate CX design and enablement to make government easy to deal with; and 3) develop a framework for digital transformation to build customer trust. The focus is on the various patient journeys (Government of New South Wales, 2019).

The patient's journey, as well as their experience of care, is influenced by both the way they are treated as a person and how they are treated for their condition. Both are important but they are delivered differently. Treatment outcomes are facilitated by the organization and delivered by the care team;

the patient experience, meanwhile, is delivered and influenced by a range of individuals, including clinicians and the non-clinical workforce with whom the patient interacts (Australian Commission on Safety and Quality in Health Care, 2018).

NSW Health maps the full customer experience of significant life journeys, such as retirement and end of life. This has led to the creation of step-by-step online information services for significant life events. Whether starting a family or planning for retirement, starting school or getting a first job, suffering a serious injury or planning a funeral, renting property or dealing with a flood, these guides improve access to the many services the government can offer during these significant life events.

New roles have been created. The patient experience officer is a non-clinical role that works principally during the peak demand times; however, the incumbent can also work a range of shifts to understand the challenges across the day and to support staff development. These people are experts in patient experience and act as internal consultants, ensuring that the target patient experience is being delivered at all times.

Airlines

Singapore Airlines is highly rated for customer experience in its core markets. It has a clear sense of purpose that shapes its behaviour and its credibility as a corporate citizen. The airline articulates its purpose in its vision statement as follows (KPMG, 2020):

> Singapore Airlines has a responsibility not only to be an excellent company, but also to be an excellent citizen of the world by enhancing the lives of the people we touch. With that aim in mind, we have made many commitments to the arts and education, to our communities, and the health and welfare of our country's citizens, and those in countries we fly to. With this goal in mind, we've also made a strong commitment to preserving the environment – and our world for future generations.

A commitment to 'enhancing the lives of people we touch' is what sets Singapore Airlines apart. It is the driving force behind innovation and experience delivery. It is rooted in the qualities of Eastern service and is reflected in every interaction, digital or physical (KPMG, 2019). Passengers notice the care and attention they receive, the help and assistance offered proactively when they have difficulties, and the overall desire to please. In the airline industry, customer patience is tested most strongly when there is disruption. Unlike many major carriers, Singapore Airlines approaches this by focusing on stress-reducing communication, ensuring that passengers are kept informed and reassured about missed connections or unforeseen overnight stays, thinking ahead and answering questions before passengers have even thought of them. Everything possible is done to put the customer back in control and reduce stress and concern. Staff are trained to de-escalate situations with emotional passengers and to show that the airline cares about the passengers' plight and is doing everything possible to put things right (KPMG, 2019).

Behind the scenes, the airline utilizes advanced systems for communication and agile crew management. Its software ecosystems work constantly to update data flow and have everything needed for crews: in-team chats, schedule tracking, task lists, issue lists and reports. Effective and quick crew communication is a vital part of disruption resolution. So, even in adversity when things are difficult and passengers are emotional and fraught, its employees are bound by its purpose to 'enhance the lives of the people we touch' (KPMG, 2019).

Emirates is a leading travel brand across the world. The airline's success is due to the company's willingness to evolve in line with the desires of its customers. Emirates is acutely aware that, for some individuals, a flight on one of its aircraft is an event-based experience – it could be a once-in-a-lifetime journey to a particular destination, or it could mark the beginning of a honeymoon for a pair of newlyweds. For this reason, Emirates is ambitious in its vision; it intends to embrace the world of big data in order to create a customer experience that can be tailored to the individual, facilitating such innovations as tailored music and film playlists so that customers can enjoy their favourite forms of entertainment once airborne (KPMG, 2017).

Aligned with its desire to keep up with escalating expectations, Emirates is not afraid to dispense with long-established conventions if they work to improve the experience for the individual. The airline has a vision to abandon traditional transportation classes (such as first class and economy) so that passengers can, instead, pick the specific services they would like to receive. For example, a customer might purposely choose an economy seat, as they are flying during the day and do not need the lie-down option, but they may also want a business-class meal. Moving forward, the idea is to provide fewer restrictions and a greater number of options, while also keeping passengers educated on what the entirety of their travel experience will look like (KPMG, 2017).

Emirates is also conscious of the restrictions that workplace functions can present, slowing down the decision making. However, with the use of cross-functional digital teams there can be a smaller number of people from myriad departments, such as commercial, IT and HR, and this is a structure that Emirates is keen to extend. Emirates is a brand that is listening to what its customers expect and is not complacent in its mission to deliver (KPMG, 2017).

Hotels

The hotel sector has long set the standard for customer service. Ritz-Carlton is often cited as the gold standard when it comes to customer experience (Ritz-Carlton, 2021). Indeed, it is so good that its training academy is responsible for teaching customer service techniques to companies around the world.

A five-star hotel and resort company with locations globally, Ritz-Carlton is renowned for its legendary services and luxury facilities creating unforgettable travel experiences in the world's top destinations. Serving the top 1 per cent of travellers, Ritz-Carlton seeks to recruit the top 1 per cent of staff. Referring to its people as ladies and gentlemen serving ladies and gentlemen, they are empowered and engaged around a strong sense of purpose, a service ethic that pervades all aspects of the employee's world. The company wants its people to feel inspired, driven and passionate about the customer, only then will they excel. In short, it puts its employees first, focusing on culture and engagement and knowing that every customer interaction is a moment of truth, a moment within which to deliver the promise of exceptional service and an opportunity to go the extra mile.

The Employee Promise, printed on a pocket-size brochure and carried by every employee at all times, was written by employees from around the world. It sets out the standards by which they treat each other. Described as the Ritz-Carlton Mystique, this exceptional experience has two underlying support structures of process and technology. Every morning at the start of the shift, employees, in what is known as the line-up, gather for 10 minutes to listen to great stories from around the world collected the preceding day to reaffirm their commitment to the company purpose, to start the day with sharing what good looks like and to inspire employees to apply the company's values in their daily work. Ritz-Carlton believes that purpose turns to passion and that passion is palpable for customers.

Supporting the approach is a technology called Mystique, an advanced CRM system that enables individual customer preferences to be collected and made available whenever that customer stays at a Ritz-Carlton hotel. If a customer prefers lime rather than lemon in their cola, then the company wants to ensure that that happens without the customer having to ask whenever they stay.

Retailers

US supermarket Wegmans, often described as a 'theme park of food', is one of the world's exceptional retailers. Famously, actor Alec Baldwin's mother refused to join him in Los Angeles because they didn't have a Wegmans there.

With stores averaging 130,000 square feet, they are three times the size of a standard supermarket. They are designed to make every shopping trip an event. From Michelin-starred restaurants to sports bars, there is something for everyone. Model trains circumnavigate the roof space to keep kids interested. But the heart of the difference is the culture and the people.

The company invests heavily in its people, the knowledge they can bring to bear and the passion they can inspire. As Chief Executive Danny Wegman put it, what point is there in having hundreds of different varieties of cheese if staff cannot explain the difference (Boyle, 2005)? To ensure they can explain the difference, staff are sent to vineyards in France, to wineries in the Napa Valley, to Europe to see how the cheese is made. Wegmans does not just sell food, it sells knowledge about how to unleash an individual's inner chef.

No customer is allowed to leave unhappy. To ensure that, employees are encouraged to do whatever is required to ensure customer satisfaction without consulting a more senior member of the team. Stories abound. It could mean sending a chef to a customer's home to clear up a messed-up food order, or cooking a family's Thanksgiving turkey in the store because the one Mom bought was too big for her oven (Acosta, 2020).

Empowering employees goes beyond making house calls, though; it also means creating an environment where they can shine, unburdened by hierarchies and lengthy decision-making cycles.

Financial services

Chief among the leading companies is the UK bank first direct. It has topped our UK Top 100 league table four times in 10 years and has consistently featured in the top three. When we account for cultural differences in how populations rate organizations, first direct is the number one brand for customer experience across the 34 countries where we conduct the research.

In Part 2 of this book we examine the Six Pillars of Experience; suffice it to say, first direct is outstanding at all of them.

first direct: putting it all together

The following is based on interviews with Joe Gordon, the former CEO of first direct (Gordon, 2020), and Chris Pitt, the CEO at the time of writing (Pitt, 2021).

first direct launched in 1989 against a backdrop of poor service in banking and was conceived to be different from day one. Now, decades later, despite the advance of technology, the rapid progress of other banks in becoming more customer focused and the new customer-oriented challenger banks, first direct continues to lead the way.

According to Joe Gordon, first direct's continued customer experience success has been driven by a fine balance of two key elements: consistency and change. 'Those two things might seem like separate bed-fellows, but they work incredibly well together,' explains Gordon. 'The consistency of focus on customer centricity internally, the consistency around the bank's mantra – pioneering amazing service – it's something everyone in the bank is bought into. That consistency of what first direct is trying to do is really important, but equally the change in how it does it is really important as well. Customer expectations change, technologies change. In 1989 first direct was set up to pioneer amazing service and the "how" back then was telephony. Then it changed to online banking, then app banking and now open banking. first direct's ability to cope with that change and understand that change in today's environment, as well as being consistent with its focus, has been key' (KPMG, 2019).

Balancing consistency and change has enabled first direct to stay both personal and relevant to its customers, meeting their expectations of a bank that is simple, easy and great to do business with.

Chris Pitt says there is now an added layer to this. The new generation of customers coming through expect more from the organizations they deal with. There is an underlying sense that this generation feels particularly strongly about fairness. Pioneering changes are now table stakes; competitive advantage can be eroded in months, if not weeks. And while customer service is as important as ever, it's harder to differentiate between brands when using an app most of the time. The special something this generation is looking for is a business that shares its values around fairness in society, that supports positive social change (including climate change and tackling discrimination), which is provable and runs deep in its values.

The building blocks

What is particularly interesting is first direct's holistic, integrated approach, which ensures all aspects of strategy are integrated and aligned. It sees the organization as a system where every component has a role in the context of the whole. Consequently, every initiative is not only mutually reinforcing but makes a clear contribution to the delivery of the company's purpose. The net result is that the whole is significantly greater than the sum of the individual parts.

Understand customers

Former first direct CEO Mark Mullen explains, 'I would encourage anyone who is leading a business, or anyone who has any involvement in business, to watch customers. People over-rationalise when you ask them questions. But when you watch how they actually behave as opposed to how they think they behave you get two very different answers. People are vastly more emotional about money, if not about banking, than they might admit to being in a rational post-purchase survey or any questionnaire or feedback group. Watching people is in my experience vastly more informative than questioning them' (Davey, 2013).

first direct uses multiple different mechanisms to understand its customers and knows them intimately:

- It knows exactly which customers it wants and which it doesn't.
- It knows what the bank does well that customers like.
- It has a clear target experience. This has six psychological factors that make each call 'amazing' – the employees know exactly how to speak with customers, the tone and the style, they know what they like and don't like.
- It is very clear on how the customer base is feeling at any point in time. (For example, when it discovered that women over 40 felt first direct was

less relevant to them than it once was, the bank co-created a new approach of going the extra step for this group.

- It aims for a 'family' rather than a 'friendly' experience.

It is the focus on the psychology of customers that makes first direct unique among banks, really getting to understand people's motivations and desires, but also their problems, inhibitions and life concerns.

Purpose and values

The offices of first direct are heavily branded; indeed, the only part of the buildings that isn't is the staff restaurant, where employees are felt to deserve some time away from all things first direct! The walls, however, scream the company's purpose – in huge letters on every wall is the mantra 'pioneering amazing service'. It is the north star, the controlling idea that shapes every action and decision.

In 1989, with a mission to change banking for the better, being a pioneer was straightforward; in these more competitive times it still inspires and motivates. A pioneer is someone who goes where others haven't gone before, it is a frame of mind that drives innovation and new thinking; amazing means to surprise, to impress, to be excellent. Something staff attempt to do every day, not just with customers but also with each other. 'Amazing' is a behavioural attribute, always seeking to surprise. It is the role of everyone to continually reset the view as to what amazing service means today.

The purpose is converted into execution through the simple rules the company describes as commercial imperatives:

- People matter more – the work starts with employees first.
- Keep the lights bright – never forget that we are in business and that commercial returns matter.
- Grow, modernize, accelerate – continue to develop and get to the future first.

Execution is shaped by the company's values, which it describes as the 'four hearts of being':

- Dare to be different – the bank looks for staff with this attribute, driving diversity and accepting that being different involves a willingness to fail but learn quickly.
- Uncommonly good sense – enabling and empowering staff to make sensible decisions.

- We're always on it – ensuring that nothing important to staff or customers falls by the wayside.

- We take money seriously, not ourselves – a blend of conscientiousness and humility that ensures that customers never feel dictated to.

All at first direct take being a 'pioneer' very seriously. It requires a high level of confidence, people who are happy with ambiguity and yet have the confidence that, despite no other role models, they will find a way. Everything is seen and filtered through a first direct brand lens, it accretes the things that add value and adds them to the existing body of knowledge: lean, agile, kaizen, value streams, all analysed, understood and adapted for first direct use.

Culture

Mark Mullen describes the culture as being so hard to verbalize but so easy to feel. And it can be felt upon walking into first direct's office – the vibrancy and friendliness exuding from those you meet. 'Culture is everything – especially in a bank that doesn't see its customers. The fact of the matter is that you probably won't speak to the same person twice if you speak to first direct. So how do you manage to create a level of consistency and reliability throughout the relationship? You can't do that if you haven't got really well-defined processes, really simple products and really consistently well-recruited and well-trained people' (Davey, 2013).

Interestingly, respondents to our research regularly observe that 'when I speak to first direct it always seems like I am speaking to the same person – regardless of gender or ethnicity, they all seem to care about me in the same way'.

first direct is very selective about who it recruits – about 1 in 100 who start the process finish it. It is very much character and values based, and much less focused on technical capabilities. This approach is then carried through the way that the bank welcomes new recruits, providing buddies and coaching support for them.

Chris Pitt acknowledges it's the people who make the customer difference, which is underpinned by a strong emphasis on the right approach to recruitment. first direct prefers not to recruit from other financial services firms, focusing instead on the caring professions, where it can find people with the right levels of empathy and care who are prepared to dare to be different.

In 2019, 44 per cent of new recruits were in fact recommended by existing employees, based on the philosophy that like tends to recruit like. In fact, while the bank opened its doors in 1989, there are several examples of three generations of a family working in different roles. Chris Pitt says, 'We know what we are looking for when we recruit people. Once we start the application process, we use people who've done the job to look for attitude and understanding. If they've got this, then we can train people how we need to do things. Looking forward to a post-pandemic world, and we're going to be able to recruit people from further afield. People who live at other ends of the country and wish to work remotely will be able to apply for roles in first direct. It's going to give us a bigger pool to fish in as we grow the bank, which is really exciting, but the challenge will be to imbue our culture in people who aren't physically in the office.'

first direct is very clear on what the culture is and strives to keep it relevant for the current challenges. It has several shaping components:

- It is not command and control.
- It is about coaching, mentoring and being supportive, tolerant of failure – unless a negative pattern emerges with an individual, then determine what coaching can achieve with the employee.
- Positive cultural messages are communicated all the time. Excellent cultural behaviours are lauded and celebrated.
- There are 'visible totems of openness' in everything from seating to how ideas are shared.
- It is about always being alive and responsive to demographic shifts – Gen Z, diversity, gender fluidity, environmental concerns.
- It believes in driving, encouraging and celebrating innovation and new ideas.
- It supports employees' involvement through the 'bubbles' approach. Employees can identify issues (bubbles), which are assessed as to whether the team can fix them themselves or whether they need to be escalated. If escalated, the change team assesses whether there is a fix planned or whether it needs to be added and prioritized as part of the change programme – the decision is fed back to the employees concerned.

Chris says, 'Maybe it came from being based in Yorkshire and Glasgow, but people in first direct are encouraged to be open to the point of bluntness. Done in the right spirit of course, with a positive irreverence, but giving and receiving feedback is vital if we're to keep improving. We're also our own worst critics. If something isn't working then we encourage people to say so.

And even if we are doing something well, such as topping a survey of customer service, we look into the metrics, where could we improve, how fast can we do this. We never want to be satisfied or complacent.'

Servant leadership

It is the role of all leaders at first direct to work to enable their people. They sit among their people, not separate in offices but where they can see, feel and hear all that is going on around them. They react quickly when issues emerge and share a collective consciousness as to where the business and its people are at any point in time. It is a style of leadership driven by a concern for people and a focus on the employee experience, to ensure it allows the target customer experience to emerge naturally.

One of first direct's core principles is building projects around motivated individuals, giving them the environment and support they need and trusting them to get the job done. first direct refers to this as servant leadership. Agile innovation depends on having a cadre of eager participants, so staff motivation and engagement is job number one at first direct.

- It is a leadership style that is non-hierarchical, open and transparent.
- It follows the 'servant leader' model. The CEO is there for a period of time – their role to leave it better than they found it.
- Leadership team meetings are held in the open office – anyone can listen in.
- The CEO and leadership team sit in the open office.
- They have stand-up meetings first thing on a Monday around their visual tracking board – 'What do we need to achieve?' – and stand-down meetings on a Friday – 'What have we achieved and who has helped us achieve this?' The tracking board which lists the team's priorities is centred in the middle of the office, there for all to see.
- Leaders are heavily ensconced in the business day to day – there are no surprises.
- It requires strong leadership due to encouraging people to be individuals and to dare to be different – a value that can present challenges.

Employee experience

The importance of their people is always on the leadership's mind. Chris Pitt says, 'It may seem like a small thing, but our employees are always referred to as people. In conversations, and in all our official communications. It's warmer and humanizing, but it also reinforces the close-knit, family feel first direct has always cultivated.'

A recent example was illustrated during the beginning of the pandemic in the UK. first direct took the decision to move all its people offsite and in a matter of a couple of weeks it had shut its doors, its people set up with all the kit they needed to be able to work safely from home. This was all achieved with very little impact on customer service. Indeed, many customers were unaware for months that there had been any change. The leadership took the decision quickly and moved decisively to protect its people, but in a controlled way which also protected its customers. The result was that the people felt supported – and safe – and appreciated the actions of the management, leaving them prepared to put up with difficult conditions in order to do what was needed for customers.

Another factor is that reward is linked to customer performance. 'It's not rocket science to understand that you are going to get the behaviours that you encourage and reward. We work hard to encourage diversity and fervently believe in providing open and transparent career paths. Our people are all different, and this is key, but they are united by their attitude, and the understanding they are rewarded for delivering amazing customer service,' says Pitt.

first direct leaders:

- are very clear on the target employee experience;
- worry about the welfare of employees – they see their role as looking after the people who look after customers;
- seek to find creative ways of reducing employee worries, e.g. the concierge service;
- ensure that everyone cares about doing their best for customers;
- emphasize the four 'hearts of being' – the first direct values;
- empower their people to make sensible judgements and to do what is right for the customer.

There is a focus on the constant development of people skills. Personal growth is a key driver of engagement and first direct is very keen that its people grow and progress. Everyone with a customer-facing role is trained to have core skills – manage a service transaction, support customers to be more digital – and this is enhanced by soft skills training as and when needed. This provides greater flexibility when the unexpected happens. For example, when a major airline failed, it caused a massive unexpected increase in calls and needed rapid flexibility to get people on the phones to talk to worried customers.

The design of the employee experience is based on creating 'skill clusters' – stepping stones for development – a double win since it ensures people have interesting jobs and first direct has flexibility when needed.

The company actively separates leadership capability from subject knowledge. It recognizes the best agents are not always the best leaders, therefore it provides an alternative career path that doesn't require progress up through the hierarchy.

Communications

Rigorous and two-way. It is all about creating understanding rather than just top-down communication. Teams get an opportunity to discuss what things mean for them and how they can respond. Feedback is encouraged and acted upon.

There's an online thank-you system through the intranet where anybody can just send a thank you to anybody for anything. Senior leaders might send five or six to different members of their wider team on any given day because their managers or team leaders passed on a note that customers provided positive customer feedback.

Mark Mullen says, 'So, at every opportunity we tried to catch people doing something right and celebrate it; we'll take that opportunity thank you very much. And that's not about selling stuff – we couldn't have cared less about that, that'll look after itself. It's that the attitude of the bank was to delight customers, and if a customer took the time to tell you that you have done that, it was a big moment. It infused the entire organisation' (Davey, 2013).

Continual circulation of what good looks like – great stories show what employees can do to make a difference. For example, one agent discovered that a young customer was away from home and feeling suicidal – a first direct agent kept them talking on the phone while another agent notified the customer's mother, checked out a taxi firm and driver and ensured the customer was taken home safely. This act of altruism was a widely lauded example of the sorts of behaviours that show caring and empathy.

- Stories show when and where employees can step outside of process.
- Managers and team leaders cascade information – so they have to understand it.

- There is a video blog from the CEO and a weekly email to outline employees' focus for the week ahead. And every fortnight there's an 'Ask Me Anything' session where people can put their questions straight to the boss.

- A bespoke app for all employees covers most social dimensions and engagement.

- When the new year's strategy is being developed, all 2,500 employees have an opportunity to work together with the strategy and the leadership team – it results in 30 meetings exactly the same, but in groups small enough that people can interact, ask questions and develop ownership.

Enterprise

first direct's adoption of 'lean agile', in a way that is consistent with its approach to servant leadership, and clear guiding values, all bound up in its mantra of 'pioneering amazing service', sees the bank split into a team of teams. People are aligned to their day-to-day teams but also form cross-functional value streams and work on projects as and when necessary. It is a loose matrix designed to deliver a continuous flow of value to a customer. Rather than the traditional waterfall project approach where a perfect solution takes a long time and things have often changed in the meantime, multiple teams work towards rapid delivery of minimum viable products (KPMG, 2019).

By taking people out of their functional silos and putting them in self-managed and customer-focused multidisciplinary teams, the value stream approach is not only accelerating profitable growth at first direct but also helping to create a new generation of skilled general managers (Rigby et al, 2016).

Vitally, adoption of a new technique such as lean agile does not mean importing a fundamentally new way of working, a new management religion or a set of do or die diktats. Far from it. It involves unpicking the key elements of agile and adding those best practices best suited to first direct to the existing canon of management techniques, born out of a similar assessment and importation of techniques from kaizen and Six Sigma.

first direct is creating its own unique management philosophy distilled from great thinking around the world. Compared with traditional management approaches, it has found that agile offers several major benefits, all of which the company has studied and improved. It increases team productivity and employee satisfaction. It minimizes the waste inherent in redundant meetings, repetitive planning, excessive documentation, quality defects and low-value product features (Rigby et al, 2016). Ultimately it has driven innovation and flexibility.

- There is a culture of continuous improvement.
- Cross-functional teams drive everything.
- There is a matrix management approach that 'just seems to work'.
- Everyone brings their own bit to the journey – no one person has ownership; the team owns.

Managing change

Connecting with the customer of the future, keeping up with the pace of change has always been key to first direct's success. It was the first 24/7/365 telephone bank in the UK, a pioneer of online banking, then mobile banking. More recently, it has partnered with fintechs such as Bud to explore what they can do around understanding open banking.

Chris Pitt adds, 'Working in new ways has always been important to staying ahead of the curve. Customers are always going to want to do things in new and different ways. But banking is still boring for most. They just want to do what they need to do quickly and easily and feel confident they are in control of their money. In terms of customer service, what customers value hasn't really changed that much in over 30 years, but in terms of what more they expect from their bank it has. People are now more challenging of the status quo, and taking action to create change around social and environmental issues. They want to deal with brands that are themselves engaged in reform and change.'

Investing in new ways of working

first direct is continually investing from a digital perspective, most recently in new technology platforms, new telephony platforms, online banking, new functionality on the app, fdpay (social media pay) and also fdesign, a customer co-creation platform (KPMG, 2019).

It's not just about technological investments for the bank, though. There is the implementation of agile ways of working, around closed-loop feedback and redesigning the bank around customer journeys and a constant flow of value. It is those kinds of investments, as well as the digital investments, that have really helped first direct to overhaul its IT estate and its ways of working. The result has been much more rapid responsiveness to escalating customer expectations:

- The change programme is 75 per cent agile; however, where it is appropriate traditional waterfall approaches are applied to the remaining 25 per cent.
- The company is in a state of regular reprioritization based on the issues that arise in the business. It works on regular release cycles. The PI (programme increment) approach schedules change – 12-week activities comprising six two- sprints.
- The change route map is in a public area, so it can be viewed by anyone. The company categorizes change across three time dimensions: 'ice' – unchangeable, baked into immediate release plans; water – more fluid, aimed for the immediate year; 'steam' – less well defined, scheduled for the next year.
- It seeks to have an end-to-end perspective on all things customer.

Critical KPIs

first direct uses a broad range of data sources to create a complex picture of the company's performance. But primarily the leadership team is focused on 'what really matters':

- How our people are feeling.
- How our customers are feeling.
- Where we are commercially – are we getting the commercial returns?

One of the benefits of a direct model is that it is infused with data and there are fewer grey areas in the customer journey. In a centralized remote environment, as opposed to a traditional branch-based model, it is more possible to gather data, whether it be via phone or online, etc, and then to reconcile that data at customer level (Davey, 2013). So customer contact histories and customer interaction metrics are abundant and technically can tell whether the bank has done a good job irrespective of whether the customer has provided direct feedback – and that includes whether they are achieving their service levels on the phone, whether they are achieving their internet banking or mobile banking or SMS response SLAs (Davey, 2013).

Chris Pitt notes, 'We know what good looks like – how good we need to be to drive the outcomes we seek by way of satisfaction metrics. We also layer on all the feedback we do receive, positive and negative. Surveys and industry feedback and reviews on sites like Trustpilot are added to post-purchase contact surveys and point-of-contact surveys. What we have is a constantly moving stream of data which shows how and when people are interacting with us, and how we're doing against our own internal measures. It's a very micro, nuanced picture which means we can very quickly tell if we're not meeting these and take immediate action.'

Physical environment

This is designed to reinforce cultural positives:

- Heavily branded, purpose and values everywhere.
- Open area for stand-up meetings.
- Designed to support agile at scale.
- Only a few meeting rooms.
- Desks not standardized in lines but offset to create team areas.

Structure: organizing the business around the customer

In the last few years first direct has reorganized the business. Historically set up on a functional basis with departments operating separately, the bank has now restructured around the key journeys for its customers. Instead of customer service being one person's job, it flows through each of the value streams. There are now people responsible for each end-to-end journey and they have access to people across the operational teams, across the marketing, commercial and risk teams too. Everyone shares the challenges around making the customer journeys as frictionless as possible.

Chris Pitt explains, 'Moving from a horizontal structure to more of a vertical stream has meant first direct is more focused on the customer than ever before. From the point where they first join first direct to the experience they have all the way through' (KPMG, 2019).

- Organized around seven value streams: Customer, People, Channels, Accounts, Lending, Mortgages and Value Added Services.
- Dedicated cross-functional teams (Business Performance, Change, Commercial, Marketing, Service Recovery) with support as required from Finance, Risk, Internal Comms and HR).

- Customer interactions managed around product journeys, e.g. mortgages (first home, move home, remortgage, simplify finances, save money, query).
- Journeys increasingly centred around emerging life needs. For example, 'I want to borrow' spans all lines of credit products.

KEY TAKEAWAYS

1 These leading companies are characterized by a strong sense of mission and purpose, thousands of people committed to the customer.

2 They think people first. What types of people will best serve our customers, promote our values and help us fulfil our purpose?

3 The leadership style is about enabling and empowering people to give of their best every time they touch the customer.

4 The culture is understood and actively nurtured. It is recognized by the leadership team as a critical part of the employee experience and carefully nurtured to ensure it continues to be relevant for today's challenges.

5 Decisions are taken with a deep knowledge of the customer and to support a clear target experience. The company knows exactly what customers are seeking physically, rationally and psychologically and is very diligent in delivering its target experience.

6 Constant physical reinforcement – symbols and totems to ensure the brand purpose is always uppermost in their people's minds.

References

Acosta, G. (2020) How Wegmans keeps winning. https://progressivegrocer.com/how-wegmans-keeps-winning (archived at https://perma.cc/G2XW-L4KC)

Australian Commission on Safety and Quality in Health Care (2018) www.safetyandquality.gov.au/sites/default/files/migrated/FINAL-REPORT-Attributes-of-person-centred-healthcare-organisations-2018.pdf (archived at https://perma.cc/ZC5V-SQ3V)

Boyle, M. (2005) The Wegmans way. https://money.cnn.com/magazines/fortune/fortune_archive/2005/01/24/8234048/index.htm (archived at https://perma.cc/LXR3-KX9F)

Davey, N. (2013) first direct: six experience lessons from the bank that bucks the trend. www.mycustomer.com/experience/engagement/first-direct-six-experience-lessons-from-the-bank-that-bucks-the-trend (archived at https://perma.cc/UF35-NK7E)

DEWA (2021) Digital DEWA. https://digital.dewa.gov.ae/ (archived at https://perma.cc/GCZ4-6DS8)

Electric Kiwi (2021) Hour of power. www.electrickiwi.co.nz/hour-of-power/ (archived at https://perma.cc/SJB6-YLTZ)

Gordon, J. (2020) Former CEO first direct [Interview], February.

Government of New South Wales (2019) Improving patient experience in NSW. www.health.nsw.gov.au/Performance/Pages/default.aspx (archived at https://perma.cc/387W-CSGW)

KPMG (2017) UK customer experience excellence analysis 2017. www.nunwood.com/excellence-centre/publications/uk-cee-analysis/2017-uk-cee-analysis/emirates/ (archived at https://perma.cc/9WG2-VK5G)

KPMG (2019) Customer first. Customer obsessed. https://assets.kpmg/content/dam/kpmg/xx/pdf/2019/10/global-customer-experience-excellence-report.pdf (archived at https://perma.cc/85P2-VYFJ)

KPMG (2020) Spotlight on: Singapore Airlines. https://home.kpmg/xx/en/home/insights/2020/01/customer-first-insights-the-power-of-purpose-case-studies.html (archived at https://perma.cc/R759-56R3)

Pitt, C. (2021) CEO first direct [Interview], March.

Rigby, D. K., Sutherland, J. and Takeuchi, H. (2016) Embracing agile: how to master the process that's transforming management. https://hbr.org/2016/05/embracing-agile (archived at https://perma.cc/X3PG-JV5D)

Ritz-Carlton (2021) Gold standards. www.ritzcarlton.com/en/about/gold-standards#:~:text=The%20Employee%20Promise-,The%20Credo,%2C%20relaxed%2C%20yet%20refined%20ambience (archived at https://perma.cc/U4GK-VYTM)

Simple (2021) Under the hood of AGL's digital transformation. https://simple.io/digital-transformation-agl/ (archived at https://perma.cc/8DWX-BZVA)

Water Online (2020) DEWA's innovative plans in providing reliable and sustainable water supplies to ensure the comfort of Dubai residents around the clock. www.wateronline.com/doc/dewa-s-innovative-plans-in-providing-reliable-dubai-residents-around-the-clock-0001 (archived at https://perma.cc/JNL9-SG6J)

PART 2

The Six Pillars of Experience: a framework for excellence

06

The Six Pillars of Experience: introduction

Over a decade of research has shown that every outstanding customer relationship has a universal set of qualities – they are the Six Pillars of experience. The Six Pillar model of customer experience best practice has been developed to provide a precise, usable definition of the kind of emotional outcome a successful experience needs to deliver. This aim was born out of a problem of definition associated with existing ways of explaining customer experiences, plus associated measures such as Net Promoter Score or customer satisfaction. While these concepts remain useful for describing the symptoms of a successful experience, most organizations found that they did little to define what a good result looked like. Understanding customer best practice was largely anchored in case studies and anecdotes rather than scientific rigour (Knight et al, 2015).

To address this problem of definition, the Customer Experience Excellence Centre's research clearly shows that there are six discrete components of an ideal experience: the Six Pillars. These have been derived from detailed customer reviews, validated in each market and modelled against the commercial outcomes of retention and recommendation (KPMG, 2019). The Six Pillars, when applied together, provide a powerful mechanism to help organizations understand how well their customer experience is delivered across channels, industries and company types. The leading organizations demonstrate mastery of these pillars and are outstanding at all of them (KPMG, 2019).

For more than a decade we have been measuring the Six Pillars of Customer Experience. Derived from millions of customer evaluations of thousands of brands, we have empirically found that they describe customer

FIGURE 6.1   The Six Pillars of Experience one

Integrity
Being trustworthy and engendering trust

Resolution
Turning a poor experience into a great one

Expectations
Managing, meeting and exceeding customer expectations

Time and Effort
Minimizing customer effort and creating frictionless processes

Personalization
Using individualized attention to drive an emotional connection

Empathy
Achieving an understanding of the customer's circumstances to drive deep rapport

experience excellence (KPMG, 2019). The leading firms demonstrate mastery of these pillars and are deliberate and purposeful in the experiences they create.

The pillars are rooted in human psychology and motivation and as such are relevant across business to business (B2B) and business to consumer (B2C) and are as relevant for employees as they are for customers. Figure 6.1 shows them as the DNA of great experiences.

- Integrity: Being trustworthy and engendering trust. Integrity comes from an organization consistently demonstrating trustworthiness. For customers, what is always top of mind is the degree to which the organization delivers on its promises. Trust and integrity are rooted in the organization's sense of purpose. They grow and bear fruit where the organization ethically, morally and socially reaffirms its purpose.

- Resolution: Turning a poor experience into a great one. Even with the best processes and procedures, things go wrong. How you recover from these situations is critical. Great companies have a process that puts the customer back in the position they should have been in as quickly as possible. But they go further. As the service recovery paradox teaches us, just fixing problems is no longer good enough – the customer must feel great about the whole recovery experience.

- Expectations: Managing, meeting and exceeding customer expectations. Expectations are increasingly being set by the best brands customers encounter. Great organizations understand that expectations are set strategically by the brand promise, then reaffirmed through everyday interactions. Some communicate clear intent through their brand communications, others set expectations accurately at every interaction and then delight the customer when they exceed them.

- Time and effort: Minimizing customer effort and creating frictionless processes. Customers are time poor and increasingly looking for instant gratification. Removing unnecessary obstacles, impediments and bureaucracy to enable the customer to achieve their objectives quickly and easily increases loyalty. Many companies are discovering how to use time as a source of competitive advantage. There is also a clear cost advantage to saving time.

- Personalization: Paying attention to people and their circumstances to drive emotional connection. Personalization is the most valuable part of most experiences. The distinguishing feature of brilliant personalization is how your customer is left feeling after their interaction. Do they feel important, valued and more in control?

- Empathy: Achieving an understanding of the customer's circumstances to drive deep rapport. Empathy is the emotional capacity to show you understand someone else's experience. Behaviours that create empathy are central to establishing a strong relationship. They involve reflecting to the customer that you know how they feel. Then going the extra mile and doing something special for them because you care.

We have observed that all great customer experience companies look alike, and all poor companies are poor in their own way. The great companies are all outstanding at the Six Pillars. Poor companies have a deficiency in at least one, more often several of them.

The opening line of Tolstoy's *Anna Karenina* is 'Happy families are all alike; every unhappy family is unhappy in its own way'. Tolstoy was seeking to show that for a family to be happy, several factors needed to be present. If there is a deficiency in one or more of these factors, the family will be unhappy (Tolstoy and Magarshack, 1961).

In science, the Anna Karenina principle is often used for significance testing. A deficiency in any one of a number of key aspects dooms a hypothesis to failure. Consequently, a successful hypothesis is one where every possible deficiency has been avoided. The Six Pillars of Experience must all be present for an outstanding customer experience. Table 6.1 shows the Six Pillar characteristics of leading firms. A company that masters the Six Pillars will achieve market-leading advocacy, loyalty and commercial returns.

The research shows that performance on the Six Pillars accounts for circa 65–70 per cent of a customer's NPS and an equal amount for loyalty. Factors outside the company's influence account for the remaining 30 per cent, for example the state of the economy, consumer confidence or the sector (e.g. financial services customers tend to be more reluctant to recommend). Price becomes less of a factor when high-quality experiences are delivered.

The Six Pillars are not simply predictors of customer experience success, but also of long-term financial value. This was powerfully apparent in work we carried out in 2016. We conducted an analysis in which customer experience performance was compared to revenues and profitability over previous years. This allowed us to contrast the performance of the CEE Top 100 brands, our 'customer champions', to the main FTSE 100 index. The difference was striking. Over this five-year period, the CEE Top 100 brands achieved double the revenue growth of the FTSE 100 – an average of 11 per cent rather than 5.5 per cent (KPMG, 2017).

TABLE 6.1   The Six Pillar characteristics of the world's leading firms

Integrity	• Active management of reputation/brand purpose and contribution to the world
	• Purpose drives internal behaviour and market ambition
	• Customer-oriented leadership behaviours – a servant leader model (there to remove problems for staff)
	• Culture of doing the right thing for customers – people empowered to do what is right
	• Memorable welcome process to set relationship tone, creates belief and trust at the outset
Resolution	• A culture of surfacing and solving customer problems
	• First point of contact resolution
	• Single point of ownership for complex issues
	• Agile response teams
	• Issue identification drives agile teams
	• Active customer recovery
Expectations	• Strong brand positioning made real
	• Clearly defined customer journeys with possible failure points and expectation reset points identified
	• Explicit strategies for exceeding customer expectations at psychologically memorable points
Time and effort	• Each journey and supporting process simplified and 'one touch'
	• Customer can choose contact method and move easily between them
	• Customer time investment recognized and rewarded
	• Continual focus on reducing customer friction points
	• Rapid time to market
Personalization	• Deep understanding of customer and their life problems across the business – circumstance-based segmentation models
	• Understand rational, physical and psychological needs arising from the customer's circumstances
	• Well-defined and understood target experiences
	• Individual customer recognized at outset and throughout journey, every customer treated as a unique individual
	• Products/solutions to resolve specific life problems
Empathy	• Entire company shows that it cares about customers
	• Able to build rapid rapport through problem recognition
	• An emotionally intelligent business
	• Reflects the diversity of its customers

The dynamics vary from business to business, of course. And it would be naive to suggest that a great experience always drives superior returns when there are other factors such as proposition and business model to take into account. But there is a clear link between customer excellence as defined by the Six Pillars and financial success. Put simply, those who master the Six Pillars also best capitalize on the economics of customer excellence and by doing so create significant shareholder value.

The Six Pillars origin

The Six Pillars were derived to solve a problem of definition. How do you codify the essential building blocks of a commercially beneficial customer experience?

In conducting millions of customer surveys we observed that customers in responding to NPS and CSAT surveys described different emotions in explaining the scores they gave. Using text analytics tools, six 'meta' categories emerged that provided a natural grouping for the multitude of emotions expressed (see Table 6.2).

TABLE 6.2   Net Promoter Score verbatim analysis

NPS score	Most frequently reported emotions	Staff behaviours	Pillars
10	Very happy, pleasure, delight, elation, proud, passionate	Caring Proactive with guidance Nothing too much trouble – going the extra mile Enthusiastic and welcoming	Empathy
9	Very grateful, valued, empowered	Understood me as a person Made me feel good about what I was doing Helped me resolve a major issue Flexibility Concerned	Personalization
8	Grateful, happy, enabled, pleased	Friendly, knowledgeable, helpful	Time and effort
7	Positive, content, satisfied, trusting	Competent, knowledgeable	

(continued)

TABLE 6.2 (continued)

NPS score	Most frequently reported emotions	Staff behaviours	Pillars
6	Helped, supported, confident	Professional, efficient	Expectations
5	Indifferent, unenthusiastic, tolerant	OK, robotic, diffident, off-hand	Resolution
4	Dissatisfied, unimportant, displeased, sad	Not taking ownership	
3	Distrust, frustrated	Repeating the company line	Integrity
2	Powerless, irritated, unhappy	Inflexible, unhelpful	
1	Annoyed, angry, mistrustful, mad	Unhelpful, passing the customer around	
0	Apoplectic, raging, upset	Rude, dismissive	

For organizations that target NPS and are concerned about how to make a difference to the number, this insight is very useful. Many companies struggle to understand the levers they have available to move their NPS scores. The above shows where they might focus their efforts.

In this chapter we examine each of the Six Pillars individually, the psychology behind them and golden rules that firms need to follow if they are going to improve each of the pillars.

Integrity

'Trust is earned in drops and lost in buckets.' What we consume says something about who we are and who we want to be. And increasingly, so does who we buy it from. Customers buy so much more than what brands do – they buy why they do it. The leading brands seek to build trust wherever and whenever possible. And they establish a two-way relationship with their customers, encouraging them to participate, to be involved as active shapers of the products and experiences that improve their lives (KPMG, 2019).

Perhaps not surprisingly, integrity is the most important pillar for driving recommendation in our research overall. Trust is in crisis around the globe. According to the Edelman Trust Barometer, which measures the levels of trust globally, it is clear that, with a few exceptions, trust has declined in nearly every major economy and many developing ones (KPMG, 2019). In fact, in 2020 it declined by five points globally (Edelman, 2021).

All brands operate within a larger narrative and the narrative of today is cynical and mistrusting. Against this backdrop, what consumers conceive a brand to be is changing rapidly. Customers form their perceptions of a brand based on their experiences. Brands are built in every interaction, at every touchpoint and in every social media post. A brand is the sum total of its words, deeds and operating philosophy (KPMG, 2019). Millennials, in particular, are drawn to organizations that display values and convictions beyond simply making money. They seek organizations that communicate their core beliefs openly and credibly; that are built around a compelling purpose, and where the 'why' and the 'how' are as important as the 'what' (KPMG, 2019).

Over time, our concept of brands has evolved through several stages: from brand as an identity, a differentiator, a quality mark and, more recently, a compelling idea. Now a brand must be linked to a philosophy containing values and beliefs and wrapped in a well-told story. The brand-building ploys of the latter part of the 20th century have left many organizations with empty marketing shells. CSR as a corporate nod to an ethical purpose is no longer good enough (KPMG, 2019). In essence, brands must have fewer tricks and more truth. There is no hiding place on the internet. The successful brands in our study have mastered the art of trust-based brand building. They have moved from an era where trust can be bought with advertising and product quality to an era where trust is built slowly over time, interaction after interaction. This is not consumption; it is a relationship. And at the heart of every successful relationship is trust (KPMG, 2019).

Customers of Lush around the world say they love the product, love the people and love the mission. It is a campaigning brand that communicates its purpose and its pursuit of ethical relationships with its people, its customers and the planet. The brand speaks to a fundamental human truth regardless of country. That is a large part of why consumers globally rank the brand top in their country for customer experience.

In China, where consumers have become wary of false advertising and false products, mobile payments platform Alipay has developed a legally protected account where customer money is held until the goods arrive in a satisfactory condition. Steps like this have helped build confidence in the platform and eased consumer fears while accelerating the adoption of online purchasing.

Brands such as USAA have become adept at 'signalling behaviours', continuously demonstrating to customers why they can be trusted. For example, at the height of the financial upselling scandal in the US, USAA ran an advertising campaign stating, 'We practice down selling, only selling you exactly what you need.' Over 70 per cent of USAA customers believe the company serves them rather than its bottom line (Chatterjee, 2017).

Our experience suggests that in every interaction a consumer has with an organization, there is a perceived moral code – a way of being that must align with the values of the consumer. The leading brands share a common characteristic: they seek to build trust wherever and whenever possible (KPMG, 2019). And they establish a two-way relationship with their customers, encouraging them to participate, to be involved as active shapers of the products and experiences that improve their lives. Without trust there is no basis for a relationship. Personally, commercially, emotionally, trust underpins every meaningful interaction we have in our lives. In today's social media world, trust and reputation are inextricably bound.

There are few CEOs who are not concerned with reputational risk; for them, integrity and trust are two sides of the same coin. Integrity is how a firm acts, trust is the outcome. When Dave Lewis, incoming CEO of Tesco in September 2014, faced multiple trust and integrity issues, his perspective was a simple one: when you face a loss of trust, you have to behave your way out of it (Tugby, 2015). Brand is what brand does.

There are trust-building events where organizations have the need to publicly react to a difficult situation, and trust-building moments where individual actions by staff add up to create trust in the organization. Trust is granular. It is made up of a multitude of small acts that build over time. This is a process you can't force or hasten. It is the natural outcome of a business whose behaviour, internally and externally, demonstrates trustworthiness through always doing the right thing for both employees and customers.

There are four critical elements that describe how an organization must act if it is to be deemed trustworthy by its customers (see Figure 6.2).

FIGURE 6.2   The Six Pillars of Experience two

Trust framework

The following trust framework illustrates the key areas for focus:

Brand principles		
Purpose	• Stand for something • Moral code • Dependable and consistent • Deliver the brand promise	

Experience interaction level		
Act in my best interest	• Show concern • My welfare is key • Act fairly	• Open and honest • Put me in control • Care about the outcomes
Ability	• Skill • Competence • Likeable • Knowledgeable	• Resourceful • Capabilities • Diagnostic capability • Demonstrate expertise
Behavioural integrity	• Credibility of communications • Deliver on promises • Commitment to standards • Congruence of word and deed	• Meeting deadlines • Consistency of interactions • Keep commitments

The science

In the first nanoseconds of meeting someone new, the human brain makes 12 different judgements about the individual in question and comes to a very quick decision as to whether the person can be trusted (Lebowitz et al, 2020). It is a mechanism formed at the outset of evolution to keep us safe. For early cavemen, faced with an axe-wielding enemy or a sabre-toothed tiger, instantaneous judgements were the difference between life and death.

Roy J. Lewicki, Professor Emeritus from Ohio State University's Fisher College of Business, is a leading expert in trust and trust management. He suggests that trust is built slowly over time, interaction after interaction: 'Trust builds along a continuum of hierarchical and sequential stages, such that as trust grows to a higher level it becomes stronger and more resilient and changes in character' (Lewicki and Wiethoff, 2000). He identifies that in the early stage of a relationship, trust is 'calculus-based trust (CBT)'. In other words, an individual carefully calculates how the other party is likely to behave in a given situation and extends their trust only so far as is necessary to achieve a positive outcome. It is a form of cognitive cost–benefit analysis tempered by the risk of extending trust. Calculus-based trust can be developed over time as the organization manages its corporate reputation, consistently delivers on its promises and behaves in trustworthy ways.

However, as the parties come to a deeper understanding of each other through repeated interactions, trust grows to a higher and quantitatively different level – identification-based trust (IBT), where each party identifies with the goals and objectives of the other. This is a more emotionally driven bond which is often difficult to break. Trust violations in the CBT phase may be highly destructive to the future of the relationship whereas they may not even be noticed in the IBT phase, such is the level of forgiveness achieved through numerous positive interactions. In this phase the trust dividend is enduring loyalty.

This has a multitude of implications for how companies 'on board customers' (Engage Customer, 2020). What happens first is the lens through which we judge what happens next. If what happens first is excellent, it is like building equity in an emotional bank account: we are more forgiving of subsequent issues. But if what happens first is poor, we magnify the emotional impact of follow-on problems.

In the UK banking market, with the advent of seven-day switching for current accounts, Santander Bank realized the importance of this and gave new customers to its 1|2|3 account what it calls the 'red carpet welcome', rapidly accumulating trust in the process (NRG, 2016). TSB Bank similarly defined what it calls internally 'the world's best welcome' (Joseph, 2013). Singapore Airlines welcomes passengers with carefully chosen fresh flower displays as they board the aircraft, the purple signifying dignity and respect – the company puts this into practice by taking great care over new or nervous passengers (Drescher, 2016). First impressions count.

The UK insurance industry has suffered a significant decline in customer trust. When Co-op Insurance sought to improve its customer experiences, it forensically examined its customer journeys for trust-eroding and trust-defining moments and then redesigned the customer journeys with trust building at the centre (KPMG, 2018). It also focused on resolution at first point of contact, knowing multiple contacts eroded trust. The net result was a 115-place improvement on our index and a 25 per cent reduction in costs.

Golden rules

CORPORATE REPUTATION: STAND FOR SOMETHING MORE THAN MAKING MONEY

Throughout Part 1, we outlined the importance of purpose based on our research. Millennials (and increasingly many consumers from other demographics) are looking for brands that have a strong sense of purpose, that stand for something, that add to the human condition, which in turn says something about the customers who buy from it.

Anita Roddick, the founder of The Body Shop, once posed the question: 'How do you ennoble the human spirit when you sell something as inconsequential as cosmetic cream?' Her answer was a simple one: by following a set of principles (Burlingham, 2013). Taking this a step further, Lush shuns the term 'ethics', preferring instead to focus on goodness, sustainability and animal welfare. Its view is a simple one: every business should be ethical – why should we talk about it (*The Guardian*, 2015)? John Spedan Lewis, founder of the John Lewis Partnership, somewhat presciently called it the 'third way': the duty a business has not just to its customers, staff and shareholders but also to make the world a better place (Bannerman, 2010).

We have consistently tracked the effect of the Marks and Spencer Plan A (because there is no Plan B) (M&S, 2017). Consumers feel more than reassured that M&S is doing the right thing; they feel personally engaged in doing the right thing.

In the world of social media, where brand behaviour is under constant scrutiny, the great brands anchor their market behaviour in a set of values and principles to guide and shape thinking in a way that ensures all behaviours are 'on brand'. Lush, first direct, John Lewis, Ocado, QVC are best-practice examples of organizations that have mastered this.

DEMONSTRABLY ACT IN MY BEST INTEREST: SHOW CONCERN FOR ME AS A PERSON

Our American research highlighted Charles Schwab, the investment bank. It first came to our attention when we noticed that an unusual number of respondents to our US study were of the view that Schwab would always act in the customer's best interest before their own. It represented an extraordinary level of trust for a financial institution.

The employees at Schwab are thinking about the customer continuously. When they realized that peer-to-peer reviews and evaluations were increasingly used as a failsafe by consumers, Schwab took the unusual step of enabling clients to leave reviews, positive or negative, on its website. An outstanding example of transparency and confidence (Schwab, 2021). At the day-to-day level, trust is built in myriad small ways. There is a range of 'signalling behaviours' which build a belief in the customer that the employee is concerned about their welfare and keen to do their best to help the customer achieve their objective. Listening intently, diagnostic probing techniques, showing understanding all signal to the customer that they are important and valued (Engage Customer, 2020).

BE COMPETENT AND LIKEABLE

Behavioural economics teaches us that we are naturally predisposed to trust experts (Bergland, 2015). Our assessment of the competence of the person we are interacting with is critical to trust building. In many cases we are likely to trust proxies for experts, whether that is technology based or even a celebrity endorsement. Increasingly, we obtain received trust as we scan reviews and referrals on the internet. The ability for customers to rapidly increase their knowledge of a topic by searching the internet has led to escalating expectations of the level of knowledge they should expect from a salesperson (Engage Customer, 2020).

John Lewis has consistently performed well in our UK index and key to achieving this was the level of knowledge displayed by its staff. They are experts in their specific category areas. Vitally, they offer their knowledge without expecting a sale in return. They see their mission as equipping the customer with everything that they need to know to make an informed decision. The customer may go elsewhere, but supported with the 'never knowingly undersold' guarantee, why would you (Engage Customer, 2020)? However, the proliferation of vendors with different pricing models over the internet is causing John Lewis to rethink this policy (BBC, 2020).

Similarly, Apple Store has pioneered the concept of the Genius. Easily accessible and available to answer any query – no matter how trivial.

Social psychologists talk about how social bonding increases social capital: we are more likely to trust someone who makes an effort to get to know us. And we know from behavioural economics that we trust people we like and we like people who like us (Bergland, 2015).

Trust is a two-way street, of course. It is one thing for a customer to trust an organization but another thing for an organization to trust its customers. Amazon trusts its customers when they report non-delivery; Marks & Spencer trusts its customers to return garments in good order. Many companies, however, do not trust their customers and put in place procedures and barriers that affect all customers rather than just the small few worthy of mistrust (Engage Customer, 2020).

DO WHAT YOU SAY YOU WILL

Behavioural integrity is the foundation upon which trust is built. Keeping promises and commitments, meeting deadlines and following through are prerequisites to a relationship based on trust in any walk of life. Congruence of word and deed is vital to employees at John Lewis – respondents frequently talk about how John Lewis employees always follow through on commitments, doing exactly what they said they would do (Engage Customer, 2020).

KLP in Norway is a life and pensions company whose entire ethos is based on ethical and responsible investing (Fixsen, 2017). It recognizes that when your focus is on doing the right thing, you need to be able to make tough choices. To help its employees live the brand, the company has developed a set of principles that it will not compromise on. It also publishes a list of companies that it will invest in and a list of those it has excluded (those whose commercial practices are outside the principles KLP espouses). In some cases, this has meant withdrawing from companies that operate in current war zones or those whose practices towards indigenous people are open to question (KPMG, 2019).

BUILDING THE TRUST AGENDA INTERNALLY

Trust is the basis of all strong human relationships. It is declining in business and public life, yet more prized than ever. In the integrity economy, the organizations that can capture trust are those that are best equipped to endure.

Trust starts with the employee. How can customers be expected to trust an organization if those inside it don't? A lack of internal trust requires a new focus on elevating trust in the workplace. According to the 2018 Edelman 'Trust Barometer' (a survey of 33,000 people in 28 countries) (Manning, 2021), one in three people don't trust their employer. Employees remarked that they trust their peers more than the CEO and upper-level executives of their company.

Mistrust occurs when large companies are perceived to be acting in their own interests first, putting shareholders ahead of customers and employees. Leaders need to demonstrate that they are trustworthy and employees need to see integrity practised daily by organizational role models. This means doing the right thing because it is the right thing to do; leading in alignment with the values of the organization; rewarding and recognizing those who act with integrity; and giving trust while asking for trust in return. Internal trust precedes external trust, and in today's world both are needed for growth (KPMG, 2019).

Trust in an organization is highly nuanced and takes many forms:

- trust in each other;
- trust in immediate manager;
- trust in senior leaders;
- trust in the organization;
- trust in how the organization relates to external stakeholders (media, regulators, customers).

M&S Food, which has consistently been one of the leading firms in our index, has laid out its ethical and trustworthiness credentials with Plan A, its commitment to the provenance of its produce and the standards by which it is created. Cleverly, it has not claimed the high ground, it has simply increased its commitment every year to doing the right thing in the right way. The result has been a significant increase in the level of trust the business enjoys from its customers. It has also resulted in considerable pride among employees (KPMG, 2019).

For millennials in particular, the sense of trust is inextricably linked to the purpose of the organization that they are dealing with, as customers and as employees. This sense of purpose doesn't necessarily have to be socially or environmentally oriented – it can be a commitment to meet the needs of a particular customer group in a special way. But it is crucial that the company clearly and unequivocally puts the needs of its customers and employees before its own (KPMG, 2019).

What our study shows is that in today's world, trust has become the imperative for staying in business and is a vital prerequisite of growth: it starts internally and radiates externally.

Resolution

The great companies can be recognized by the way they fix things when they go wrong. Even the best companies realize that from time to time unexpected things will happen and they need to have a plan B, a contingency for resolving customer issues when things go adrift. What is critical, though, is not that they fix things, but how they leave the customer feeling when they put things right. Companies such as John Lewis and Waitrose describe it as 'heroic' recovery, ensuring the customer feels better about the organization because of the way they have handled things (Cooper, 2013).

Known as the 'service recovery paradox', it is a phenomenon we have observed frequently in our client research. It is reflected most clearly in Net Promoter Scores. If something goes wrong and it is fixed adequately – that is, the customer is returned to the position they were in pre-issue – the individual's NPS score tends to drop by an average of 10 points. If it continues to be a problem, the score drops to minus 45. But if it is fixed brilliantly, then the score rises to plus 10 points.

The best companies don't try to solve problems for customers. Instead, they solve problems with customers. They learn about problems customers want to solve and outcomes they want to accomplish. They use these insights to shift their focus from products to customer solutions.

When Anne Mulcahy took over as CEO of Xerox in 2001, she faced an all but insurmountable task: she was being urged to declare bankruptcy, debt was mounting, the stock was sinking and the bankers were calling in loans. By the time she relinquished her role in 2010, the company was vibrant, profitable and revitalized. When asked how this was achieved, she said, 'I focused on impact, solving problems with people around the world.' Famously she offered to fly anywhere any time to save a Xerox customer (Wijeseri, 2019).

Problem solving is a mindset. The approach is the same whether it is solving customer life problems or problems caused by organizational pain points. Great companies do not leave problem solving to complaints or customer services; they are constantly looking for new customer problems to solve, and that requires closeness to the customer and highly developed empathy.

Problems rarely occur in isolation – there is often a series of problems that gets in the way of what the customer perceives to be a successful outcome. Problem mapping based on the customer's objective is useful both for removing internal pain points and for developing commercially viable solutions.

Consider the following. Fitbit is a product many people use as a fitness aid. However, for an individual seeking to get in shape to run a marathon (event), it is only part of what they need. Alongside their Fitbit, they will need to assess their current level of fitness (circumstance), they will want gym membership, a geolocation device, a heart monitor, a guide on diet and a structured eating programme that suits their level of fitness and calorie consumption (jobs to be done). They will want to know the progress they are making towards their goal (motivation) and ideally to have all of this in one place (solution). They will want to share their experiences in a learning environment with others (connection) and deal with companies that reflect their values and support their motivations (purpose).

This, then, is the entirety of an experience. It is a series of hurdles and obstacles, all of which can be removed with a solution to the experience need. It is not just about friendly service or a great product, it is about how you work back from the customer's life to deliver impactful solutions.

When problems are caused for customers by internal failings, customer recovery is highly important. Even with the best processes and procedures, things will go wrong. Great companies have a process that not only puts the customer back in the position they should have been in as rapidly as possible but also makes the customer feel really good about the experience.

The science

At the heart of resolution lies the human desire for peace of mind, the satisfaction that arises from the absence of anxiety and worry.

- When issues occur, customers can feel out of control, have a fear of unplanned consequences and find their stress and anger levels increasing.
- A contingency plan for avoiding these negative feelings reduces anxiety; having that plan associated with the brand over the long term builds confidence. It is believed that one very poor experience requires five positive ones to overwrite it in memory (Tugend, 2012).
- The Service Recovery Paradox describes the impact on the customer of how a problem is fixed. Earlier in this section we looked at the quantitative NPS impact but, done well, heroic recovery equips and motivates customers with positive stories to tell friends and colleagues. The Jet Blue pilot who bought delivery pizzas for passengers subject to a lengthy tarmac delay is an oft-repeated tale.

For the top organizations, a problem-solving mindset focused on resolution is more than a protective response to the great amplifier of social media and resultant reputational risk. It is based on a genuine desire to make things right for the customer and to ensure the brand promise is consistently delivered each time, every time.

John Lewis and Waitrose refer to it as 'heroic recovery'. Amazon refers to this process as 'inverting the turtle'. When a turtle falls on its back, it cannot get back on its four legs again without intervention. Amazon assumes end-to-end responsibility for anything that goes wrong under its brand and it is the epitome of successful resolution. Respondents to our Customer Experience Excellence study provided case study after case study of how Amazon has successfully resolved problems, many of which were not of its own making.

Apple Store has realized that encouraging customers to interact with a Genius is a key resolution point for both user- and device-related issues. Apple has even gone as far as developing its own positive language around resolution. Apple products do not crash – they simply 'stop responding'. At Apple, employees are advised to be careful in how they phrase things. If an account or client is difficult, employees replace words such as 'annoying' or 'too much work' with 'opportunity to get better' or 'chance to learn what we did wrong'. Positivity is contagious and every failure is seen as an opportunity to improve service to customers (Richardson, 2017).

Nationwide Building Society has climbed inexorably up our UK Customer Experience Excellence league table, breaking into the top 10 in 2014. Resolution is key to its experience strategy. Encouraging customers to share problems and issues enables root-cause analysis and resolution action planning. Resolution at first point of contact and first-contact ownership have driven dramatic improvements in service. A closed-loop, voice-of-the-customer system supports issue identification and ensures that customers who have an issue are immediately re-contacted.

Ocado has driven its superior customer experience by empowering its drivers to immediately deal with any issues customers may have with breakages or substitutions, thus ensuring rapid resolution at point of need.

Ritz-Carlton is renowned for 'legendary service'. Like Ocado, resolution is achieved through staff empowerment. Every employee is empowered to spend up to $3,000 without having to seek management approval to put something right for the customer. But at Ritz-Carlton it is more than just fixing things; it is about anticipatory service, getting to the customer with solutions before the customers themselves realize they have an issue or a problem.

Joshi the giraffe became famous when a seven-year-old boy left his favourite stuffed toy behind after a family visit to the Miami Ritz-Carlton. The good thing to do was to reunite boy and giraffe as rapidly as possible. The great thing to do was to spend an hour photographing Joshi enjoying the delights of the hotel, having a massage in the spa, resting by the pool, in the bar with other stuffed toy guests and driving a buggy along the beach. (Who knew a stuffed giraffe could drive?) Joshi was indeed returned rapidly but with a photo album showing that Joshi had really enjoyed his extended holiday. At Ritz-Carlton, resolution is definitely effected with style and élan.

Golden rules

ASSUME MY INNOCENCE – SEE MY POINT OF VIEW

It is difficult enough trying to resolve a problem without having to prove you are innocent at the same time. The new breed of online retailers (Amazon, AO, Zappos) has completely redefined the starting position for resolution, designing their process for the satisfaction of the 99 per cent who are not trying to rip them off rather than the 1 per cent who are.

A WARM AND SINCERE APOLOGY

The psychology of sorry is an interesting one. Psychologists David De Cremer and Chris Reinders Folmer report that people who have a complaint believe that an apology will help, but when they actually get one, it doesn't seem to live up to expectations (De Cremer et al, 2010). That is often because, although well intentioned, the apology fails to show empathy for the resulting customer situation and a clear stated intent to put things right. So feeling heard and acknowledged is a key part of the apology process. It is vital that the customer feels listened to.

One of our respondents recalled that when ringing John Lewis to report a faulty kettle which leaked steam, the agent's response was, 'Oh my goodness, I am so sorry to hear that – are you OK?' The agent's primary concern was for the customer. A new kettle was delivered the following morning.

Professor De Cremer suggests that his results indicate that a sincere apology is a first step in the reconciliation process, but you need to show that you will do something else (De Cremer et al, 2010). Leaving the customer feeling satisfied with the situation and the organization requires action or substance.

OWN THE RESOLUTION – FIX WITH URGENCY

Poor or slow response can do swift damage to a company's reputation. Responding rapidly and keeping customers informed helps remove the emotion and can also leave customers feeling positive. The speed with which RBS and NatWest responded to their well-publicized banking platform outages in 2012 and their rapid remediation actually saw an increase in the banks' NPS scores.

SURPRISE ME IN HOW WELL YOU FIX MY ISSUE

Is there a Joshi moment? Can the issue be fixed with style and élan? Appliances Online came fifth in our survey; two of our respondents told us that when a cooker failed to arrive from the manufacturer, AO sent pizzas to keep its customers fed. Also, when a washing machine could not be delivered to a new mother, the company sent baby clothes.

GO THE EXTRA MILE IF REQUIRED

One of our respondents recalled how impressed he was by the way an Emirates hostess in the Dubai airport lounge reacted when he mentioned to her that the bathroom had run out of towels. She ran to the service area to fix the issue. She was showing that she realized that time was a vital commodity in an airport: it was important to her that the issue was fixed as quickly as possible.

GIVE ME OPTIONS GOING FORWARD

It is rare that there is one course of action leading to rectification. It is helpful to give the customer options to see which suits them best. One of our respondents described how when John Lewis were unable to deliver an item to them 'not only did it offer an alternative date but the option of it being delivered to my local Waitrose (only a mile away) or my office, asking the question: which would suit me best?'

The service recovery paradox works in specific circumstances. It isn't always true that great recovery will repair the damage to the relationship, but the great organizations have learned they can benefit enormously in terms of customer satisfaction, advocacy and loyalty when they put things right with style.

Expectations

Meeting or, where possible, exceeding customer expectations.

The third pillar is expectations (Engage Customer, 2020). They can be described as the pre-experience beliefs about how a product or service will be delivered that serve as a standard or reference point against which the performance of an organization will be judged. Knowing what the customer expects is the first and possibly most critical step in delivering great experiences.

It has been widely accepted that exceeding customer expectations is key to customer satisfaction, delight and loyalty. More recently research has shown that the very minimum for customer satisfaction is meeting expectations. Accordingly, it is critical for organizations to try to find out in advance what their customers' expectations are, because a failure to meet or exceed those expectations could lead to dissatisfaction and defection (Engage Customer, 2020).

In a world where expectations are a moving target, accurately setting and then meeting expectations has to become a core competence. Consequently, world-class organizations pay attention to two things: how expectations are formed and then how they meet those expectations. Amazon, for example, strives to ensure that it delivers products within three days. It sets the expectation and then uses a range of delivery methods to exceed it (*Daily Mail*, 2019). At the very least, it expects to meet the expectation it has set.

When Zappos started trading, it had a choice: invest in advertising or invest in the experience and drive word of mouth. It chose the latter, really wowing its customers by shipping products by air overnight. Customers' expectations at the time were for a three-day delivery; in fact, if they ordered before midnight, they were likely to get their products by 8.00 am the following morning. Zappos didn't reveal how it achieved this miracle and its customers, duly excited, told their friends and colleagues about this amazing service, fuelling the Zappos word-of-mouth marketing strategy (Hsieh, 2010).

Expectations can be set explicitly or implicitly. Some brands embed achieving the expectation in their brand promise: motoring rescue company Green Flag (we get to you within 60 minutes or you receive £10 compensation) (Green Flag, 2021); Premier Inn (a great night's sleep or your money back) (Premier Inn, 2021); Ibis hotels guarantee to resolve any issue you may have with the service received in the hotel within 15 minutes or your stay is free (Ibis, 2021).

For other organizations the expectations are set implicitly. Ritz-Carlton, for example, delivers on multiple small expectations knowing that cumulatively these add up to the brand promise: 'where the genuine care and comfort of our guests is our highest mission'. In fact, at Ritz-Carlton, managing each individual guest's expectations is a science and provides the basis for a highly personalized service to its customers. In each hotel within the chain, a special organization exists called guest recognition. This special function uses the CLASS database to remember over 800,000 guests and generate information for all appropriate staff. It stores likes/dislikes, previous difficulties, family interests, personal interests, preferred credit card, frequency of stay, lifetime usage/amount of purchase. In this way staff are able to understand what is 'new or different' about an individual customer. Staff carry special notebooks to capture insights on each guest and then input the information into the database. It ensures that Ritz-Carlton is able to continually meet and often exceed guests' expectations. They call it the Ritz-Carlton Mystique (Michelli, 2013).

Great organizations manage both explicit and implicit expectations. In particular they focus on how expectations are formed and develop their strategies accordingly. They ask themselves the following questions:

- How does word of mouth shape expectations?
- What are the explicit and overt promises or commitments that we can make to our customers?
- What are the small ways in which we set expectations day to day? Do we set expectations accurately?
- What are the intensifiers – those things that load our customers' expectations with emotion?
- Who is setting our customers' expectations for service? What do we need to do to respond?

Not all expectations are equal. Organizations have choices about the expectations they meet, the expectations they exceed and how they might delight the customer. In many instances, a customer will have a range within which their expectations can be met. For example, some customers will be willing to wait for 60 seconds for the phone to be answered and their satisfaction will not change if the phone is answered within 120 seconds. This is known as the zone of tolerance and is vital for planning response times and optimizing resources.

The science

Expectations are how we make sense of the world and understand what will happen next. Daniel Kahneman describes how our brains have two systems which view the world through our network of expectations. System one is our monitoring system, which enables us to operate on automatic for much of the time. As long as everything meets our expectations, we can do things without consciously thinking about them. However, when our expectations are not met, system two is activated, which brings the failure to meet the expectation to our conscious attention. It activates our emotions and we become fearful if we can no longer accurately predict what will happen next (Kahneman, 2013).

So we like it when things happen the way that we expect. We like it even more when we're not sure that things will happen as well as we expect and they happen that way anyway. We particularly like it when our expectations are exceeded in a pleasurable way. The brain is continually forecasting and reforecasting what is likely to happen next. This process happens below the level of consciousness and uses heuristics and shortcuts to save computational effort. This is why expectations are such a vital part of customer experience.

The Kano model

Professor Noriaki Kano, Professor Emeritus of the Tokyo University of Science, anticipated the rise of expectations in business science and developed a widely recognized customer satisfaction model which shows that what was once unexpected becomes expected through familiarity. It is this effect that has driven the escalation in expectations and the phenomenon of expectations transfer, where our best experience in any category sets our expectations for a similar experience in another category.

Golden rules

SET MY EXPECTATIONS ACCURATELY

AO is a good example of an organization that manages expectations very skilfully. As long as you order from the appliances company before 8.00 pm, it will deliver the following day, at a time slot of your choosing. This approach to expectation management is carefully orchestrated. Setting and meeting the logistical expectations of the customer is the first step – the way in which staff deal with the customer, the care they take and the friendliness of their people then exceeds expectations, leading to a delighted customer.

AGREE TIMINGS WITH ME

Being clear on the plan and what the customer needs to do is vital to successful expectation management. AO has been successful because it is absolutely clear on timings and requirements of the customer. Being able to set a convenient time is a key first step.

The advent of tracking technology has changed consumer expectations around being kept informed. Ocado set new standards in this area, texting customers in advance with information about the delivery vehicle – its colour and driver name and contact details, overcoming any concerns as to whether the person at your door is from Ocado or not. An estimate of the delivery time and any substitutions are also conveyed, all of which builds trust.

RESPOND MORE QUICKLY THAN I ANTICIPATE

A rapid response to queries, issues or complaints is what customers expect: the company should see the situation from the customer perspective and act accordingly. Rapid response is a hygiene factor rather than a delight factor. It provides reassurance that the company takes the situation seriously.

USE PLAIN ENGLISH – NO JARGON

The language used is also very important. Vague promises lead to frustration. Clear promises, such as those made by John Lewis Partners ('never knowingly undersold') and Premier Inn ('a good night's sleep or your money back'), establish the ground rules from the outset. Customers have become adept at spotting obfuscation and hidden get-outs.

FULFIL OR EXCEED YOUR PROMISES

Failing to meet an overt promise is worse than not making a promise at all. We saw, above, that AO has a process for dealing with customers when it is just not possible for it to meet its promise, sending takeaway pizza when a cooker could not be delivered, etc. Exceeding the expectation even after failing to meet an expectation.

GUIDE ME THROUGH THE PROCESS

By guiding the customer carefully through the process, expectations can be accurately set and then delivered against. Customers often have no idea how long it might take to meet their objective. A process that sets expectations ensures the organization is not caught out.

Time and effort

Minimizing customer effort and creating frictionless processes.

The next pillar is valuing time and effort (Engage Customer, 2020). When we ask a customer to invest their time with us to achieve an objective, we should recognize that investment and show that we are thankful for it. It is also about making things as simple as possible, so the customer time investment is minimized. Essentially it is about how the customer feels about the time investment they have made.

Time poverty is a feature of modern-day lives. Customers gravitate towards companies that make life easy for them and reward them by choosing to spend time (and money). By understanding and examining these 'effort components' it is possible to break down and understand the customer journey from a different perspective. It enables us to see where we can take effort out of the process for the benefit of the customer.

There are two effort areas that can then be used to guide customer experience design:

1 The removal of 'non-added-value time' waiting periods that cannot be transformed into adding value for the customer through education, information or entertainment. Lidl, for example, has re-engineered its checkout procedures so that the big delay with customers repacking their shopping after scanning is done away from the till. It reduces the delay impact of a major bottleneck.

2 The focus on minimum viable actions, a concept borrowed from Six Sigma (Wendell, 2021). It seeks to creatively design experiences that ensure that customers can achieve their objectives in the minimum possible number of steps.

Amazon has taken this to heart. In fact, its mantra is 'the best service is no service – when things just work' (Price and Jaffe, 2008). By systematically removing impediments to the customer achieving their objective, Amazon has driven up satisfaction and revenue. One-click ordering is a good example of ensuring nothing gets in the way of a customer making a purchase.

The Transportation Security Administration in the US is modifying its queuing system at airports based on the amount of help a passenger needs, streaming customers not by the order they have presented themselves but by whether they have children, are infrequent flyers and need help, or are frequent flyers and know the procedures backwards. This ensures each group clears security with the minimum viable number of steps given their level of knowledge or number of children.

Telecoms company BT's 'Customer Effort' research indicated that effort really is a key measure of customer loyalty and it does have an impact on perceived value for money (only 5 per cent of customers who had a difficult experience said they felt they had got good value for money). Customers who said BT was an easy company to do business with were 40 per cent less likely to go to a competitor than those who ranked BT as difficult (Steers, 2012).

Research by the Corporate Executive Council estimates that in any experience, how a customer feels about the effort they expend represents 65 per cent of their total assessment of the experience (Dixon et al, 2010). We know that what happens first (law of primacy) in an experience sets the tone for the remainder of the experience; a good start and the customer will be more forgiving of future transgressions. What happens last is what the customer remembers (law of recency). The combination of these two is known as the serial position effect. If the first impression of an experience is a long, unproductive wait followed by a high-effort interaction, no matter how well the experience ends, the memory will be a poor one. Managing waiting time and effort is therefore critical to positive memories of the event.

Computer science researcher Don Norman in his paper 'The psychology of waiting lines' identifies eight principles that govern how we should think about waiting time (Norman, 2018):

- Emotion dominates.
- Eliminate confusion (provide a clear model of how the queuing system will work).
- The wait must be appropriate.
- Set expectations, then meet or exceed them.
- Keep people occupied (filled time passes more quickly than unfilled time).
- Be fair.
- End strong and start strong.
- The memory of the event is more important than the actual experience.

The top organizations in our research programme observe these eight principles, but in assessing how they deliver against them they pay attention to three important things:

1 What was actually done to or for the customer.
2 What was perceived by the customer.
3 What the customer expected.

CASE STUDY
Zalando

Started in 2008, Zalando has a market capitalization of $11.85 billion, employs 15,000 staff and is building an 'operating system for fashion', providing logistics, technology and marketing solutions to brand partners across its business. It is a 'consumer platform' aimed at fashion. Starting in the Netherlands, Zalando subsequently expanded to 15 European markets in 24 months.

Central to its differentiation is convenience. From the outset, the founders of Zalando believed that they should be focused on a great experience in terms of delivery and the opportunity to return and call customer service, which required them to own the logistics, the customer service interface and the online experience. They invested heavily in front- and back-office technology to ensure it was all aligned and connected. They foresaw the world of platforms. For example, there is one app for transport (Uber), one major app for entertainment (Netflix) and one app for music (Spotify). They wanted to be the app for fashion.

David Schneider, co-founder of Zalando, describes the objective as being to create a destination for consumers and a platform for brands, an integrated marketplace dedicated to fashion. A single app for fashion. The founders looked at best practice from Zappos, Alibaba and WeChat, which had developed ecosystems by platforming their assets. They recognized that there are huge inefficiencies in online retail and specifically in fashion. Potentially warehouses full of inventory if you get things wrong – building an operating system for fashion helps de-risk the enterprise and enables those closest to the trends to market their products in a conducive market environment. This requires making everything accessible, convenient and personalized. Such a platform helps companies digitize, bring their products to market and reach new customers (KPMG, 2019).

The science

Our brains consume roughly 20 per cent of the body's energy. Psychologists have long recognized this with the 'law of least effort'. Our brains are 'cognitive misers' and will do the easy thing rather than the complex thing that requires thought and thus energy. Even though we have intricate minds, we don't want to think too hard, or too much, if we don't have to. If there are several ways to do something, we choose the course of action that's the least cognitively demanding. And this is often done without conscious thought (Lanoue, 2015).

The principle of cognitive efficiency says that individuals are unlikely to expend any more cognitive effort than necessary to attain the objective they are pursuing. Thus, they use the procedure or judgemental criterion that is easiest to apply. The principle of knowledge accessibility says that individuals typically use only a small subset of the relevant knowledge they have acquired as a basis for comprehending information – generally the knowledge that comes to mind most quickly and easily (Boyd, 2013). When something is unexpectedly easy, the 'fluency effect' describes how we ascribe much greater value to the activity and the firm that provides it.

Golden rules

Key parts of the customer experience (often because they happen first) are the time we spend waiting and the effort required to achieve our objectives. Our studies show that in both of these it is not the actual experience that counts, it is how customers feel about the experience that matters. Indeed, we would go further – it is the memory of the experience that counts. Positive memories are created when the following golden rules are applied.

MAKE MY TIME INVESTMENT PLEASURABLE

Disney theme parks are probably the champions at handling the frustration of queues. When people are asked what they disliked the most, the answer is immediate: the lines, the queues and the waiting. People dislike the queues. But when it comes to the question of whether they would go again, the answer is a resounding yes. It is the memories that count. For many rides, Disney has cleverly incorporated the queue into part of the experience, as a briefing or an orientation exercise, which makes them feel more appropriate, fair and manageable. More recently the Disney wristband and FastPass have removed the need for extensive waits (Walt Disney World, 2021).

GIVE ME SIMPLE, CLEAR INSTRUCTIONS (ENGAGE CUSTOMER, 2020)

Albert Einstein remarked that 'a thing should be made as simple as it can be but not simpler' (Sessions, 1950). The balance between too much information and too little information is a fine one. Apple is celebrated for its design-led approach to simplicity; the 'start-up' guide to a new phone or iPad ensures that the customer can get started and become productive immediately.

MINIMUM VIABLE STEPS TO MY OBJECTIVE – MAXIMUM OF THREE

What is the irreducible number of steps required for the customer to achieve their objective? A much publicized advert from Lidl dramatized how much easier Lidl is to do business with than Morrisons. The ad listed the 44 steps you needed to undertake to achieve lower prices via rival supermarket Morrisons' loyalty card. Or, the ad said, 'You could just go to Lidl' (Ehrenberg, 2014). Our research shows that any more than three steps begins to irritate or confuse. NPS scores tend to drop at step 4.

NO LONGER THAN TWO MINUTES WAITING

Psychological research has shown that when forced to wait, our minds turn towards things that are troubling us or that we are preoccupied with. The net result is that our mood state deteriorates (Tartakovsky, 2016). Typically, we see NPS scores drop when people are forced to wait beyond two minutes. In Australia, the banks have moved to a two-tier contact centre model, an immediate answer (almost like a switchboard) and then being routed to the necessary area of expertise. They have seen significant improvements in satisfaction. There is something about the immediacy of speaking to a human being, removing many of the negative waiting effects, even though the elapsed time to resolution is the same.

PROVIDE THE ANSWERS I NEED WHEN I CONTACT YOU

In a world of ubiquitous information, we expect the first person we contact to have all our relevant information to hand and to have a level of competence in the subject matter that exceeds our own. Prudential moved over 100 places up our UK Top 100 in 2014 after huge investment in training its people and the deployment of CRM and knowledge systems that supported first point of contact resolution (Knight et al, 2015).

ADVISE ME OF PITFALLS AHEAD

Staying a step ahead of the customer and recognizing potentially negative situations before they develop is important. One respondent to our survey described asking a bank call centre agent to enable debit card usage in Paris. The agent completed the task and then offered a phone number that could be reached via the customer's mobile phone from the till in Paris, which would immediately authorize the transaction in the event of any problems.

Increasingly, speed and ease are becoming a source of competitive advantage: we desire instant gratification and are often willing to forego greater rewards in the future for immediate rewards now. Kindle, for example, has revolutionized book reading: see it, buy it, read it, transact in seconds, and all from the comfort of your own home. AO, in our most recent experience excellence survey, was lauded for its rapid approach to appliance purchasing: order before 7.30 pm and the appliance will be delivered free of charge the following day. The effortless speedy experience is becoming a key differentiator.

Personalization

The fifth pillar is personalization – using individualized attention to drive an emotional connection. For many companies this involves getting the right information to the right customer at the right time, and that is certainly important. But true personalization comes from a deep understanding of the customer's circumstances, the tailoring of the experience to meet those circumstances and how the customer is left feeling about themselves after an interaction. Do they feel important, valued, has their sense of self-worth improved because they know more, feel more in control and better equipped to deal with the world?

In the new post-COVID-19 world, knowing and recognizing a customer is no longer enough: customers now expect firms to understand them as well.

Personalization involves demonstrating that you understand the customer's specific needs and circumstances and will adapt the experience accordingly. Use of name, individualized attention, knowledge of preferences and past interactions all add up to an experience that feels personal. It makes the customer feel important and valued and begins to build an emotional connection. A great personalization experience plays to the ego and leaves the customer with an elevated sense of self-worth. Among the Six Pillars, personalization has the most significant impact on advocacy and loyalty.

Thanks to technological advances, much of the work on personalization done by organizations has been 'inside out': for example, the deployment of web content, based on explicit preferences, implicit behaviour or previous history and the ability to target customers with the right offer at the right time in the right place.

If we step into customers' shoes and take an 'outside in' approach, then personalization is more about how an organization responds to a range of emotional needs: the desire to feel unique, an individual – valued and important.

The science

As consumers we are attracted to personalized experiences because they make us feel recognized: feeling significant is more important in today's marketplace where we can feel like just another consumer. We want to behave and be appreciated as an individual, with our unique wants, needs and desires.

In their 2002 paper, researchers Pelham, Mirenberg and Jones argue that people have a basic desire to feel good about themselves and behave according to that desire. These automatic positive associations would influence feelings about almost anything associated with the self (Pelham et al, 2002). 'Implicit egotism' refers to the psychological phenomena which combine to give us the unconscious component of our sense of self-esteem – the hypothesis is that humans have an unconscious preference for things they associate with themselves.

A personalized experience gives the impression that we matter to the companies that are serving us: understanding personalization is increasingly important to businesses seeking customer loyalty and advocacy.

Golden rules

GREET ME

How we are greeted sets the tone for what happens next. Call centres have long acknowledged the power of the opening and encourage employees to put a smile in the voice. Some even go as far as putting mirrors on desks so employees can see themselves smile!

Ritz-Carlton has a mantra of 'Radar on – Antenna up', ensuring staff are attentive to acknowledging every guest and identifying the unexpressed needs that can make a difference to a guest's stay (Robertson, 2021). Premier Inn in the UK has learned much from this approach. All staff smile, make eye contact and have personal greetings for guests. More importantly, they are willing to engage and help wherever they can.

SHOW ME YOU KNOW ME

We all like to be recognized – the maître d' at a restaurant that remembers our name and our favourite table by the window is a movie trope but still effective. So it is with companies – we like to think we matter to our suppliers and at the very least they should recognize us.

The famed British Airways 'Know Me' programme addressed this head on (Business Traveller, 2021). Using digital technology, onboard tablets were uploaded pre-flight with information on individual passengers so the crew could welcome them by name. For example, if a Silver Executive Club member is flying in business class for the first time, the technology enables the crew to welcome the passenger and articulate the benefits of the cabin. Or if a frequent flyer has had problems on a previous flight, the crew recognize the issue and use it as an opportunity to go the extra mile and help the passenger on their forward journey.

RECOGNIZE OUR HISTORY TOGETHER

When we meet someone we have any form of relationship with, we know we have a shared history, a series of previous exchanges that shape the tone of any interaction. It enables us to pick up where we left off last and is the essence of any relationship. Technology can now appear to replicate this at scale. Our research suggests that Amazon does this better than most, using your name, showing your history together, reacting to your preferences and providing little moments of delight as its recommendation engine finds something unique to you.

The professionalism and responsiveness of staff set one of the largest European opticians, Specsavers, apart from its competitors. Respondents to our survey talked about feeling that when dealing with Specsavers staff, they were all that was important. Many respondents highlighted the patience of staff as they tried on frame after frame to get the right look. They also cited a sense of collaboration, that staff worked with them to make sure their needs were met.

MAKE ME COMPETENT

Increasing a customer's knowledge improves their sense of self-worth and puts them in control.

In Taiwan, Taishin Bank developed digital bank Richart with the goal of providing the best financial customer experience through mobile banking. A favourite of young Taiwanese, Richart has as its goal to teach young Taiwanese residents how to effectively manage their wealth at an early age. Richart has been conducting campus lectures in universities and schools across the country. Richart is the first digital banking product in Taiwan to undergo the social return on investment (SROI), an internationally recognized project performance evaluation approach, to provide insight into

Richart's influence on society. It showed that every NT$1 of investment into Richart has the potential to create NT$5.5 of societal value – which is 1.5 times (KPMG, 2020).

Staff training is deep rooted in Lush's customer experience strategy to ensure the right products are prescribed. Lush staff are trained to ask diagnostic questions and provide demonstrations, samples and testing. Staff won't attempt to prescribe a product until they have a deep understanding of a customer's needs. Do they have problems with skin conditions? What works or doesn't work with their beauty regime? These are key questions which highlight underlying issues or problems that the staff can fix. Through cultivating this deep understanding, Lush has delighted customers – and it also sells considerably more products.

The need to feel in control is a powerful motivational driver. Appliances Online cleverly puts customers in control in many different ways. They can choose delivery times and read detailed descriptions and website reviews of individual products. Choice is a key element of control – too wide a choice breeds confusion, too small a choice and customers feel railroaded. According to customers, AO gets it just right, enabling them to choose from a range that's neither too large nor too small (Engage Customer, 2020).

SURPRISE ME WITH SOMETHING RELEVANT

Black Tomato is one of the UK's fastest growing online travel companies yet to make it into the CEE Top 100. However, its approach is remarkable. Customers choose their destination not by selecting a location but by how they want to feel on holiday. They receive a small, but uniquely relevant, gift on departure, an 'arts of travel' kit, which can include everything from relevant literature to music inspired by the destination to get the traveller excited and in the pre-adventure frame of mind, and a 'return to reality' kit containing a bottle of wine and vouchers for a takeaway when they return. Black Tomato recognizes the emotional highs and lows of a holiday and architects customers' experiences accordingly (Scheffler, 2016).

UNDERSTAND MY NEEDS AND CIRCUMSTANCES

In Chapter 2 we identified that 'understand me' is as important as 'know me'. It is the essential precursor to empathy and the first step in tailoring an experience.

In the US, the number one customer experience company USAA examines its customers' lives forensically, regularly bringing customers into its offices for 'encounter sessions' during which members of staff can hear first hand what is important to a customer and what is going on in their lives. By focusing on life events USAA is able to understand how a customer going into a life event is likely to be feeling and what is needed to successfully navigate that life event. It is a method of mass individualization as every customer experiencing a life event will feel the help, support and guidance that USAA provides is unique to them (Solomon, 2018).

INDIVIDUALIZE WHAT YOU DO

It is said that great radio broadcasters speak as if to an audience of one. Each listener feels they are the only one being addressed. Great customer experiences are the same. Stitch Fix is an example of how a customer experience can be individualized at scale. Highly individualized clothing selections are provided to each individual client. Data science, algorithms and artificial intelligence are used to match the right clothes to the right person. CEO and founder Katrina Lake describes the interaction process as an ongoing conversation, a mechanism by which the company and the customer understand each other more. Customer responses indicate their needs and preferences, whether the items are right for their body shape or their lifestyle or their overall taste. It is all useful information used to help recommend exactly the right products for their customer.

Customers complete an 80-question survey at the outset and then 85 per cent of customers in the US give feedback to Stitch Fix on whether they like or dislike items they have been sent, as well as advising on how well they fit. More than 75 per cent have played the company's Style Shuffle game, which encourages customers to like particular styles and clothes and then generates product ratings to fuel algorithms that will pair up customers with an item that fits them perfectly and suits their tastes (Pithers, 2019).

Empathy

The final pillar is empathy, seeking to understand the customer's emotional circumstances and create deep rapport. Empathy lies at the heart of how human beings relate to each other. We are naturally herd animals and the desire to affiliate is one of the basic human drivers. Successful herding and affiliation means being able to accurately read the intentions of others. Nature has equipped us to do this through empathy and the ability to put ourselves in another's shoes, see the world from their perspective and, by doing so, infer their motives. It also enables us to relate to them, to vicariously experience the emotions of others and use this to moderate our own emotional response (Net MBA, 2002). Unfortunately, large organizations seem to drive this out of us.

In today's world, empathy should be a core organizational competence: being able to intuit customer psychological and physical needs at point of contact and at the corporate level helps drive innovation. Empathy is the art of letting the customer know that you can genuinely understand what it is like to be in their shoes. Empathy-creating behaviours are key to establishing a strong relationship. They involve the telling of personal stories that reflect back to the customer how you felt in similar circumstances. Then going the one extra step because you understand how they feel.

At the corporate level, empathy seeks to answer the question, 'Do we walk in the shoes of our customer, and do we really understand what it is like to be a customer of our company?' At the day-to-day level, it is the emotional intelligence with which the company deals with the customer, showing that the company cares about its customers. Empathy is more than just seeing the world from the customer's perspective. It is having the emotional intelligence to choose the right response from a range of potential emotions in order to improve things for the customer.

Organizations may tend to believe that empathy, as a soft skill, is the preserve of customer-touching staff. Yet empathy for the customer, as a core organizational capability, is as relevant for marketing, HR and the leadership as it is for those who directly serve customers. Being able to put yourself in your customers' shoes, see the world from their various perspectives, is essential for proposition development, innovation and effective strategizing. In fact, empathy is a source of customer advantage that less successful organizations often fail to embrace (Engage Customer, 2020).

The science

Some neuroscientists hypothesize that mirror neurones allow us to replicate in our head what we see others doing as well as the emotions they are likely to be feeling (Thomas, 2012). While it is not uncontroversial, mirror neurones are associated with the ability to detect tacit information about other people, how they are feeling or even maybe what they might be thinking or sensing. They enable us to relate to each other, providing us with a possible window into other people's experiences.

Dev Patnaik in his book *Wired to Care* (Patnaik, 2009) observes that humans seem to lose this ability when in groups or organizations. He explains that empathic organizations such as USAA create an environment in which mirror neurones are activated so that staff are able to react with the appropriate emotional response to any given customer situation.

Golden rules

Our research shows that organizations which prosper through embracing empathy follow these golden rules.

INVEST IN TIME TO LISTEN

Psychologists through time have known about the power of feeling understood. American psychologist Carl Rogers was one of the founding fathers of person-centred therapy and he describes it thus: 'When I have been listened to, I am able to re-perceive my world in a new way and to go on. It is astonishing how elements that seem insoluble become soluble when someone listens. I have deeply appreciated the times that I have experienced this sensitive, empathic, concentrated listening' (Rogers, 1959).

Lush has operationalized empathy in the way it approaches the customer. Staff are encouraged to use the products on sale, to even participate in making them so they know the ingredients. By asking customers a series of open diagnostic questions, they are gradually able to home in on products that are exactly right for each customer. The commercial outcome of this is astonishing, with high NPS scores and high levels of cross-sales. All because they are prepared to listen (Lush, 2021).

PROVIDE THE APPROPRIATE EMOTIONAL RESPONSE

Emotional intelligence is the ability to choose how you respond emotionally to a given situation. When a banking customer has lost their debit card, they do not want sympathy, they want reassurance – they want to know that the card will be stopped and a new one issued as soon as possible; they do not want to be made to feel stupid.

Leading organizations like Google now rely more on the emotional intelligence of the candidate than on grades or experience when selecting new recruits. They are looking for 'Googliness', a way of being that could be described as empathetic. While there are no specific tests for this, recruiters are trained to look for specific characteristics in how the candidate conducts themselves through the recruitment process (Moran, 2020).

SHARE YOUR SIMILAR EXPERIENCES – MAKE AN EMOTIONAL CONNECTION

Online shoe retailer Zappos identifies as one of its key differentiators the ability to establish a personal emotional connection (PEC) and leave a lasting memory. This supports its marketing strategy of relying exclusively on positive word of mouth. The company recruits people who are naturally empathetic and then trains them how to connect.

Its basis for call quality evaluation are the following questions:

- Did the agent try to make a personal connection with the customer?
- Did they keep the connection going if the customer responded?
- Did they discover the customer's real motivation for buying shoes (e.g. going to a wedding, party, special event)? Did they ensure that need was met emotionally and rationally?
- Was it a 'wow' experience?

The company uses a number of different ways of engaging with the customer. Staff talk about the weather, sports or pick up on clues from the customer. More recently, they have routed calls to an agent who has lived or worked in the same state. So they start with something in common. The company has also learned that staff sharing their own experiences helps frame the interaction as a discussion between equals (Zappos, 2021).

TREAT ME AS YOUR PRIORITY

Empathy-rich experiences occur when the staff member demonstrates a personal interest in the customer. It requires a set of behaviours that combine into a narrative takeaway that says: I am interested in you as a person; I want to be friendly towards you; you are important to me and my organization. You are valued.

TAKE OWNERSHIP OF MY ISSUE

When customers share an issue, they want the certainty of knowing that someone in the organization owns their problem and will take personal responsibility for seeing it through to a successful conclusion. first direct often leads our excellence survey and much of the respondent feedback related to how good first direct employees are at taking ownership. They listen carefully, probe gently, then take ownership to resolve the query.

SHOW YOU CARE

Respondents in our research talk about staff members showing they care in three different ways:

- Pays 'special' attention to me.
- Goes out of his/her way.
- Gave me something extra that I might not expect but will appreciate (e.g. a cup of coffee).

Body language, tone of voice and enthusiasm all play their part in showing that the staff member cares about achieving a good outcome for the customer.

Empathy is a way of addressing other people's feelings in a way that helps them feel good about themselves – and feel good about you. Responding to customers' emotional situations takes strong detection skills as well as highly developed emotional intelligence. Taking the problem off customers' hands when they want reassurance, responding with urgency when something untoward has happened and providing sympathy and understanding when they are needed are frequently mentioned attributes of first direct staff (Engage Customer, 2020).

KEY TAKEAWAYS

1 The Six Pillars are the defining characteristics of great experiences.

2 You cannot pick and choose, all six are required for excellence.

3 They are rooted in human psychology so play out in any human-to-human or human-to-digital interaction.

4 The pillars are mutually interdependent and intertwined – it is how they connect that delivers the totality of the customer experience.

References

Bannerman, L. (2010) Socialism meets middle England: inside the John Lewis miracle. www.thetimes.co.uk/article/socialism-meets-middle-england-inside-the-john-lewis-miracle-h7j5grwv26m (archived at https://perma.cc/3CDP-PCLK)

BBC (2020) John Lewis to pull 'never knowingly undersold' pledge. www.bbc.co.uk/news/business-53881214 (archived at https://perma.cc/RBM2-G6N3)

Bergland, C. (2015) The neuroscience of trust. www.psychologytoday.com/us/blog/the-athletes-way/201508/the-neuroscience-trust (archived at https://perma.cc/F8PC-ULX8)

Boyd, D. (2013) The path of most resistance. www.psychologytoday.com/us/blog/inside-the-box/201305/the-path-most-resistance (archived at https://perma.cc/42MP-K4ZQ)

Burlingham, B. (2013) This woman changed business forever (1990 profile). www.inc.com/magazine/19900601/5201.html (archived at https://perma.cc/9PEH-G49N)

Business Traveller (2012) BA to roll out 'Know Me' initiative. www.businesstraveller.com/news/2012/07/02/ba-to-roll-out-know-me-initiative/ (archived at https://perma.cc/8E8E-56M5)

Chatterjee, D. (2017) Three emotional territories that winning brands get right. https://go.forrester.com/blogs/3emotions/ (archived at https://perma.cc/D8V9-K5W2)

Cooper, L. (2013) Customer experience rankings: power to the people. www.marketingweek.com/customer-experience-rankings-power-to-the-people/ (archived at https://perma.cc/YF8F-RZ2Y)

Daily Mail (2019) Amazon will give one day delivery to Prime members around the globe. www.dailymail.co.uk/news/article-6961703/Amazon-aims-bring-one-day-delivery-Prime-members-globe.html (archived at https://perma.cc/ESS2-358F)

De Cremer, D., Pillutla, M. M. and Reinders Folmer, C. (2010) How important is an apology to you?: forecasting errors in evaluating the value of apologies. https://journals.sagepub.com/doi/abs/10.1177/0956797610391101?journalCode=pssa& (archived at https://perma.cc/ZW5W-LDPE)

Dixon, M., Freeman, K. and Toman, N. (2010) Stop trying to delight your customers. https://hbr.org/2010/07/stop-trying-to-delight-your-customers (archived at https://perma.cc/9PS7-MU46)

Drescher, C. (2016) Rose, orchid, plumeria: the significance of signature flowers. https://runwaygirlnetwork.com/2016/11/17/rose-orchid-plumeria-the-significance-of-signature-flowers/ (archived at https://perma.cc/ABJ3-B2CD)

Edelman (2021) Edelman Trust Barometer 2021. www.edelman.com/sites/g/files/aatuss191/files/2021-01/2021-edelman-trust-barometer.pdf (archived at https://perma.cc/75QE-4SZL)

Ehrenberg, B. (2014) Store wars: Lidl attacks Morrisons with combative ad campaign. www.cityam.com/supermarket-price-war-lidl-attacks-morrisons-combative-ad-campaign-in-store-wars/ (archived at https://perma.cc/5BGB-GA2R)

Engage Customer (2020) The golden rules to the Six Pillars: integrity. https://engagecustomer.com/the-golden-rules-to-the-six-pillars-integrity/ (archived at https://perma.cc/XR9A-8HUC)

Fixsen, R. (2017) Norway: ahead of its time. www.ipe.com/norway-ahead-of-its-time/10019227.article (archived at https://perma.cc/6JC7-MYG6)

Green Flag (2021) UK breakdown and recovery. https://mayday.greenflag.com/pdfs/PolicyTAndC_26.pdf (archived at https://perma.cc/T3R3-N2VU)

Hsieh, T. (2010) How I did it: Zappos's CEO on going to extremes for customers. https://hbr.org/2010/07/how-i-did-it-zapposs-ceo-on-going-to-extremes-for-customers#:~:text=In%20search%20of%20high%2Dcaliber,to%20Las%20Vegas%20in%202004 (archived at https://perma.cc/65YP-C2JC)

Ibis (2021) Your 15 minute guarantee. https://ibis.accor.com/promotions-offers/special-offers/owm005720-001-15-minute-guarantee.en.shtml (archived at https://perma.cc/C6NZ-WWC6)

Joseph, S. (2013) TSB launches by 'welcoming customers back to local banking'. www.marketingweek.com/tsb-launches-by-welcoming-customers-back-to-local-banking/ (archived at https://perma.cc/N4AG-S3EB)

Kahneman, D. (2013) *Thinking, Fast and Slow*. 18th ed. New York: Harvard.

Knight, T., Conway, D. and Jenkins, T. (2015) A new era of experience branding. https://assets.kpmg/content/dam/kpmg/pdf/2016/04/a-new-era-of-experience-branding.pdf (archived at https://perma.cc/2PJ7-7YFP)

KPMG (2017) The connected experience imperative. www.nunwood.com/excellence-centre/publications/uk-cee-analysis/2017-uk-cee-analysis/ (archived at https://perma.cc/ZKX4-68AF)

KPMG (2018) Ignite growth: connecting insight to action. https://colleaguestories.coop.co.uk/2018/11/28/co-op-insurance-moves-up-119-places-in-the-uk-kpmg-nunwood-customer-experience-excellence-rankings/ (archived at https://perma.cc/R8ZV-U4XM)

KPMG (2019) Customer first. Customer obsessed. https://assets.kpmg/content/dam/kpmg/it/pdf/2020/01/Global-customer-experience-excellence-2019.pdf (archived at https://perma.cc/VQE8-RMYU)

KPMG (2020) Customer experience in the new reality. https://home.kpmg/xx/en/home/insights/2020/07/customer-experience-in-the-new-reality.html (archived at https://perma.cc/C5VK-XLH5)

Lanoue, S. (2015) Cognitive psychology for UX: the principle of least effort. www.usertesting.com/blog/principle-of-least-effort (archived at https://perma.cc/PUC6-RTZA)

Lebowitz, S., Akhtar, A. and Hroncich, C. (2020) 12 things people decide within seconds of meeting you. www.businessinsider.com/things-people-decide-about-you-in-seconds-2016-11?r=US&IR=T (archived at https://perma.cc/KK5N-VVHR)

Lewicki, R. J. and Wiethoff, C. (2000) Trust, trust development, and trust repair. https://ombudsfac.unm.edu/Article_Summaries/Trust_Trust_Development_and_Trust_Repair.pdf (archived at https://perma.cc/Y8NP-LFYK)

Lush (2021) Lush people. https://uk.lush.com/article/lush-people (archived at https://perma.cc/CDH9-42UD)

M&S (2017) Plan A report. https://corporate.marksandspencer.com/documents/plan-a/m-and-s_planareport_2017_fullreport.pdf (archived at https://perma.cc/8UR9-KM99)

Manning, B. A. (2021) 5 steps for building trust in the workplace. www.td.org/insights/5-steps-for-building-trust-in-the-workplace (archived at https://perma.cc/T2Z3-YVQ6)

Michelli, J. (2013) Customer service is not enough. www.businessknowhow.com/marketing/crmaction.htm (archived at https://perma.cc/3HBH-3NT9)

Moran, G. (2020) 4 ways Google looks for emotional intelligence in job candidates. www.fastcompany.com/90471177/4-ways-google-looks-for-emotional-intelligence-in-job-candidates (archived at https://perma.cc/753U-NQZU)

Net MBA (2002) McClelland's theory of needs. www.netmba.com/mgmt/ob/motivation/mcclelland/ (archived at https://perma.cc/5UN8-JPZY)

Norman, D. (2018) The psychology of waiting lines. https://jnd.org/the_psychology_of_waiting_lines/ (archived at https://perma.cc/L5Z4-PHTX)

NRG (2016) Meet the stars – Santander's operational division. www.nrgplc.com/news-insights/insights/meet-stars-santanders-operations-division-previously-geoban-uk/ (archived at https://perma.cc/TP6Z-P2JM)

Patnaik, D. (2009) *Wired to Care: How Companies Prosper When They Create Widespread Empathy*. 1st ed. Upper Saddle River, NJ: FT Press.

Pelham, B. W., Mirenberg, M. C. and Jones, J. T. (2002) Why Susie sells seashells on the seashore: implicit egotism and major life decisions. *Journal of Personality and Social Psychology*, 82(4), 469–87.

Pithers, E. (2019) Could Stitch Fix solve your wardrobe crisis? www.vogue.co.uk/article/katrina-lake-stitch-fix-interview (archived at https://perma.cc/Q7TN-K3QY)

Premier Inn (2021) A good night's sleep guaranteed. www.premierinn.com/gb/en/why/sleep/good-night-guarantee.html (archived at https://perma.cc/E76Q-9EPC)

Price, B. and Jaffe, D. (2008) *The Best Service Is No Service: How to Liberate Your Customers from Customer Service, Keep Them Happy and Control Costs*. 1st ed. San Francisco: Wiley & Sons.

Richardson, D. (2017) What we can learn about customer service from Apple's training manual. https://riseperformancegroup.com/what-we-can-learn-about-customer-service-from-apples-training-manual/ (archived at https://perma.cc/6BJ2-NDBX)

Robertson, G. (2012) Ritz-Carlton case study: meet the 'unexpressed' needs of guests. https://beloved-brands.com/2012/10/25/ritz-carlton-2/ (archived at https://perma.cc/9MZC-KCND)

Rogers, C. R. (1959) *A Theory of Therapy, Personality, and Interpersonal Relationships as Developed in the Client-Centered Framework*. 1st ed. New York: McGraw-Hill.

Scheffler, D. (2016) Why millennial luxury travellers are harder to please – and how the industry is rising to the challenge. www.scmp.com/magazines/style/article/1939112/customised-travel-experiences-incorporate-tech-elements-and-local (archived at https://perma.cc/3EGY-LA27)

Schwab (2021) Customer ratings and reviews – publishing guidelines. www.schwab.com/reviews/publishing-guidelines (archived at https://perma.cc/ZJ3C-JJC9)

Sessions, R. (1950) Albert Einstein. http://en.wikiquote.org/wiki/Albert_Einstein (archived at https://perma.cc/R5SX-BFWW)

Solomon, M. (2018) How USAA bakes customer experience innovation into its company culture. www.forbes.com/sites/micahsolomon/2018/09/30/how-to-build-a-culture-of-customer-experience-innovation-the-usaa-way/?sh=42d6167a2378 (archived at https://perma.cc/Z4WS-2A7U)

Steers, N. (2012) Warren Buckley, BT: how measuring customer effort saved our service operations. www.mycustomer.com/service/channels/warren-buckley-bt-how-measuring-customer-effort-saved-our-service-operations (archived at https://perma.cc/KW39-8DCX)

Tartakovsky, M. (2016) What to do when you have to wait – and can't stop worrying. https://psychcentral.com/blog/what-to-do-when-you-have-to-wait-and-cant-stop-worrying#1 (archived at https://perma.cc/422H-6KA4)

The Guardian (2015) Don't brand your business with the label 'ethical'. www.theguardian.com/media-network/2015/mar/26/brand-business-ethical-lush#:~:text=Handmade%20cosmetics%20retailer%20Lush,fact%20it%20does%20zero%20advertising.&text=Lush%20shuns%20the%20word%20%E2%80%9Cethical,about%20laying%20its%20products%20bar (archived at https://perma.cc/VXZ2-UB2L)

Thomas, B. (2012) What's so special about mirror neurons? https://blogs.scientificamerican.com/guest-blog/whats-so-special-about-mirror-neurons/ (archived at https://perma.cc/2ZTX-HL5F)

Tolstoy, L. and Magarshack, D. (1961) *Anna Karenina*. New York: New American Library.

Tugby, L. (2015) Tesco boss Dave Lewis: we'll behave our way out of trouble. www.retail-week.com/grocery/tesco-boss-dave-lewis-well-behave-our-way-out-of-trouble-/5074261.article?authent=1 (archived at https://perma.cc/42FJ-LSZZ)

Tugend, A. (2012) Why people remember negative events more than positive ones. www.nytimes.com/2012/03/24/your-money/why-people-remember-negative-events-more-than-positive-ones.html (archived at https://perma.cc/94Y3-C5SG)

Walt Disney World (2021) Unlock the magic with your MagicBand or card. www.disneyworld.co.uk/plan/my-disney-experience/bands-cards/ (archived at https://perma.cc/879U-AUB9)

Wendell, S. (2021) Designing for behavior change. www.oreilly.com/library/view/designing-for-behavior/9781449367947/ch04.html#:~:text=The%20Minimum%20Viable%20Action%20is,assumed%20impact%20on%20behavior)%20works (archived at https://perma.cc/MS4S-Q9PM)

Wijesiri, L. (2019) Anne Mulcahy – Xerox CEO knew what it takes to win against all odds. www.dailymirror.lk/business-news/Anne-Mulcahy-Xerox-CEO-knew-what-it-takes-to-win-against-all-odds/273-177225 (archived at https://perma.cc/CAF2-RG84)

Zappos (2021) Zappos customer service forms. www.zapposinsights.com/clt-forms (archived at https://perma.cc/VZA2-HSF2)

07

Applying the Six Pillars to the organization

In this chapter we explore the Six Pillars of Experience, the key characteristics of successful customer experiences. Now used across the world from Russia to Brazil, the Six Pillars are a way of inculcating best practice not just into change management but into every fabric of organizational life. They provide a mechanism for answering organizational questions and bring a connected rigour that aligns organizational effort around a common language and approach.

Success requires that the pillars are seen as a set. Eliminate one and the others become less meaningful. They can be developed sequentially or concurrently, but competitive value emerges when firms manage the interconnectedness. Focusing on one or two may provide a short-term benefit, but ultimately over the long term this will not guarantee success. As we will see, there is a natural hierarchy to the pillars that aids both focus and prioritization.

Purpose, brand and the Six Pillars

Converting the brand into an experience, as opposed to a set of communications, is not always straightforward. For many organizations, attempting to bring the brand alive in every customer interaction is haphazard at best. This chapter will demonstrate the process and show how the Six Pillars help ensure completeness and consistency. Every aspect of the customer and employee experience can be carefully orchestrated to be on brand without any dissonant notes.

TABLE 7.1   Six Pillar golden rules and brand

Pillar	Brand manifesto	Experience golden rules
Personalization	The offer can be tailored to me Comms are relevant to me, e.g. Burger King 'Have it your way' (The Drum, 2019)	Recognize me Show me you know me, recognize our history together Make me competent, put me in control Surprise me with something relevant Understand my needs and circumstances Individualize what you do Make me feel valued and important
Resolution	Public commitments to being exceptional and, if not, to putting things right, e.g. Green Flag (Green Flag, 2021), Premier Inn (Premier Inn, 2021)	Take ownership First-time resolution Assume my innocence – see my point of view A warm and sincere apology Own the resolution – fix with urgency Surprise me in how well you fix my issue Go the extra mile if required Give me options going forward
Integrity	Our reputation: what we stand for as a business over and above making money for stakeholders, e.g. 'We embrace the very highest standards of honesty, ethical behaviour, and exemplary moral character' (Eli Lilly, 2021); 'fighting animal testing in the cosmetic industry' (Lush, 2021)	Competent at what you do Keep promises Demonstrably act in my best interest Show concern for me as a person Do what you say you will Keep me informed Be likeable
Time and effort	Public commitments to being easy or simple, e.g. US: Geico: '15 minutes or less can save you 15% or more on car insurance' (Forbes, 2018)	Make my time investment pleasurable Give me simple, clear instructions Maximum of three steps to my objective No longer than two minutes waiting Provide the answers I need when I contact you Advise me of pitfalls ahead

(continued)

TABLE 7.1 (continued)

Pillar	Brand manifesto	Experience golden rules
Expectations	The brand promise, e.g. first direct being 'the unexpected bank' (Vizard, 2014); 'To embrace the human spirit and let it fly' (Virgin Atlantic, 2021)	Set my expectations accurately Agree timings with me Respond more quickly than I anticipate Use plain English – no jargon Fulfil or exceed your promises Guide me through the process Provide information openly and honestly
Empathy	Public commitments to being helpful, friendly or understanding, e.g. 'low friendly fares' (Jet2, 2021); NatWest helpful banking and 'You are what you do' (RBS, 2021)	Invest time to listen to me Provide the right emotional response Share your similar experiences Treat me as your priority Take ownership of my issue Show you care

In a purpose-fuelled world, experience branding has to go much deeper than just cleverly presented products: it is aimed at people who share the same values, who see aspects of their own personality, real or aspirational, within the brand. These experience traits need to infuse every product, every communication, every experience and every touchpoint.

The brand personality arises naturally from a clearly defined set of brand values and a detailed brand manifesto that clearly articulates a set of beliefs to guide and shape brand behaviours. These values and beliefs inspire actions and activities that span all Six Pillars.

Defining the brand experience

In the previous chapter we identified the golden rules, the factors that drive success in each pillar. By aligning the brand manifesto to the Six Pillars, the golden rules show how that manifesto can be converted into day-to-day experiences. Some examples are shown in Table 7.1.

CASE STUDY
Lush

Lush provides an excellent example of a firm whose coverage of the brand basics can be mapped onto the Six Pillars.

Integrity: Lush is a business that stands for something and believes that actions count. It is genuinely concerned about being a good, morally guided business that, as its brand states, will make their 'mums proud'. It is the campaigning nature of Lush that excites the passions of its people. Lush avoids the word ethical, but does describe itself as sustainable, responsible and good. Lush shuns animal testing, needless packaging, excessive executive pay, donates extensively to aligned causes and pays its suppliers a fair price.

Resolution: Lush has an instant, no quibble returns policy. Its mantra is 'the customer is always right'; it wants customers to be completely happy with their product purchase and will exchange or refund the product, no matter what the reason. Often customers receive a range of free samples as recompense for their trouble.

Expectations: The Lush brand promise is a clear one: fresh handmade cosmetics. Every dimension of the Lush experience serves to deliver on this explicit pledge. Implicitly, customer expectations are met by the behaviours and personality of its staff – passionate, enthusiastic fans of the products they sell.

Time and effort: In most organizations, the focus is on how you save customers time, how you make the organization easy to access and to engage with. At Lush, all of these are true. But Lush is remarkable for focusing on how you spend time. How you create the Lush experience at home. How you unwind and de-stress. The return on this time is hugely valuable and restorative – it is 'me time'. A time for indulgence and contemplation, all made easier by a clearly signposted set of products to create the type of 'me time' experience you need.

Personalization: This starts with the way that staff interact. No attempt to sell, just a series of diagnostic questions to understand more about the customer's specific needs before prescribing the right type of products. Lush achieves the ultimate prize of personalization: customers who feel their self-worth has been increased because of their association with Lush and other 'Lushies'.

Empathy: Lush has operationalized empathy in the way it approaches the customer. Asking a series of open diagnostic questions, it is gradually able to home in on products that are exactly right for the individual customer. The commercial outcome of this is astonishing, with high NPS scores and high levels of cross-sales – all because it is prepared to listen. (KPMG, 2016)

Looking to a digital future

We are entering a world where we will manage our lives on technology platforms, portals that are gateways to resolving innumerable life issues, making purchases and managing and scheduling our everyday lives. With the information we offer through these platforms firms will be able to predict our needs and prepare us to meet them before they arise. Automated concierges and bots will provide a linguistic gateway into an advanced world of consumer technology where AI and machine learning-based functions get to know more and more about us so that they can anticipate what we will need next and make sure it is at our fingertips when required.

There is no doubt that technology will be both a disruptor and an enabler. Successful companies are those that start with a customer problem first and then apply technology, innovation and ingenuity to fix it.

Using the Six Pillars for trend analysis will surface future opportunities for improving the customer experience. Identifying the cutting-edge players allows a firm to modify actions and ensures that any technology is rooted in experience improvement rather than being pursued for its own sake. An analysis of new technologies suggests that the biggest impact (shaded areas) is likely to be in personalization and time and effort, as Figure 7.1 shows.

Personalization

Central to a personalized experience is context, the ability to relate the product or service to the customer's life and being there when they are ready to make a decision – this means not just pushing the firm's story and not just being there when a sale is likely.

Personalization plays to a customer's sense of self-worth. At one level, this is about being made to feel valued and important. At another level, it is about shared values and brand personality. It requires understanding how organizations play a role in the customer's personal brand – retailers such as Ralph Lauren and Calvin Klein show the importance of people being able to see their own personalities or characteristics they aspire to in a company's brand (KPMG, 2017).

So, the brand experience, digital or human, must amplify and reflect self-perception; this is leading towards 'hyper-personalization', uniquely curated products and services exemplified by organizations such as Zappos and Netflix as they strive to find exactly the right product for the individual. More unusually, at the Dubai Future of Government Services Exhibition in

FIGURE 7.1 Six Pillars and technology

	Personalization	Integrity	Empathy	Time and effort	Expectations	Resolution
Blockchain						
API						
Mobile						
Internet of things						
3D printing / adv. manufacturing						
Cloud						
Drones						
Data and analytics						
AI / cognitive automation						
RPA						
AR VR						
Cyber						
Voice / NLP						

2015 there was a pop-up café known as the Pharma Café. When dining at the café, visitors were given a bespoke drink based on their own DNA, which was obtained by a hand scan at the entrance (Ross, 2015). A concept taken to the next level by the wellness industry where DNA testing is used to prescribe a range of supplements and exercises and wellbeing activities that are unique to every individual.

Resolution

This is about fixing the basics, the problems that organizations just live with and expect customers to live with. But social media amplification has caused organizations to become much more circumspect about issues that have social implications. Experiences are increasingly socialized. Negative reviews trigger an 'it could happen to me' response in existing and potential customers and can severely damage a business. It requires the ability to turn negative perceptions into positive ones and in the process rebuild social capital.

Anticipation of likely customer issues is a new science. It involves understanding the obstructions and issues a customer may face in their particular circumstances and fixing them before they arise, ensuring that the customer is put in control when things go wrong.

Customers of USAA involved in an accident can use their car insurance app. If you have an accident, you simply dictate what happened into your phone and take a photograph of the scene. An augmented reality screen enables the customer to pinpoint key aspects of the accident. The app adds the GPRS co-ordinates of the accident and the weather conditions at the time. Press a button and the claim is initiated – no forms, no paperwork. A replacement car can be delivered to the scene in one hour (USAA, 2021).

In Sweden, Swedish Rail uses predictive analytics to identify potential delays on public transport before they happen and texts customers with alternative routes. The model, called the Commuter Prognosis, applies a prediction model to visualize the rail system as it will be two hours into the future. Using the predictions, Stockholmstag can forecast disruption in its service and, more importantly, its traffic control centre can prevent the ripple effects that cause most delays (Spring Wise, 2015).

Integrity

Ninety per cent of significant purchase decisions are subject to social influence. Research by Google shows that consumers, on average, consult 11 information sources before making a decision. Decisions may start in a search engine, but increasingly customers refer to their social networks for insight and direction. Organizations need to be able to join their customers' circle of social trust if they are to be relevant and connect emotionally (Google, 2011).

Firms are beginning to understand that their target audience also has an audience, and both need to be satisfied as to the firm's integrity. Firms approach this in different ways, but being a good corporate citizen is now central to how they communicate.

In the US, Ally Bank responded creatively to the backlash against banks following several mis-selling issues in the industry. It initiated an advertising campaign about setting new standards of behaviour in banking and doing what is right for customers (Ally, 2011).

For Coca-Cola it is a commitment to sustainability. The drinks company has made stretching commitments such as minimizing what goes to landfill, and demonstrates its progress towards these targets (Coca-Cola Company, 2019).

Time and effort

This means being able to respond to the urgency of now. Social media units that operate 9–5 are no longer acceptable: communication is now a 24-hour operation. This means being present and available when needed. For example, KLM was the first airline to make all flight documents digitally available in one place and use messenger bots to provide updates in the event of delays (KLM, 2017).

Firms are recognizing that touchpoints can be designed so human interaction is no longer required. For example, Starbucks' mobile app manages loyalty points and pre-ordering. Now nearly 28 million users make purchases through the app at least once every six months – 25 per cent of all customers now avoid having to queue (Campbell, 2020).

Nimbl is a mobile ATM operating in New York. Customers simply use the app to specify the amount of cash they need and it is hand-delivered to their desk or home (Zaleski, 2014). Nordstrom trunk club is a monthly delivery of male clothing items that learns what is right for the individual through what is returned (Nordstrom, 2020). Amazon provides one-hour delivery in city centres and till-free stores where you don't have to queue to pay – the system automatically makes the right charges based on what you have picked from the shelves (Forest, 2021).

Expectations

Organizational agility is becoming critical to responding to escalating expectations: silo-based business models are no longer fit for purpose. Big data is being used as a way to exceed expectations.

There are apps that sense when you are bored and send personalized content to you. Telefonica conducted research into boredom and how it could be detected. By monitoring use of its phones and accessing over 40 million data points, it devised Borapp. This data allowed the Borapp to predict boredom with 82 per cent accuracy and send tailored content to the phone (Gershgorn, 2015).

The smart home and the internet of things are applying technology in a way that is moving mundane tasks like fridge restocking to a new level of automation. Devices in the home are linked to mobile delivery services which in the process learn about likes and dislikes, so ordering exactly what the customer might want on a particular day (Samsung, 2021).

Empathy

In a social world, people's attention is attracted towards those who demonstrate an awareness and understanding of their interests, challenges and options. A sense of belonging comes through feeling understood. Empathy is detectable and vital for psychological satisfaction, but how do you deliver human empathy through technology?

At one level there is the increasing adaptation of companion robotics to customer service. In Japan, with a rapidly ageing population, the use of robots as carers has grown rapidly. Learning from empathetic robots that are able to recognize and respond to basic human emotions is beginning to move into customer service, accelerated by developments in artificial intelligence (Softbank, 2021). Amazon is designing interfaces that subtly emulate human behaviour to appear more engaging, more psychologically satisfying and more connective (The Manifest, 2019).

Prioritization

Most organizations overestimate their capacity to implement initiatives. For organizations of any size, the number of 'in flight' initiatives at any one time can be several hundred. Many of these are departmentally initiated; they

FIGURE 7.2   Six Pillars prioritization

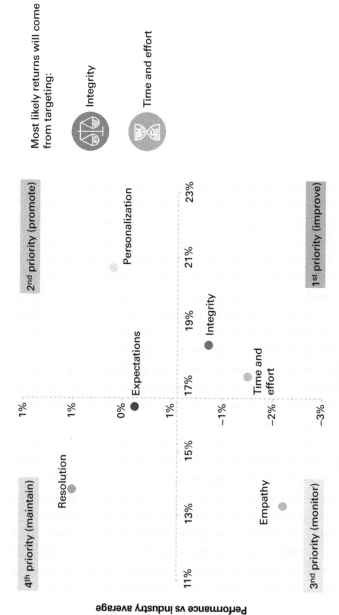

serve to improve the department's functioning capability in a business model that may already be unsuitable for customer centricity. It is rare that the sum total of these initiatives adds up to a positive overall end-to-end experience for the customer.

In numerous case studies we have found that only a very small number of these initiatives will make a meaningful difference to the customer. With a major bank, which had 433 initiatives in play, only 11 in fact would make a major difference to the customer. Over 100 could be stopped as they only fulfilled departmental silo objectives that would no longer be required in a customer-centric world, freeing up resources to ensure the success of the 'hallmark' 11 projects.

The problem is that non-aligned initiatives consume time, resources and effort – resulting in suboptimal support for those that will make a positive difference. Prioritization and sequencing are therefore critical, but deciding what is really important and whether it can be adequately supported is a key leadership task.

In determining where to focus first, many firms use a statistical technique known as performance importance regression analysis. This is used to gauge how satisfied people are with the quality of service they have received and the relative importance of certain characteristics of that service (see Figure 7.2).

This approach can work well with the Six Pillars, enabling a clear view of which pillar will have the most impact on improving service. However, firms need to be careful to construct an analysis of drivers of detraction as well as drivers of promotion as each of these can lead to different results.

Research by the London School of Economics shows that companies achieve four times the commercial benefit by removing detractors than they achieve by creating promoters (Marsden et al, 2005). The reasons for detraction are different from the reasons for promotion; consequently there is a Maslovian hierarchy to take account of when focusing on the pillars. There is little value in focusing on developing personalization or empathy if there is poor lower-order performance that creates detraction.

The hierarchy (see Figure 7.3) spotlights where organizational efforts can be best expended. Removing the causes of mistrust, unresolved issues and mis-set expectations fixes the basics. Advocacy is driven when the customer finds the organization easy to use, suited to their personal circumstances, and has a sense that the organization cares about them.

FIGURE 7.3   The Six Pillar implementation sequence

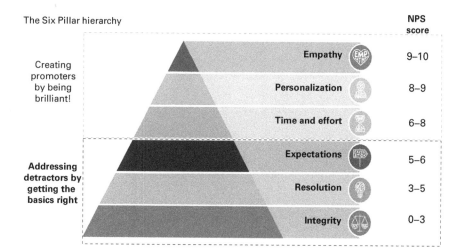

Assessing initiative efficacy

Table 7.2 gives a scoring system-based method of validating the contribution that individual initiatives might make. Initiatives that do not contribute on either scale should be considered as superfluous and stopped.

Aligning the employee experience with the customer experience

The Six Pillars are equally important in the employee sphere and provide a natural bridge to align the employee experience with the customer experience. In Chapter 3 we examined the new employee and the connection with customer experience.

Transforming the CX requires firms to adopt an equally methodical approach to the employee experience (EX). Those that seek to change the world recognize that they must first change themselves. To achieve this, these organizations are looking at their people through the same lens as they do their customers and are applying the same engagement strategies to improve attraction, motivation and retention. It spans propositions, experiences, journeys and personal growth and manifests itself in a customer-obsessed culture (KPMG, 2019).

TABLE 7.2 Six Pillars and initiative prioritization

Score each initiative between 1 and 5 based on impact

	Integrity	Resolution	Expectations	Time and effort	Personalization	Empathy
Consequences of inaction						
Financial ROI						
Ease of implementation						
Risk compliance						
Benefit to customer						
Criticality to strategy						

FIGURE 7.4 Aligning customer and employee experience

Employee experience

Empathy
- I am able to bond and affiliate with my colleagues
- Issues are dealt with sensitively and with emotional intelligence
- **Leaders react positively and in line with our values when under pressure**

Personalization
- Help me develop as an individual – be the best I can be
- A job role that enables me to utilize my unique talents
- **An environment that promotes continuous learning and improvement**

Time and effort
- My time and extra effort are recognized and appropriately rewarded
- **Employee journeys to achieve a personal objective are clear and straightforward**
- Leaders and managers show respect for my time

Expectations
- The organization has stretching objectives
- **Leaders are clear on their expectations**
- Leaders provide helpful and constructive feedback

Resolution
- Personal concerns are dealt with, with urgency
- I am able to participate in decisions that affect me and my team
- **I am supported by leaders to learn from mistakes without blame**

Integrity
- The business has a higher purpose than just making money
- **Interpersonal relationships are based on trust**
- Communications are consistent, open and explanatory

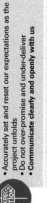

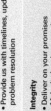

Customer experience

Empathy
- Invest quality time to really understand us
- Show that you care about our business and us as individuals
- **Do not leave us feeling hard done by**

Personalization
- Make us feel important to you as a client
- **Make us feel special as individuals and more confident about being successful**

Time and effort
- Maximize the value from our time investment
- **Show a desire to reuse existing assets**
- Find ways of saving us costs by thinking cleverly

Expectations
- Accurately set and reset our expectations as the project unfolds
- Do not over-promise and under-deliver
- **Communicate clearly and openly with us**

Resolutions
- **Fix problems rapidly when they arise**
- Senior people should be visible, not invisible, when things get difficult and lead the resolution
- Provide us with timelines, updates and plans for problem resolution

Integrity
- Deliver on your promises
- **Make it clear how you have added value**
- **Be transparent and open**

DIFFERENTIATORS	
Achieving an understanding of the customer's circumstances to drive deep rapport
Using individualized attention to drive an emotional connection

BASIC	
Minimizing customer effort and creating frictionless processes
Managing, meeting and exceeding customer expectations
Turning a poor experience into a great one
Being trustworthy and engendering trust

Our research shows that the Six Pillars can be universally applied to both customer and employee relationships. By seeing all people (and their digital counterparts) through this singular lens, organizations can remove disconnection and unify their colleagues around common ways of thinking. Looking at both employee and customer experiences through the same framework, we can achieve several advantages (see Figure 7.4): a single, coherent internal language for experience excellence, whether customer or employee; a model for defining how to deliver customer outcomes by showing the precise employee experiences needed to create the right behaviours; the foundations for defining customer-centric capability and recruitment frameworks; a basis for more joined-up analysis of customer and workforce insights, linking the voice of the customer with employee feedback (KPMG, 2019).

In Chapter 3 we introduced the concept of the 'human equity continuum', the link between employee, customer and commercial outcomes. The Six Pillars of employee experience are a useful tool for assessing what best practice across this model looks like (see Figure 7.5).

For aligned organizations there is no distinction between brand values and internal values. The culture is the brand and the brand is the culture; they are synonymous. The customer experience is rooted in the employee behaviours that emerge from the culture. The following illustrates how two top US businesses achieve employee and customer experience alignment (KPMG, 2017).

FIGURE 7.5   The Six Pillars and the human equity continuum

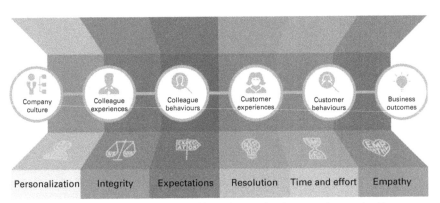

The Six Pillars of Experience provide an integrating framework, ensuring the employee experience is architected to deliver an excellent customer experience

CASE STUDY
USAA

Culture:

- Built around empathy – no organization understands its customers better.
- Care about customers and each other.
- Obsessed with customers and delivering an outstanding service.
- Stringent employee recruitment and on-boarding.
- Customer-oriented metrics drive focus, e.g. making a positive difference to customer lives.
- 'Servant' leadership model – to serve first.

Employee experience:

- Inclusive, diversified with considerable opportunities for growth.
- Empathy for customers through 'living as a customer'.
- Regular customer encounter sessions: 'customer surround sound'.
- Ongoing customer service training.
- Ninety-two per cent of staff agree it is a great place to work (Great Place to Work website).

Employee behaviour:

- Serve customers 'fabulously well'.
- Go the extra mile willingly.
- Show they care deeply about the customer.

Customer experience:

- Strong sense of trust.
- Innovative products that solve life problems, developed with customers in USAA labs.
- Sense of belonging – but retaining individuality.
- USAA as duty and patriotism.

Customer behaviour:

- Extraordinary loyalty (97.8 per cent customer retention rate).
- High levels of multiproduct ownership.
- High levels of recommendation.

Commercial outcomes:

- Willing to sacrifice short-term profits for customer benefit, e.g. refund of premiums for military serving in Iraq.
- Net worth growing 4 per cent annually.
- Assets growing 7 per cent annually.
- $1.8 billion returned to members as dividends.

(KPMG, 2017)

CASE STUDY
Air New Zealand

When in 2005 Air New Zealand posted the largest loss in the country's corporate history, the company's future seemed particularly bleak. But that was when Air New Zealand staged one of the most customer-centric turnarounds in world history. It identified an 'essential Kiwiness' – a pride in all things New Zealand. From that point onwards, its people, its communications and virtually every facet of every touchpoint radiated pride in its country of origin. Today, it is one of the most consistently profitable, full-service airlines in the world.

The catalyst for this change was Sir Ralph Norris, a well-respected New Zealand banking CEO, who was called in to transform the business. Sir Ralph's customer-centric leadership and customer-focused strategy were embodied in the mindset change from 'we fly planes' to 'we fly people'. One of the first things Sir Ralph did was to engage the top 800 leaders at Air New Zealand in thinking about, discussing and acting on insights from customer feedback and observations. He wanted them to find out what customers valued and what they hated about the flying experience. What they learned was that customers loved the friendly, outgoing and slightly tongue-in-cheek humour that typifies Kiwis and this provided the platform for change. Staff were encouraged and empowered to exhibit their Kiwi personalities and to engage customers in a warm, welcoming and friendly way. All of this customer knowledge is embodied in their 'essential Kiwiness'. You can see it when you fly with Air New Zealand – even the safety announcements are engaging and feature some of New Zealand's star rugby players, spectacular scenes of the country and references to some famous movies made in the country.

> *We have a really clear internal sense of purpose which is to supercharge New Zealand's success. Our purpose is bigger than flying people from point A to point B – it's about connecting New Zealand with the world.*
>
> Anita Hawthorne, General Manager of Customer Experience, Air New Zealand (KPMG, 2019)

It starts with leadership

If the roots of excellence sit in culture and employee experience, then it is here that leadership is needed the most.

There are many leadership models, but when it comes to outstanding customer and employee experiences there is one model that dominates: the servant leader model. Robert K. Greenleaf, who coined the phrase, outlines that a servant leader should be focused on helping individuals grow as people, enabling them to become fuller, more rounded individuals capable of self-management. 'A Servant Leader shares power, puts the needs of the employees first and helps people develop and perform as highly as possible' (Greenleaf, 2007). Servant leadership inverts the norm; customer service employees become the main priority. Instead of the people working to serve the leader, the leader exists to serve the people.

Fundamentally the leadership role is no longer about command and control but employee enablement. When we find high trust, high employee engagement and low turnover, it is most often driven by a servant leadership style where people are treated with respect and dignity yet challenged to perform at the highest level.

Nordstrom, the US department store, performs well in our US index. It has institutionalized servant leadership as its dominant style through its inverted pyramid. In this model leadership is at the bottom of the pyramid and the employee is at the top. This is not just a clever ploy to make employees feel good – it is a real approach to the role of leadership. Even the three original Nordstrom brothers started out in the stock room. Nordstrom relies heavily on servant leadership in order to enable customer-focused teams and inspire every colleague to create excellent customer service.

Truett Cathy, the founder of Chick-fil-A, the US fast-food group and a leader in our US index, was one of the original servant leaders, long before the term existed. He grew a $10 billion business through his humility, his concern for his employees and customers, and his commitment to making the world a better place. He set the tone for the business: there to make employees' lives easier and better and in so doing deliver great experiences for the customer. He believed that employees deserved one day every week that they could count on as not being a workday. To this end Chick-fil-A does not open on a Sunday.

His humility has given rise to a unique culture. Employees describe the company culture as being built on relationships and valuing one another. Despite controversy around the organization's involvement in political and social causes, its culture is often seen as bringing out the best in people, fulfilling leadership potential and delivering great business performance.

In her book *It's My Pleasure: The Impact of Extraordinary Talent and a Compelling Culture* (Turner, 2015), Dee Ann Turner identifies that the Chick-fil-A culture is perpetuated through three pillars (Kruse, 2015):

1 **Finding people who fit.** Chick-fil-A's staff selection process focuses on three Cs: character, competency and chemistry. The company looks for individuals with character who will treat everyone they come across with respect and kindness, no matter their position.

2 **Nurture talent by telling the truth.** Providing constructive feedback Chick-fil-A believes is the kindest thing you can do for an employee and creates a culture of trust that prizes individuals and relationships.

3 **Chick-fil-A guests also experience the company's compelling culture.** Customers can expect to be treated with honour, dignity and respect. Chick-fil-A employees have helped the company become known for its 'second-mile service' and delivering the signature response of 'It's my pleasure'.

Servant leaders are not only close to their employees and the challenges they face, they are also close to their customers and encourage other leaders to do the same. Walt Disney was famous for experiencing life as a customer: he would regularly don a disguise and wander through his theme park, listening to customers observing what they liked and what they didn't like. He scolded his leadership team when he discovered they were leaving the park for lunch, insisting they were missing opportunities to see and feel what customers experienced.

Justin King, former CEO of the UK supermarket chain Sainsbury's, would arrive unannounced at stores three or four times a week and simply wander the aisles, observing what was working and not working. Not for him the royal visit but seeing Sainsbury's as his customers saw it. His view was that the only way to see how the strategy formulated in the boardroom was transmitted to customers was to see it in action in real life (Thompson, 2011).

Starbucks is known as a servant leadership company. Chairman and CEO Howard Schultz believed that the only way to build a great company that would endure for the long term was by linking shareholder value with value for employees. During his time in charge, Starbucks grew from 11 stores to 28,000 in 78 countries, but what was important to him was the type of company he was creating, one that takes care of its employees, giving them access to tuition, free education and healthcare. It is a business that he described as elevating humanity. For him the two pillars of humility and servant leadership are the essence of great leadership (Dahlstrom and Warnick, 2018).

Servant leader behaviours

So, what do we conclude from studying the leaders of the world's best brands? If servant leadership is one proven way to the employee culture needed for growth, what are the leadership traits that today's executives must exemplify?

- **Listening:** Top leaders listen more than they speak. They listen to all employees, customers and stakeholders. They are focused on understanding first and foremost.

- **Healing:** To be able to resolve conflict in a way others respect and value. Being able to solve emotionally intense problems and encourage others to collaborate and value each other.

- **Awareness:** Continuous scanning of key trends and new thinking and the ability to inculcate relevant parts of these into their body of knowledge of how the business can operate better.

- **Persuasion:** Not manipulation, but the ability to encourage others to see a better way. To create unity and focus rather than discord and busy-ness.

- **Conceptualization:** The ability to carry and communicate a bigger picture, one that is driven by purpose and mission and communicated through vision.

- **Foresight:** Anticipating problems before they occur, learning from mistakes in the past and helping others to ensure they are not repeated.

- **Stewardship:** Recognizing they are in a role for a period of time and seeking to leave it in a better position than they found it.

- **Emotional intelligence:** The ability to see the world from different perspectives and put themselves in the shoes of others, but most importantly they show that they connect emotionally with others.

Of these traits, based on our experience speaking to the leaders of many of the excellent organizations that lead in the global indices, this last quality is the most important. Emotional intelligence is nothing new. However, it is the catalyst that makes everything else possible. For when we look at the engines of value – the continuum from culture to experience – we are essentially looking at clusters of complex human interactions. None of these is first and foremost a rational situation: we are, after all, emotional animals ruled by caprice and instinct. It is the leaders who can read, anticipate and react to these situations who are best equipped to create the connections that every business requires to thrive.

This emotional intelligence needs to be coupled with a tacit admission that businesses are not simply rational, empirical and financial edifices. They are not money-making machines. Rather, they are factories for experience, for human emotion. Traditional business management, especially in many Western markets, has been designed to squeeze out emotion and reward austere rationalism. In many failing organizations, the few departments that get close to human emotions, be they branding, learning or design, are derided. They are seen as lightweight, as 'fluff', in comparison to the 'hard' disciplines of finance, systems or operations.

Yet it is these very disciplines, those closest to human nature, that tend to nurture the kind of leaders tomorrow's enterprises need. It is those leaders most in tune with humanity's emotional nature who are best positioned to foster a culture of internal service. By doing so, they are able to start the journey to excellence.

CASE STUDY
Servant leadership in electronics

Some years ago, we were working with a company that specialized in supplying businesses with electronic components. While assessing its cultural attributes we encountered a true customer-centric leader in the unlikely area of the loading dock. The individual was responsible for several packing teams, employees whose role was simply to pick stock from shelves in the warehouse and pack it carefully to protect the fragile components in transit.

The manager, when he took over the team, faced high staff turnover due to the mundane nature of the job. He decided to overcome this by challenging the team to think more deeply about what they were doing and how they could add more value. What did the components do? Why were some on emergency delivery, who were the customers they were sending these parts to and what was their experience? The walls soon became covered with diagrams as the team sought to understand what the components did and how they fitted into bigger systems. They had competitions to identify individual components and the roles they played and they discovered that these components were used in life-saving equipment, used by the emergency services, kept radar installations going and were used by defence forces to protect the country.

They began to contact customers and find out the problems they had with component deliveries. They identified when pack sizes were wrong, requiring multiple orders, or when the failure rate of a component meant that the first replacement might fail so a second was placed on emergency order. The retention problems stopped, people were keen to join the team, it was a fun and inspiring place to be, employees felt empowered, supported and linked with a higher purpose. All because the manager had created line of sight between the loading dock team and their customers.

Table 7.3 shows the link between the Six Pillars, the employee experience and the leadership behaviours required to ensure that the Six Pillars are reflected naturally in employee behaviour.

TABLE 7.3   Six Pillars and organizational behaviours

Pillar	Employee experience	Customer-oriented leadership behaviours
Personalization	• Help me develop as an individual – be the best I can be • Enable me to improve my sense of self-worth – make me feel my contribution is valued and that my work is meaningful • A job role that enables me to utilize my unique talents • An environment that promotes continuous learning and improvement	• Focus on the customer as an individual • Aim to make the customer feel special and important • The target experience for customers is articulated and understood • Empower people and encourage creativity in everyone
Time and effort	• My time and extra effort are recognized and appropriately rewarded • Leaders and managers show respect for my time • Employee journeys to achieve a personal objective are clear and straightforward	• Look to minimize the effort a customer must make to engage with us • Show the customer that we value their time
Expectations	• Leaders are clear on their expectations • Leaders provide helpful and constructive feedback • The organization has stretching objectives	• Ensure we accurately set the customer's expectations • Objectives are clearly communicated • Acknowledge when we don't deliver against our commitments

(continued)

TABLE 7.3 (continued)

Pillar	Employee experience	Customer-oriented leadership behaviours
Integrity	• Business has a higher purpose than just making money • Fairness is key • Interpersonal relationships are based on trust • The environment is safe for me to be myself • There is consistency between word and deed • Communications are open and explanatory • Rules are applied consistently • There is trust between and across teams	• Convey what we stand for to the customer • Leaders inspire trust • Leaders role models the organization's values • Teams are able to see how they impact the customer • Doing the right thing for customers is the top priority here
Resolution	• There is support when I need it • Personal concerns are resolved with a sense of urgency • I am able to participate in decisions that affect me and my team • Leaders look after my interests • I am supported to learn from mistakes without blame • I am empowered to make sensible decisions	• Promote a problem-solving mindset • React rapidly when dealing with a customer issue • Ensure that after an issue we leave the customer feeling better about the organization
Empathy	• The organization and its leaders care about me • I am able to bond and affiliate with my colleagues • Issues are dealt with sensitively and with emotional intelligence • Leaders react positively and in line with our values when under pressure • Leaders show sensitivity and concern over needs and feelings	• Demonstrate that the organization cares about its customers and employees • Leaders start by considering the customer when making decisions • Foster passion for the customer

SOURCE KPMG, 2019

KEY TAKEAWAYS

1   The Six Pillars are a useful mechanism for guiding brand behaviours and the nature of customer behaviour through applying the golden rules.

2   They also provide a lens for conducting an environmental scan, especially a technology review, but also of political, environmental, social, legal and economic aspects.

3   They form a Maslovian hierarchy which aids sequencing and prioritization.

4   They enable the cross-mapping of the employee experience to the customer experience and pervade all aspects of the employee experience.

5   They inform leadership behaviours that enable Six Pillar behaviours to emerge naturally.

References

Ally (2011) Ally Bank launches new 'people sense' ad campaign. https://media.ally. com/press-releases?item=122832

Campbell, C. I. (2020) Starbucks says nearly a quarter of all US retail orders are placed from a phone. www.theverge.com/2020/10/30/21540908/starbucks-app-q4-earnings-mobile-payments

Coca-Cola Company (2019) Sustainable business. www.coca-colacompany.com/ sustainable-business

Dahlstrom, L. and Warnick, J. (2018) Schultz to employees: 'This has been the dream of a lifetime'. https://stories.starbucks.com/stories/2018/schultz-to-employees-this-has-been-the-dream-of-a-lifetime/

Eli Lilly (2021) Tireless discovery and a force in the community. https://careers.lilly. com/why-lilly

Forbes (2018) Is the claim Geico saves you 15% actually true? www.forbes.com/ sites/priceonomics/2018/09/21/is-the-claim-that-you-save-15-with-geico-actually-true/?sh=513aaa1a4e93

Forest, A. (2021) 'It's scary': shoppers give verdict on Amazon's futuristic till-free supermarket. www.independent.co.uk/news/uk/home-news/amazon-fresh-supermarket-ealing-london-b1812423.html

Gershgorn, D. (2015) Smartphone app can detect when you're bored. www.popsci. com/smartphone-app-can-now-tell-when-youre-bored-and-suggests-buzzfeed-as-cure/

Google (2011) The zero moment of truth macro study. www.thinkwithgoogle.com/ consumer-insights/consumer-journey/the-zero-moment-of-truth-macro-study/

Green Flag (2021) UK breakdown and recovery. https://mayday.greenflag.com/pdfs/PolicyTAndC_26.pdf

Greenleaf, R. (2007) Start here: what is servant leadership? www.greenleaf.org/what-is-servant-leadership/

Jet2 (2021) Jet2. www.jet2.com/

KLM (2017) KLM welcomes BlueBot (BB) to its service family. https://news.klm.com/klm-welcomes-bluebot-bb-to-its-service-family/#:~:text=KLM's%20new%20service%20bot%20is,intervention%20of%20a%20KLM%20agent.&text=KLM%20is%20well%20known%20for%20its%20personal%20approach

KPMG (2016) Lush. https://nunwood.com/excellence-centre/publications/uk-cee-analysis/2016-uk-cee-analysis/lush/

KPMG (2017) Engineering a human touch into a digital future. https://assets.kpmg/content/dam/kpmg/uk/pdf/2017/05/US-customer-experience-excellence-analysis-report.pdf

KPMG (2019) Customer first. Customer obsessed. https://assets.kpmg/content/dam/kpmg/it/pdf/2020/01/Global-customer-experience-excellence-2019.pdf

Kruse, K. (2015) How Chick-fil-A created a culture that lasts. www.forbes.com/sites/kevinkruse/2015/12/08/how-chick-fil-a-created-a-culture-that-lasts/?sh=724f7e633602

Lush (2021) Lush people. https://uk.lush.com/article/lush-people

Marsden, P., Samson, A. and Upton, N. (2005) Advocacy drives growth. https://digitalwellbeing.org/wp-content/uploads/2015/05/Marsden-2005-06-Advocacy-Drives-Growth-Brand-Strategy.pdf

Nordstrom (2020) Your personal styling team, upgraded. www.trunkclub.com/blog/personal-clothing-stylist

Premier Inn (2021) A good night's sleep guaranteed. www.premierinn.com/gb/en/why/sleep/good-night-guarantee.html

RBS (2021) What does 'we are what we do' mean? www.rbs.com/rbs/news/2016/09/natwest-_-what-does-we-are-what-we-do-mean-.html

Ross, C. (2015) DNA dining. www.lsnglobal.com/news/article/17251/dna-dining

Samsung (2021) Smart fridge freezers. www.samsung.com/uk/refrigerators/family-hub-fridge-freezers/

Softbank (2021) Pepper. www.softbankrobotics.com/emea/en/pepper

Spring Wise (2015) Algorithm predicts and prevents train delays two hours in advance. www.springwise.com/algorithm-predicts-prevents-train-delays-two-hours-advance/

The Drum (2019) Have it your way. https://hookagency.com/medical-pharma-digital-marketing/have-it-your-way/#:~:text=Burger%20King%20came%20out%20with,pop%20culture%20and%20on%20individuality.

The Manifest (2019) Amazon's user experience: a case study. https://medium.com/@the_manifest/amazons-user-experience-a-case-study-fb567f79b51f

Thompson, J. (2011) Justin King: Sainsbury's growth king in no hurry to check out. www.independent.co.uk/news/people/profiles/justin-king-sainsbury-s-growth-king-no-hurry-check-out-2264258.html

Turner, D. A. (2015) *It's My Pleasure: The Impact of Extraordinary Talent and a Compelling Culture.* 1st ed. New York: Elevate

USAA (2021) File an auto claim. www.usaa.com/inet/wc/auto-insurance-claims?akredirect=true

Virgin Atlantic, 2021. Virgin Atlantic. www.virgin.com/virgin-companies/virgin-atlantic

Vizard, S. (2014) first direct takes brand to high street for the first time. www.marketingweek.com/first-direct-takes-brand-to-the-high-street-for-the-first-time/

Zaleski, A. (2014) A start-up that wants to make ATMs obsolete. www.cnbc.com/2014/11/07/a-start-up-that-wants-to-make-atms-obsolete.html

08

The Six Pillars and memorable customer experiences

Companies around the world are striving to achieve 'memorable experiences', yet few companies understand how to create memorability. The Six Pillars provide a mechanism for ensuring memorability by incorporating the latest insights from neuroscience and psychology into experience design.

The decisions we make in life are based on our memories of experiences, not our actual experiences. Memories are malleable and flexible and therefore this distinction, between experience and memory, is vital as it requires experience designers to consider what will be remembered and how these memories drive commercially beneficial behaviours.

With new experiences we amend, rather than maintain and protect, our past memories, occasionally changing them beyond recognition. The newly stored information is altered, forming new and modified representations of events. For companies this means that marketing effort has to be expended to crystallize the memory of the brand and influence how it is stored and retrieved in the human brain. This is one of the reasons why we see firms increasingly marketing the experience of dealing with them rather than the products themselves (KPMG, Nunwood, 2016).

Neuroscientist Daniel Kahneman explains the process of memory using the concept of the 'two selves': the 'experiencing self' and the 'remembering self'. The experiencing self lives in the present, processing current inputs and information from the physical and social environment. Once these moments have passed, however, most are lost for ever. Kahneman estimates the average retention of an experience is about three seconds (Kahneman, 2011).

The remembering self recalls experiences which are defined by change, specifically experiences that are new, novel or personally meaningful, providing emotional peaks in a stream of experiences. Neurochemical tags are added to memories that are emotionally important to aid retrieval and influence our future behaviour. As humans, this has a profound effect on our behaviour. Subconsciously we will 'approach' situations that are likely to recreate existing emotionally positive memories and 'avoid' situations that reactivate emotionally intense negative memories (KPMG, Nunwood, 2016).

We remember negative emotions much more strongly than positive ones. Indeed, we remember the emotion first, then the event itself. This has led some to speculate that it can take as many as five positive memories to over-write one powerful negative memory (Thompson, 2007).

There are also generational differences in how emotion affects memory, which experience designers should consider. Older people show a tendency to retain emotionally positive memories over negative ones, while young adults are the reverse: it seems that younger people find negative information more compelling and memorable (Gutchess et al, 2019). Thus the challenge for loyalty-fixated CEOs is to ensure their business satisfies the needs of the experiencing self, so that consumers are drawn to them, while they also provide experiential moments that the remembering self can use to create memories that will bring consumers of all ages back again and again (KPMG, Nunwood, 2016).

Most companies are engaged in the wholesale improvement of customer experiences through large-scale transformative projects. But Kahneman's 'two selves' suggests that firms should focus on understanding where it is appropriate to be good enough (meeting the needs of the experiencing self) and where they need to excel (activating the remembering self). For many, this will lead to a programme of prioritization and focus, not necessarily wholesale change.

Small-scale memorable experiences can be cemented in the customer's psyche through repetition. Signature actions such as Chick-fil-A employees saying 'It's my pleasure', Apple Store's Genius, Hollister's video screen and Starbucks' name on the cup reinforce the brand through memorability and anticipation. In addition, companies such as AO.com and Lakeland show that a memorable experience doesn't have to be a premium one – it's enough to meet customer needs at a particular price point for a particular segment. In some cases, it just requires staff to have the desire and the autonomy to craft memorable events.

The memorable experience architecture: the serial position effect

In the UK, Emirates, Lush, Apple Store, giffgaff, AO.com and others have consciously or intuitively focused on how memories are created. They concern themselves with which specific parts of the experience are particularly memorable and why. They are clear on where they have to be exceptional and where being okay is good enough (KPMG, Nunwood, 2016).

The key to memorable experiences is embodied in the psychological term 'the serial position effect'. This highlights where and when to make experiences memorable:

1 first impression;

2 emotional peak;

3 last impression.

A great start, experiences that are new, novel or personally meaningful, provide emotional peaks in a stream of experience. Our remembering self also likes endings, how experiences conclude – the big finish.

The truth of the serial position effect is a profound one: if you manage these three parts of an experience, whatever goes on between these key points, as long as it isn't horrible, probably won't be remembered. This focus prevents over-engineering and wasted investment in non-essential parts of an experience (KPMG, Nunwood, 2016).

First impression

The first impression relates to what is known in psychology as the law of primacy. The first thing that happens shapes our view of what happens next: it is a process of priming. If the initial experience is outstanding, it is like

FIGURE 8.1 The serial position effect

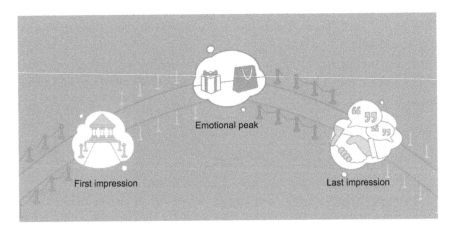

placing a large deposit in an emotional bank account. If what happens next is positive, it benefits from confirmation bias: we look for reasons to validate and justify the decisions we have made (KPMG, Nunwood, 2016). If, however, it isn't quite as positive, subsequent issues are more likely to be forgiven. But if the initial experience is poor, the reverse becomes true and we tend to magnify the negative.

A first impression doesn't have to be memorable in its own right. Brands that deliver a good first impression do this by delivering or even exceeding expectations, beginning the process of trust creation and starting a positive disposition to the brand. It is no accident therefore that organizations focus on 'the welcome'.

Who does this well?

- Santander – providing a 'red carpet welcome'.
- British Airways – with a clear focus on greeting, the captain comes out to welcome passengers on board.
- TSB – as soon as you enter a branch, a staff member comes to you with a smile and a willingness to assist.
- first direct – always greeted by a warm friendly voice, not a computer.
- Jaguar – designers focus intently on what happens when you enter the car.
- Aston Martin – orchestrates an emotionally intense experience when revealing a new car to its owner.

What is the impact on the customer? A great first impression creates an environment where future positive memories can be stored.

Emotional peak

In designing the emotional peak, we can look at the role of emotion in an experience in three ways:

- Where the customer is emotional and where our emotionally intelligent response will be memorable. For example, urgency, sympathy, understanding, reassurance.
- Where the customer can be made emotional. For example, first car, first joint account, or where the experience is personally meaningful.
- Where the transaction must happen as quickly and expediently as possible and there is no emotional content. The emotional peak can be something

tangible, such as a gift or added extra, or intangible, in the way a staff member deals with you and the personal attention and warmth they exude.

Whatever the emotional peak, it is typically something a customer is not necessarily expecting (KPMG, Nunwood, 2016).

Tapping into customer 'firsts' provides a great opportunity to deliver an 'emotional peak' – customers buying a first house, a child on its first flight abroad, etc. It is an opportunity to educate, show care and attention and become a trusted ally (KPMG, Nunwood, 2016).

Who does this well?

- Emirates: taking photographs of families on board and providing them in a souvenir folder (KPMG, 2016).
- Ritz-Carlton: staff seem to care personally and anticipate customer needs ahead of the customer themselves (Robertson, 2021).
- Nationwide: providing a welcome hamper for mortgage customers at their new home (Sammi, 2017).
- Doubletree by Hilton: providing warm cookies at check-in (Hilton, 2021).

What is the impact on the customer? From an emotional peak, a positive memory is created. As discussed above, the human brain creates a desire to repeat such memories, increasing loyalty to the brand.

Last impression

Last impressions are about making the customer feel good and leaving them on a positive note. The psychological law of recency applies. We recall our memories through the last thing that has happened in an experience (peak-end theory).

Who does this well?

- Apple Store: learned from Four Seasons the power of creating a last impression, encouraging team members to ensure a warm, friendly finish and an invitation to return (Gallo, 2021).
- Airlines such as British Airways and Virgin America: with the captain leaving the flight deck to say goodbye and thank you for your custom, as well as opening new arrival lounges in key airports to extend the lasting impression of care and concern for the passenger.

Brands need to recognize that it's the small touches which can leave a good last impression. Examples of such touches include:

- Use the customer's name.

- Summarize what has been achieved, e.g. 'So this is what we have done for Mr Smith ...'.

- Warm the customer of anything that might go wrong and what to do if it does, e.g. 'We have activated your debit card for use overseas. If for any reason something goes wrong, please call this number and they will be able to sort things out immediately for you.'

- Reference any previous personal discussion, e.g. 'Good luck with the wedding!'

- Send them away with a warm goodbye and an invitation to return: 'Pop back and tell us how it went.'

- If the customer says 'thank you' then it is best practice in the hospitality industry to respond with 'It was my pleasure', not 'You are welcome'.

- Ask 'Have I done everything you need today?' (rather than 'Is there anything else you need today?') as it gives them a chance to say yes and leave on a positive statement.

What is the impact on the customer? The small touches demonstrate empathy with the customer and leave them with a warm feeling towards the brand. Last impressions don't have to be spectacular, but they end that memory and as long as the gist of the memory is positive, it will leave the customer wanting to return (KPMG, Nunwood, 2016).

Applying the Six Pillars to memorable experience design

The Six Pillars are helpful in experience design to ensure memories are retained and crystallized in a positive way.

Examples of memorable experiences

Ritz-Carlton has 40,000 'memory makers' – every employee is charged with creating something memorable for each individual customer. The company has pioneered the art of memory making, offering guests various opportunities:

- Let us make you the captain of your own ship for a day.

- Let us show you the view from the 110th floor.

- Let us invent a drink in your honour.

These are 'big' memories, but staff are charged with creating great memories at every touchpoint. At Ritz-Carlton, this means a 40,000-strong army of memory makers are working every day to create those special touches that customers will not just remember but will return to enjoy again.

Customers are invited to share these memories on social media. Behind the scenes, every single day, the memory makers share new ideas and insights

TABLE 8.1   Six Pillars and memory

Pillar	Memory impact
Personalization	We retain memories that are personally meaningful, that reflect things we care about. We are concerned also about things that affect our sense of self-worth and self-esteem. We are more likely to retain memories where we have been made to feel better about ourselves.
Resolution	Errors, problems and issues will be retained as powerful negative memories with a strong influence on future avoidance behaviour. Our research has shown, however, that when a poor customer situation is retrieved brilliantly then it sticks in the memory because it meets the emotional story criteria – the service recovery paradox.
Integrity	Behavioural economics teaches us that we like people who are like us and we trust people who we like. Likeability is a key part of gaining trust. We are more likely to remember people we like.
Time and effort	The more the cognitive effort, the more likely the brain is to retain the memory (deep processing theory) – but this has to happen in a good way, otherwise it is retained as a negative memory.
Expectations	The brain is an expectation engine. Daniel Kahneman defines two 'selves' as brain systems: system one and system two. System one is the fast processing part of the brain that allows us to function on automatic; however, it relies on expectations being met. When an expectation is not met, it invokes system two, which is slower and more reflective, and allows us to consider the implications of an unfulfilled expectation.
Empathy	How we are dealt with when we are emotional sticks in our memory for good or for bad. It is vital to get this right. Organizations that have made significant progress in customer experience often do so simply by restoring humanity to the experience.

SOURCE KPMG, Nunwood, 2016

about how they can make the Ritz-Carlton experience memorable (KPMG, Nunwood, 2016). A series of videos describes that the group is in the business of creating indelible memories that last a lifetime and that a significant amount of dedicated care and craftsmanship goes into making memories for the discerning world traveller (Hospitality.net, 2012).

Some other examples of organizations achieving this well are:

- In the UK, M&S CEO Steve Rowe rebranded staff internally as 'Moment Makers' and staff are charged with creating emotionally connective memorable moments for customers (M&S, 2019).

- Looking to the leaders in the US, both Disney Parks (Walt Disney Parks, 2020) and Ritz-Carlton offer the services of a professional photographer to capture special moments (Ritz-Carlton, 2021).

- AO.com enables reviews to be streamed across its site, realizing that the memories of others can become an individual's impetus to act (AO, 2021).

- Lush uses its website Lush Kitchen as a way of cementing memories of a particular product experience in the customer's mind (Lush, 2021).

- Eurostar has used an advertising campaign with the line 'Stories are waiting', inviting potential passengers to create their own stories and memories by using Eurostar. The company sees its role as inspiring a connection between people and places, as a facilitator of future memories (Eleftheriou-Smith, 2013).

- One of the most remembered financial services adverts of recent times was the NatWest advert for emergency cash. Why? Because it immediately tapped into negative emotions we could all relate to but delivered a positive outcome. It told an emotional story with a happy ending (CliveandJerryTV, 2012).

- Singapore Airlines uses a specially developed scent called Stefan Floridian Waters. It is worn as perfume or cologne by the cabin crew and permeates the hot towels. It is the neuroscience behind its development that is interesting – it has been specially formulated to influence the pleasure centres of the brain and tap into positive memories. Smell is the most powerful of the senses in evoking memories. As soon as you walk onto the aircraft, positive memories of service are evoked, accumulated and more deeply imprinted (Chang, 2018).

- Virgin Group's airline brands around the world have long known the power of creating emotional memories. One of our research respondents talked about mentioning to the cabin crew that she and her partner had just got married and were travelling on their honeymoon. Fifteen minutes later, the captain paid them a visit with a bottle of champagne signed by each of the crew and invited the whole aircraft to celebrate with a round of applause. An emotionally rich, memorable experience shared among 155 people.

- Hollister provides a unique multisensory experience showing the power of ambience. The smell (olfactory), the loud music (auditory), the nature of the lighting and the video of Huntington Beach (visual) combine to create a highly memorable experience (*European Journal of Marketing*, 2017). These are all connected through the Hollister brand story. This describes the brand as being founded in 1922 in Huntingdon Beach by John Hollister, selling artifacts collected on his travels. When these ran out, he started selling surf wear. The Hollister store experience reflects each aspect of this story (KPMG, Nunwood, 2016).

Customer journey design

The Six Pillars play a considerable role in experience and interaction design across customer journeys. Journey maps are now a regular feature of organizational life. But identifying what really matters to customers and when to make this explicit are often unanswered questions.

Personas are often used in experience design. They are distilled essences of real users. In user experience (UX) design, you use personas to build empathy with target users and focus on their world. You should always create personas from observations about real users – personas should never be invented out of your assumptions or what you think you know about your users. They are a vital tool when it comes to experience design. They are the target that the design is being readied for and need to be grounded in fact. The Six Pillars can be used to extend the use of personas and ensure they are comprehensive and insightful.

The following illustrates the different types of passenger that an airline might design experiences for:

- CEOs and senior executives who use being unreachable on a flight as 'me time'. As such they want to be recognized, cosseted and then left to watch films/read with minimum fuss.

TABLE 8.2 Customer experience needs by Six Pillars and segment

	Integrity	Resolution	Expectations	Time and effort	Personalization	Empathy
Senior executives	Treat me with the respect for my position as a top executive	Predict problems and prevent them, present me with solutions, not problems	'Me time', out-of-contact catch-up time	Meals when I want them	Tailor the experience to my schedule Recognize me as a frequent flyer	Be attentive to my needs, show that you care Make me feel important to you
Consultants, IT specialists	Keep your promises – I need to be certain of my schedule	Predict and resolve problems in advance	Set and reset my expectations accurately	Maximize my laptop time on the flight Enable me to arrive meeting ready	Recognize my frequent flyer status, make me feel valued	Make sure I am not sitting near children
Empty nesters	Minimize disruption – I only have a few days to spend at the destination	Let me know in advance of any problems and how to get around them	Set my expectations about the destination, tell me things I might not know about that will exceed my expectations	Give me shortcuts to save time	Share your knowledge of destinations with me Let me chat with you	Listen to me and pay special attention
Families	Keep your promises, e.g. taking a stroller on board	Quickly resolve any issues, reassure me	Tell me about family-friendly hacks at my destination	Make it easy for me to travel quickly with children	Help me with my children	Show you care about me and my family having a good time

FIGURE 8.2   Six Pillars and the customer journey

Designing a Six Pillar-compliant customer journey

The impact of a recall on the psychology of the customer can be substantial. The customer concern 'antenna' will be very active and it is vital that the customer journey is designed carefully to ensure that it delivers the brand principles and also embraces global best practice by being structured in a way that maximizes the contribution of the Six Pillars.

World-class journeys reflect the Six Pillars at each touchpoint.

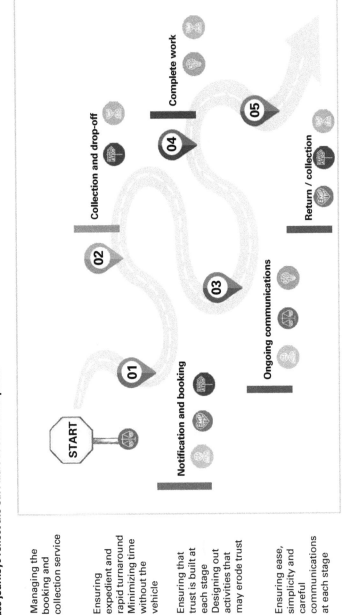

 Managing the booking and collection service

Ensuring expedient and rapid turnaround Minimizing time without the vehicle

Ensuring that trust is built at each stage Designing out activities that may erode trust

Ensuring ease, simplicity and careful communications at each stage

FIGURE 8.3 Emotional interaction design

 Priming

- Key emotions
- Up-front cues
- Customer circumstances
- Barriers

 Welcome

- Smile (in the voice)
- 4-second rule
- Voice performance (pitch, pace, inflection, vocabulary)
- Personal greeting
- Establishing credibility
- Use of name

 Engage

- Subtle discovery
- Purposeful small talk
- Active listening
- Questioning techniques / laddering
- Key needs identification
- Empathy statements
- Personal storytelling

 Solve

- Positive language
- Reciprocity
- One additional thing
- Confirming questions
- Product, process knowledge

 Close

- Strong summary
- Next step commitment / education
- Next issue avoidance
- Time estimate
- Thank by name
- Invitation to return

- Consultants, IT specialists, executives flying on business who want to arrive at meetings ready. They want to sit away from children and use their devices for as long as possible with minimum disturbance.

- Older empty nesters who are going on a city break or short holiday. They want to engage with cabin staff, gain knowledge about the destination and share experiences.

- Families on a special holiday. They want to be helped with their children and with settling into the flight. They want their children to be made to feel special.

The Six Pillar Persona Framework can be used to design future journeys which ensure that the critical dimensions of a world-class experience are covered in a way that is tailored to each persona. In Table 8.2 we have applied the framework to the above airline personas.

Figure 8.2 is based on a manufacturer recalling cars for an important post-purchase fix, a frustrating inconvenience for the customer. The Six Pillars play an important role in getting it exactly right at each touchpoint. In this example we can see that at each stage of the journey the Six Pillars are prevalent in different combinations. At the outset it is about establishing confidence and trust, personalizing the experience to the customer. During the journey, time and effort becomes an area for focus. Finally it is once again about putting the customer back in control.

Interaction design

Every interaction, whether human to human or human to digital, can be broken down into its constituent parts and, using the Six Pillars, optimized using best practice. The Six Pillars and the golden rules provide a checklist to ensure the interaction is as emotionally connective as possible. Figure 8.3 demonstrates the interaction process.

PRIMING

The first stage in the process is the pathway to making contact with an organization, which shapes the customer's mindset before they speak to a member of staff. Have they had to wait, did they find it difficult to get through, what is the firm's reputation, what have internet reviews said about them? This sets expectations for the customer which need to be either fulfilled or reset.

WELCOME

Second, welcoming is key. The hospitality industry has learned that how you say hello makes a significant difference to how the guest feels about their stay. Ritz-Carlton is so focused on this that when one of its cars picks you up at the airport, the driver texts your name to the doorman so they can greet you personally.

First impressions count and organizations are increasingly fixed on them. Some describe it as the 'red carpet welcome', others strive to achieve the 'world's best welcome'. Retailers, restaurants and hospitality sectors are generally best at welcome.

Online, Amazon ticks the psychological welcome boxes: it uses your name, recalls your history together and aims to make suggestions only someone who knows you really well would be able to make. Zappos uses call line identification to route customers to agents who have lived in the same town so they can build rapport.

Some contact centres have taught their people to identify the customer's personality type either directly or from previous interactions. They can then adjust their behaviour accordingly, either controlling the conversation because this customer prefers it that way or letting the customer control the conversation if that suits them better (KPMG, Nunwood, 2016).

ENGAGE

There are few companies that go to such lengths as USAA to teach their employees listening and rapport-building skills. Staff are trained for months in what it is like to be one of their customers. Listening well is one thing, but listening so that you understand, because you can put yourself in their shoes, is quite another.

For USAA the focus on empathy is all-embracing: knowing the customer, their circumstances and their likely needs defines every aspect of the experience. Contact centres are organized around life events so that staff build up a deep understanding of exactly what their customers are going through: they can relate to the event and offer useful life advice (Solomon, 2018). The customer feels important and valued (KPMG, Nunwood, 2016).

SOLVE

How an agent responds to a query has an immediate impact on the customer. Positive language and emotional intelligence are important. If the customer requires urgency, then the agent should reflect that need; if they require reassurance, then a 'we can do this together' attitude is needed. The customer needs to feel heard and understood.

Solving customer problems doesn't have to be a dour affair. JetBlue, Disney and Southwest Airlines have become known for their outgoing, assertively customer-friendly behaviour.

Anecdotally, when recently getting a disappointed tweet from a customer after an unexpected charge, JetBlue staff went onto the customer's Facebook profile so they could recognize him, searched the airport until they found him and then resolved his issue face to face. This type of occurrence isn't rare with JetBlue. In another instance, one JetBlue customer jokingly tweeted that she expected a 'welcome parade' at the gate when she arrived in Boston. The person who responded to the tweet informed the JetBlue staff at Boston and the staff took it upon themselves to greet the woman with marching band music and handmade signs (Cox, 2014; KPMG, 2018).

The crucial point of all this is empowerment and enablement, giving employees the freedom to make sensible judgements and do what is right and then allowing them the means to fix customer issues.

CLOSE

The final point is the anchor that we use to retrieve the memory in future. Apple Store has long known this and staff are very prescriptive about how they say goodbye. When you have finished talking with an Apple Genius they will walk with you to the door, find something personal to say based on their earlier conversation with you, bid you a warm farewell and invite you to return in the future (KPMG, 2018).

Companies are now starting to focus on next issue avoidance (NIA), thinking ahead about what may happen next to the customer, the issues they may encounter, and taking proactive action to help them avoid the problem before it happens. For example, in 2012 British Airways launched its 'Beyond the Flight Deck' programme, making flight crew more accessible to passengers. A key part of this was having the captain say goodbye to passengers as they left the aircraft in the belief that the way you say goodbye makes a difference (Eden, 2015), but also ensuring that any transfer delays or issues were quickly dealt with as the passengers left the aircraft so they were equipped to deal with any possible further travel problems.

FOLLOW-UP

Follow-up communication protocols govern how the relationship is extended after the contact centre interaction, by email, letter or check-in call. One financial institution has what it calls its 2,2,4,6 approach. After a customer takes a new product, they get a follow-up call two days later to ensure everything is happening as it should, after two weeks to check the customer has no queries about using the product, at the end of the first month to check in, then after six months to check whether the customer has any further needs.

Even a great interaction fades in memory. Regular check-ins sustain the benefit and generate positive customer feelings towards the brand.

CASE STUDY
A.P.P.L.E.

Apple Store employees are told (and trained) not to sell but rather to help customers solve problems. Their job is to understand the needs, often unexpressed ones, that the customer may find difficult to articulate. The Apple standards of service lay out exactly how a customer should be treated: its use of Apple as an acronym provides an easily memorable sequence for how to approach any customer situation.

- **A**pproach customers with a personalized warm welcome.
- **P**robe politely to understand all the customer's needs.
- **P**resent a solution for the customer to take home today.
- **L**isten for and resolve any issues or concerns.
- **E**nd with a fond farewell and an invitation to return.

(Gallo, 2021)

Digital design

As companies further embrace digital, enabling customers to personalize their end-to-end experience has become mainstream. This shift, however, led to a fragmentation of the purchasing experience. Now platforms are emerging in response, as companies seek to own a particular purchasing area and enable their customers to select suppliers in a single environment. Zalando and Amazon Marketplace are examples of how the purchasing experience is being reconfigured to make life easier for customers and enable them to assemble suitable combinations of products.

Consequently, customers are increasingly 'mixing and matching' as they unbundle and then reconfigure their buying experience to suit their individual needs. Firms that react to the connected consumer and enable customers to re-bundle in unique and personalized ways are beginning to achieve a market advantage.

The internet has enabled customers to create their own customer experiences. It has been particularly true of the travel industry, where customers have long been able to unpick components such as flight, hotel, car hire and transportation. More recently, customer configuration has also hit the retail sector. Customers may walk into a physical store for information but then purchase online and have the product delivered and installed (if necessary), all at a time of their choosing.

The process may involve several different entities, but it is seamless to the customer. The reality is that this digital democratization of the purchasing process is fragmenting what has historically been a stable and predictable process. The leading firms in our research are those that are connecting their customer in unique and exciting ways by developing a network of ecosystem partners that enables and empowers the customer to bundle services and products in ways that suit them best. These firms realize they cannot do everything themselves, but they can create an integrated environment where consumers can construct seamless journeys using the power of connected digital technology.

Singapore Airlines (SIA), for example, took top spot in our Australian survey because customers there assessed that it had the ability to get closer to them and understand their needs and requirements at each stage of the travel life cycle. This has meant looking beyond the touchpoints that are managed or controlled by SIA to understand how value is being added to the end-to-end experience regardless of who actually delivers that experience. The company's investments into a customer experience management (CEM) system allowed it to listen and react to the customer's voice as it moved through this unbundling and re-bundling process. This, in turn, uncovered opportunities to improve passengers' experience across multiple touchpoints. One of the areas SIA identified was a need to catch up with its digital experience. It set about creating an app that reconnected and re-bundled different components of the on-board and pre-boarding travel experience for the benefit of its customers (Singapore Airlines, 2021).

In New Zealand, New World is a food retailer that aims to integrate both online and in-store shopping. Examples include delivering healthy dinner kits and in-store demonstrations with competitions to inspire and incentivize customers to participate with the brand. Customers in New Zealand note that the brand demonstrates its integrity through fair trade and a strong environmental focus.

Rebuilding and integrating customer journeys is a process of aggregation, selecting appropriate partners, orchestrating them and then presenting the options to customers in new and exciting ways. Many of the leading firms in our research are using this re-bundling process to create a cohesive whole that delivers on the brand promise.

Chinese firm Alipay is a mobile and online payment platform. When it realized that its customers were holding balances in their accounts, it put this money into a money market fund and started paying its customers a level of interest that often exceeded the level paid by banks. Alipay also provides direct links to more than 65 financial institutions (including Visa and Mastercard) to facilitate payment services for more than 460,000 online and local Chinese businesses (Fernandez, 2017). QR codes can be used for local in-store payments. Customers can use the Alipay app to make credit card bills payments and for bank account management, P2P transfer, prepay mobile phone top-up, bus and train ticket purchase, food order, ride hailing, insurance selection and digital identification document storage. Alipay also allows online checkout on most Chinese-based websites such as Taobao and Tmall (Ant Group, 2019; KPMG, 2019).

The measurement framework

Having designed end-to-end experience, firms need to measure their performance across touchpoints. It is in this area that the Six Pillars prove particularly useful, especially when integrated with other key performance indicators into a measurement framework.

The measurement framework is the mechanism by which multiple different data sources and measurement approaches are integrated and aligned to make sense of the voice of the customer. At its most mature, it links the day-to-day experience being delivered at each touchpoint with the impact this has on the overall customer relationship to predict the resultant financial outcomes.

Leading organizations are rapidly embracing this new insight paradigm. They are anchoring primary research with social, operational and financial data in order to support multiple stakeholders in making data-led decisions. These are designed to improve the customer experience, create value and realize operational efficiencies (KPMG, Nunwood, 2018). Figure 8.4 shows the relationship between journey KPIs, product KPIs, marketing and brand KPIs, the Six Pillars and the higher-order metrics such as NPS or CSAT.

FIGURE 8.4   Measurement framework

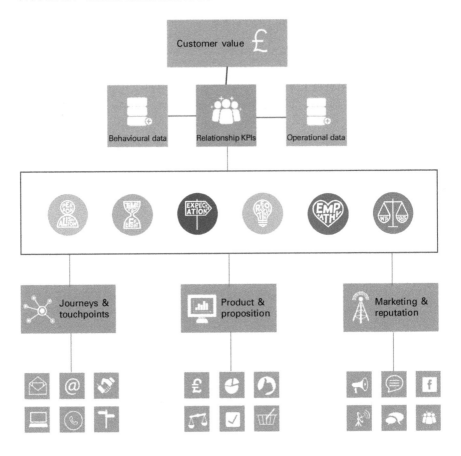

Customer journey analytics

Firms are increasing their analytic focus on customer journeys. Journey analytics is a new form of analysis that combines both quantitative and qualitative data to understand consumer behaviours and motivations across touchpoints over time. It enables analysts to achieve a deep understanding of customer activities at different stages of the journey and provides rich insights as to how the journey can be improved to both deliver a better experience for the customer and improve the commercial returns for the organization by removing unnecessary costs and finding opportunities to increase revenues (KPMG, Nunwood, 2018).

Amazon obsesses about customer journey analytics, constantly looking to innovate and remove obstacles for the customer and improve the quality of the experience by making each journey easier to navigate to a successful conclusion. Analytics also enable the organization to intercept the customer, when necessary, with something of value. For example, next issue avoidance, or next best action, technologies enable contextual engagement with the customer, increasing personalization and relevance (KPMG, Nunwood, 2018).

- Traditionally KPIs are focused on the internal mechanisms of the organization (process lead time, passing stage gates, etc).

- But truly customer-oriented organizations align their metrics to customer outcomes.

- This creates a culture that becomes 'customer obsessed' since employees are then being measured by benefits to the customer rather than the business.

- It also drives a decision-making process that puts the customer first.

- This in turn drives the benefits already described in the manual – loyalty, acquisition, etc.

KEY TAKEAWAYS

1 In this chapter we have examined how the Six Pillars can be seen as a management system, a mechanism for uniting several facets of a customer experience programme.

2 From looking across the customer life cycle to the design of individual customer journeys and interactions within journeys, through to measurement and improvement, the Six Pillars act as a golden thread, a set of design criteria that ensures consistency, cohesion and integration.

3 Consistency is one of the key issues companies face when designing customer experiences. Using the Six Pillars as a guide can give firms line of sight across touchpoints and ensure that best practice is being employed where possible and also that the areas that will have the most positive impact on customers are being attended to.

References

Ant Group (2019) How Alipay changed the way China invests. https://medium.com/alipay-and-the-world/how-alipay-changed-the-way-china-invests-and-helped-a-fund-grow-400-times-over-9c13f77af4b6

AO (2021) Read what our customers are saying. https://ao.com/customer-reviews

Chang, I. (2018) Scentsational brands: three companies using scent branding and ambient scent. https://reedpacificmedia.com/scentsational-brands-3-companies-using-scent-branding-and-ambient-scent/

CliveandJerryTV (2012) NatWest emergency cash. www.youtube.com/watch?v=QgqFB2U-cBE

Cox, L. K. (2014) Delighting people in 140 characters: an inside look at JetBlue's customer service success. https://blog.hubspot.com/marketing/jetblue-customer-service-twitter

Eden, P. E. (2015) BA first officer Kate Laidler talks success of Beyond the Flight Deck. https://runwaygirlnetwork.com/2015/07/11/ba-first-officer-kate-laidler-talks-success-of-beyond-the-flight

Eleftheriou-Smith, L.-M. (2013) Eurostar encourages people to share Parisian experiences. www.campaignlive.co.uk/article/eurostar-encourages-people-share-parisian-experiences-major-brand-push/1216877

European Journal of Marketing (2017) An embodied approach to consumer experience: the Hollister brandscape. *European Journal of Marketing*, 58(9), 1–51.

Fernandez, A. (2017) What can PayPal learn from Alipay's business model? www.kapronasia.com/asia-payments-research-category/what-can-paypal-learn-from-alipay-s-business-model.html

Gallo, C. (2021) The Apple Store's secret sauce. www.inc.com/carmine-gallo/5-steps-apple-retail-employees-use-to-sell-iphones-create-loyal-customers.html

Gutchess, A. et al (2019) Age differences in the relationship between cortisol and emotional memory. www.ncbi.nlm.nih.gov/pmc/articles/PMC6682424/

Hilton (2021) The cookie is only the beginning. https://doubletree3.hilton.com/en/about/cookie.html

Hospitality.net (2012) Ritz-Carlton reveals 'the art of the craft'. www.hospitalitynet.org/news/4057594.html

Kahneman, D. (2011) *Thinking, Fast and Slow*. New York: Farrar, Straus and Giroux.

KPMG (2018) Know me: the key to an individualized, personal customer experience. https://assets.kpmg/content/dam/kpmg/campaigns/global-cee-project/pdf/CEE-Know-me-US-2018.pdf

KPMG (2019) Tomorrow's experience, today: harnessing a customer first approach in a changing world. https://assets.kpmg/content/dam/kpmg/ie/pdf/2019/03/ie-tomorrows-experience-today-harnessing-a-customer-first-approach.pdf

KPMG, Nunwood (2016) Making memories. https://assets.kpmg/content/dam/kpmg/uk/pdf/2016/09/making-memories.pdf

KPMG, Nunwood (2018) Ignite growth: connecting insight to action. https://nunwood.com/media/2336/2018-uk-customer-experience-excellence-analysis.pdf

Lush (2021) Lush encyclopedia blog. https://lushalot.com/category/lushkitchen/

M&S (2019) Sourcing Christmas moment makers. https://jobs.marksandspencer.com/sourcing-christmas-moment-makers

Ritz-Carlton (2021) Photography concierge. www.ritzcarlton.com/en/hotels/naples/naples-beach/area-activities/photography-concierge

Robertson, G. (2021) Ritz-Carlton case study: meet the 'unexpressed' needs of guests.

Sammi (2017) Unboxing my Nationwide mortgage hamper. www.youtube.com/watch?v=22Zs6oDEW0U

Singapore Airlines (2021) A seamless and safe journey with SingaporeAir mobile app. www.singaporeair.com/en_UK/us/mobile-app/

Solomon, M. (2018) How USAA bakes customer experience innovation into its company culture. www.forbes.com/sites/micahsolomon/2018/09/30/how-to-build-a-culture-of-customer-experience-innovation-the-usaa-way/?sh=42d6167a2378

Thompson, A. (2007) Bad memories stick longer than good ones. www.livescience.com/1827-bad-memories-stick-good.html

Walt Disney Parks (2020) Disney stories. https://disneyparks.disney.go.com/blog/2020/02/introducing-capture-your-moment-a-new-disney-parks-photo-experience-at-magic-kingdom-park/

PART 3

The 90-day plan: achieving a quantum leap

09

Preparation

In his book *The First 90 Days: Critical Success Strategies for New Leaders*, Michael D. Watkins observes that 'aligning an organization is like preparing for a long sailing trip': you need to be clear on your destination, the mission and goals of the organization, have a route defined and planned (strategy) and only then determine the structure, processes and skills required for the voyage. He also counsels potential travellers to 'watch out for reefs that are not on the charts' (Watkins, 2003).

This is excellent advice, to which we add purpose as the north star to guide you. When considering potential reefs, it is helpful to evaluate what has failed in the past, the endemic shortcomings of the organization that will delay or even curtail the voyage. In this third part of the book we lay out the 'navigation' process for a radical shift in customer experience delivery.

If the answers to the following questions are in the negative, then this is the section for you:

- Is our business structured to withstand disruption?
- Do we have the flexibility and agility to compete effectively with new forms of competition?
- Do we get to market rapidly and successfully?
- Does our culture and internal environment support the long-term achievement of our strategy?

Winston Churchill once remarked, 'Never let a good crisis go to waste' (Gruère, 2019). It is much easier to make change when the odds are stacked against you, when there are compelling reasons for change and there is empirical evidence for all to see that the ways of the past have failed.

We live in a time where there is a unique opportunity to reset business to meet the challenges of the future. Technology change, disruption, post-COVID-19 response, new ways of working, global competitors – there are enough imperatives for senior executives to really think the business through from the ground up. There is never a good time to consume a considerable amount of senior executive time, but if you don't do it now, maybe those executives won't have jobs in the not too distant future.

The parable of the frog comes to mind: when placed in a pan of cold water which is slowly heated, the frog will stay still and die. But throw the frog into a pan of boiling water and he will jump out and escape.

For many organizations, change is a slow, incremental process. For others, perhaps those faced with an impending cliff edge, it can take the form of end-to-end transformation. It is most difficult to effect extensive change when business performance is acceptable, when the business is trading as it always has, when the early warnings of seismic industry change seem far into the future. For many organizations in this steady state, change is piecemeal and often glacial. Individual initiatives pile up as well-meaning departments establish their own change programmes. But rarely does this array of initiatives result in a quantum improvement in the customer experience.

Organizations are adept at generating almost invisible resistance to discontinuous change. To overcome this requires a sustained, well-thought-through and rigorous execution. The impact of COVID-19, huge technological disruption and rapidly changing patterns of consumer behaviour are now there for all to see. These are no longer early warning signs. They present a real and present danger. This is now a crisis. Don't waste it.

Over the years we have seen the power and catalytic effect of a 90-day senior leadership strategic programme to reconceive and reinvent the business. This is not a traditional long-term planning session, where a financial outcome for functional plans is usually the driving force and where the majority of the discussion is all about budgets. We are not talking about the traditional, annual senior executive strategic away days. This is a proven methodology for rebasing the business, for really getting to grips with thorny problems that have been consciously or unconsciously avoided. It is a process that gets all the elephants out of the room and subjects the business to forensic scrutiny.

Achieving this requires a new way of harnessing executive thinking power. It isn't just a longer meeting where views are exchanged. This is an event-based process, where strategic decisions are made, where substantial change is an inevitable outcome. It is also a profound experience where the change is as much inside the minds of the executives as it is in reconceiving the business.

We need to see the organization as a system – but what sort of system? It is important to differentiate between complicated systems and complex systems. Complicated systems have a defined output (e.g. the engine of a car). They can be defined and managed piece by piece: every problem has a solution. Complex systems meanwhile (e.g. a business) can generate unintended consequences and need guidelines and checklists and behavioural criteria to shape outcomes in the right way.

The process we outline in the following chapters aims to help create the platform by which the problems of a complex system are shaped to move in the right direction, where the outcomes are more cohesive and consistent. We aim to address the fundamental gap in most business approaches to the customer.

The process has five component parts: three 30-day sprints, preceded by a period of input preparation and followed by a period of consolidation. It is a process with clear inputs and outputs, with key sessions divided into a series of considerations. The use of the word 'consideration' is deliberate: these are not agenda items. A consideration is an open question, it requires careful thought, structured inputs, investigation of options and alternatives, and it is made over time as new information is made available, mulled and investigated until it reveals a useful truth. We have found that 90 days is sufficient to give real depth to the considerations and results in a high-quality output.

Our experience of working this process with some of the biggest companies in the world is that it drives a strategic quantum leap. Pivotal discontinuous shifts occur when executives have time to think deeply about the problems at hand in a structured and considered way rather than when they are on the constant hamster wheel of reactive decision making.

Rules of the game

Success requires seeing the organization as a complex system. It requires a holistic approach to considering the business and how it works. It runs for 90 days and requires careful facilitation. The following guidelines on running the 90-day programme are drawn from our experience of this process. We recommend that you use them in creating your own process.

How much time is allocated depends on the company. Ideally, for each 30-day period it should be at least two days a week, or a single intense week. The numbers of people involved will depend on the company. We have seen these programmes run with as few as 12 and as many as 60.

The programme must be championed by the leadership team and led by the CEO – handing it over to a transformation director or allocating it to the change team guarantees failure. We should not be surprised that the organization tends to pay real attention only to the things the CEO pays attention to.

Bring in external speakers. Get the input of thought leaders. This doesn't necessarily have to be empirical or based on primary research: it is about insight from wherever it comes. One exec briefing we ran had an expert who focused entirely on the ages and career aspirations of the CEOs in the industry. He predicted a number of acquisitions and mergers that would meet their aspirations rather than any strategic logic. He turned out to be right: it played out exactly as predicted.

This will not work with a dry submission of board papers. This has to be an experience: proper facilitation; real customers talking; real employees talking (or at the very least on video). The environment needs to be carefully prepared to enable everything necessary for supporting the considerations to be in the room, creatively displayed.

The process requires provocations, challenges and facilitation to encourage non-linear thinking and reduce the tendency to reinvent the past. The failure audit is a crucial device for ensuring the team does not slip back into old ways.

Use external benchmarks and case studies to aid understanding of best practice and remove 'can't be done' challenges. For example, when running such a programme with a restaurant chain concerned about achieving consistency of employee behaviour towards customers, we used the example of Chick-fil-A to show that the mass delivery of outstanding customer behaviour in an environment of significant employee turnover was eminently possible. You just had to work out how.

Ban any 'we tried this before, and it didn't work' responses. Why did it fail? What is required to make it work?

Do not be seduced by the wholesale import of the latest management fad. first direct looks at each new set of thinking and picks out the really relevant insights that will work for the company. It strips away the zeal and isolates the unique truth at its heart that made it resonate in the first place and adds that to its canon of knowledge about how it can manage its business (Gordon, 2020). We have often felt that the children's poem 'How to eat a worm' (https://100.best-poems.net/nobody-likes-me-guess-i039ll-go-eat-worms.html) contains exactly the right prescription for getting the best from a prevailing management fad: 'Bite off the heads, suck out the juice and throw the skins away.'

Finally, beware of the 'quick wins' trap. There is a quite understandable tendency among managers to do the nine easy things with low chances of success before the one big thing that guarantees success. Quick wins give the illusion of momentum, yet all they do in reality is clog up the works. The history of failed businesses is full of companies that picked off quick wins and then failed to deal with the substantive issues that drive survival.

Pre-90 days: preparation

In his seminal book *Good to Great*, Jim Collins observed, 'You must have the discipline to confront the most brutal facts of your current reality, whatever they might be' (Collins, 2001). The pre-90 days should be spent preparing the inputs, including the 'brutal facts'. The quality of the considerations made through this process are a function of the quality of the inputs. Instruction should be given not to sugar the truth, no matter how difficult it might be. This process requires brutal honesty.

In our experience this is a six-week exercise best allocated to dedicated cross-functional teams to collate and visualize. These are inputs designed for consideration and deliberation. These are not final presentations asking for a decision. It is important that the facts are not diluted or 'interpreted' for the audience; in fact, the rawer the inputs, the better. Polished presentation materials confine thinking. We are looking to expand it.

KEY TAKEAWAYS

1 Every industry is facing seismic change. Organizations need to prepare now to ensure they are 'future ready'.

2 It requires executives to detach themselves from the day to day, determine what the future is likely to hold for their industry and really think through what their organization needs to do to succeed in a very different reality.

3 It requires levels of honesty that organizations seldom achieve – every closet needs to be devoid of skeletons, every room elephant free.

4 Prepare for an immersion session with the executive team by accumulating as much insight as possible in a single location and look for engaging and creative ways to bring it alive.

References

Collins, J. (2001) *Good to Great*. 1st ed. Chicago, IL: Random House

Gordon, J. (2020) Former CEO first direct [Interview], February.

Gruère, G. (2019) Never let a good water crisis go to waste. www.oecd.org/agriculture/never-waste-a-good-water-crisis/

Watkins, D. M. (2003) *The First 90 Days: Critical Success Strategies for New Leaders*. Boston, MA: Harvard Business School Free Press.

10

The first 30 days

In this chapter we outline the tasks required to get the 90-day process under way, the engagement with the data and the necessary considerations to move the organization forward based on a deeper knowledge of both the customer and the internal capability for change. The first 30 days should involve total immersion in all things external and in particular all things customer.

We recommend two sprints, looking first externally and second internally. This builds in a period of reflection based on a new understanding of the customer and the impact of environmental shifts. Executives can use the time between the two sessions to think through what it means for them personally and for their area of responsibility.

Days 1–15: opening the window to the outside world

At the heart of this process is an understanding of the customer, the market and competitors. It requires more than a hastily prepared SWOT analysis for the annual planning process; it means really getting under the skin of the factors that can accelerate or inhibit progress. It requires 'wallowing' in the data, an immersion approach whereby executives really learn to see the market through a different, more objective lens.

Table 10.1 lays out the key customer, market and competitor elements that need to be considered.

TABLE 10.1   First 15 days considerations

Input	Considerations	Output
Driving forces of structural industry change External speakers	Where will our industry be in three years' time?	Clarity on the future of the industry Clarity on the structural drivers of environmental change
Six Pillars PESTLE analysis External speakers	What are the important environmental and social implication of this change?	
Six Pillars future impact projections External speakers	What will affect customer needs, desires and wants over this period? What circumstances or events in our customers' lives give rise to these needs?	Clarity on how customer needs are changing
Real customers talking about their relationship	Who are our best customers? What do they say about us?	
Analysis of customer value	Which customers and products drive our economic engine? What really makes us profitable? What loses us money?	Clarity on what makes the business work commercially
Competitor assessment, benchmarking across the Six Pillars	What do our competitors do better than us? What do their customers think of them?	Learning and opportunities
Six Pillar interaction model	What do we want our customers to think and feel when they interact with us?	Target customer experience
Opportunities and threats analysis	What are the opportunities and threats that arise from this?	Input to next session

Days 16–30: internal reflection

For the second sprint it is time to consider the internal capabilities, the organizational wherewithal that supports future success. This involves immersion in deep understanding of the current position, being brutally honest about the current state and striving for complete clarity on what drives the company's economic engine.

TABLE 10.2   Second 15 days considerations

Input	Considerations	Output
Opportunities and threats arising from first 15 days Previous purpose, mission, vision and values	What does the external analysis mean for our purpose – do we need to redefine? Is it compelling enough to act as a north star? What would the world miss if we didn't exist?	Validated/redefined purpose statement
Map of culture to understand the values currently guiding behaviours	Does our current culture support our future strategy? Identify the values that bring the new purpose to life. Who needs to be disempowered or empowered?	Simple rules that will guide future behaviour
Failure audit – identify the reasons for past failures	Analyse reasons for past failure (why have we failed to …) and develop mitigations	Failure future-proofing
Six Pillar leadership model	Does our leadership style and behaviour model what we need to achieve our strategy? Are we command-and-control bosses or servant leaders?	Leader behaviour framework
Six Pillar analysis of employee experience	What is our current employee experience? What future changes do we need to take into account? How will this affect the employee life cycle?	Employee understanding Employee life cycle design implications
Employees in their own voices	What do our employees say about us?	
Evaluation of structural changes to the employee experience over time (e.g. new working patterns, new technologies)	Define future employee experience	Target employee experience
Human value chain – how employee behaviours drive customer experience	What do we need to do to ensure that the employee experience and the customer experience are aligned such that the target customer experience naturally emerges from our culture?	Company-specific human value chain
Employee customer skills match	What drives our economic engine? Which employees make this work?	Right employees in the right places
Six Pillar maturity model Journey- and needs-based design options	What are the organization design implications? Do we need a new way of working?	What is the transition plan to a new design?

Start with an inside-out look at your core purpose, your reason for existing as an organization. Where have we come from? Why were we created? Where do we have the biggest impact socially and environmentally? What are our authentic values? How do these map onto the values of our customers? Then redefine or amend as necessary. This process can take some time: it is important to get it right. Purpose is the north star, the compelling reason why customers and future employees will be attracted to you. It also provides a motivational fuel for engaging existing employees.

Table 10.2 shows that some often ignored facets of the company such as culture need to come under the microscope. Culture is the filter through which all change is executed, it has the power to shape, undermine or accelerate what is required. An understanding of culture and what it takes to modify or harness its strengths is missing in most organizations.

There is no reason why every business cannot be like first direct, the company we profiled in detail in Chapter 5. first direct has no inherent technical advantage (in fact, it uses the systems and IT infrastructure of its parent HSBC), it has no geographic or structural advantage. The difference lies in how it is guided by its purpose and the impact its purpose has on the organizational mindset. Every component part of the business comes together to be mutually self-reinforcing because it is thoroughly thought through and designed to dovetail with everything else. This is what we are doing over these 30 days, creating the conceptual pillars that will drive cohesiveness and integration.

They may be old fashioned now, but the PESTLE and SWOT techniques are still valuable means of interpreting structural changes occurring in the industry. Bringing the customer to life for all members of the programme is a critical success factor. Path-to-purchase analysis or customer life cycle maps can be used to show how the new customer is emerging, to identify their changing purchase and engagement criteria and their network of influencers. What is important is that all those involved can put themselves in the shoes of their customer. Think QVC, where every employee can see the world through the customer's eyes. In the very early days of its transformation in 2010, it was empathy-driven customer insight that drove QVC's cultural change programme.

CASE STUDY
Economic engine: airline

The power of this 30-day focus was evident when working with a premium airline which was under considerable pressure from low-cost competitors. It had reached a crossroads: compete with the low-cost airlines on their terms or continue as a premium carrier. It had some critical decisions to make.

The start point was being clear on the current situation, the brutal truth, while understanding what drove its economic engine. A handful of its routes drove a substantial proportion of the profit. Its desire to keep up standards across the entirety of its route portfolio meant that there was no money available to invest and protect the core passengers and routes that drove its economic engine.

It also surfaced that the least trained staff often were rostered to care for the most profitable and demanding customers. A quick decision was made to roster those staff with at least two years' experience and well-developed passenger care skills.

Tough decisions had to be taken to protect and invest in its profit driver funded from reduced service in non-critical areas. Once the decisions were implemented the airline saw its profitability grow by 30 per cent.

CASE STUDY
Purpose: utility

When using this process with a major utility, executives freely admitted that they did not have the time to 'think customer'. Most of their meetings were operational in focus and if they spent 5 per cent of their time on the customer then that was it. The 90-day process opened their eyes to what their customers needed and what the 'connected home' might mean for their business in future.

More important than this was realizing that customers wanted to see them playing a much bigger role in the environment: this made them take a step back and radically re-examine the company's purpose. They realized it was not enough to set sustainability objectives for themselves – even industry-leading objectives. The process – listening to the customer voice – allowed the executives to see that, as an industry leader, the company could take its place and influence an entire industry, and peripheral industries as well.

CASE STUDY
SunTrust Bank

SunTrust Bank has systematically and inexorably moved up the US league table (+137 places). It is the systematic, purposeful nature of its approach that makes it stand out. Its 30-day start point involved adopting an outside-in approach, really getting to understand the difference it makes to customers' lives and answering the question, 'Why is it that SunTrust exists?'

So began an intensive and rapid 30-day immersion in the past and a detailed examination of the historical customer base and values. It discovered that SunTrust (which subsequently merged with BB&T to create Truist) is a bank rooted in its communities – an organization which in times of discord has historically focused on building personal relationships with its customers to help restore financial confidence and wellbeing. 'That is how we found our authentic purpose. We believe everyone can achieve the financial confidence to live a life well spent. That became our rallying cry, the stand we were taking, and the movement we were launching,' said Jeff VanDeVelde, Chief Customer Officer (Trevail, 2017).

From this point, the bank focused on how it personalizes its relationship with customers, looking at how individual customer journeys and its relationship with communities help it fulfil its purpose. Removing pain points, putting customers in control and creating community links paved the way for a significantly improved customer experience. It has focused on making change happen: 'outside in – delivered inside out'.

There is a strong link between the improvements in experience and the financial ratios of the bank. In a news release subsequent to the rediscovery of its true purpose, CEO William H. Rogers said, 'SunTrust revenue is up 7 per cent and our efficiency ratio and tangible efficiency ratios have improved by 90 and 100 basis points, respectively' (Trevail, 2017).

Culture

An examination of culture and its ability to accelerate or inhibit the successful achievement of the strategy is something that executives rarely indulge in. However, it is a vital component of the overall organizational capability and should be made real for executives as they go through the first 30-day sprint. This involves some preparatory work in understanding and documenting the core aspects of the organization's culture.

Culture is the invisible operating system of the organization. In most businesses it is given scant attention, though 'culture' is often blamed for derailing key initiatives. first direct shows that knowing the culture, its strengths and shortcomings is a vital management input. It is the role of its leaders to keep the culture relevant and to nurture it for future leaders. There are myriad ways to measure and understand culture. One of the most powerful is an unwritten rule analysis, a mechanism for really understanding why the organization behaves as it does.

In his book *The Unwritten Rules of the Game*, Dr Peter Scott-Morgan explains that corporate culture is subliminally controlled by a series of unwritten rules (Scott-Morgan, 1994). These rules can often be the unanticipated consequences of written rules. For example, 'spend your budget this year or you won't get it next year' is prevalent in many businesses – the unintended consequence of the budgeting process which goes on to create a set of employee behaviours that is not beneficial to the business.

In one company that prided itself on cross-training employees by moving them between jobs every 18 months, the unwritten rule was 'be a hero in your first three months (often by dismissing what has gone before), and do not leave anything in place that might benefit the next incumbent'. This drove a culture of short-term thinking and unhealthy competition rather than the intended culture of highly trained, multidimensional staff.

One simple way to quickly get to grips with culture and surface some of the critical unwritten rules is through interviewing recent recruits. New employees must go through an often subconscious process of acculturation. They have to adapt their behaviour to those around them. They intuit acceptable or successful behaviour by observing those around them. By simply asking new staff about their experience in the first few months – what they found odd, or how behaviour differed from that in their previous companies – real cultural insights can be surfaced.

Organization design: customer journeys

Buinesses everywhere are struggling to come to terms with the twin concepts of agile at scale and customer journey management. Dealing with this issue requires clarity on the customer journeys that the business is managing, the role of cross-functional working and the way in which an agile methodology can be adapted to suit a particular business.

In Chapter 4 we explored the migration options for a customer-centric organization design. The senior leadership needs to think through their migration plan and have a clear view of what the ultimate destination might look like.

Failure audit

We are frequently told that more than 70 per cent of change programmes fail. Based on our own observations we wouldn't dispute this. But few organizations really learn from their past failures, which means they probably continue to repeat them.

In a failure audit, the business has to take an honest look at its recent past, identify which programmes have failed to achieve their goals and ask the fundamental question why. Beyond the management of the programme, what systemic organizational factors, beliefs or ways of working have doomed the initiative to failure from the outset? What are the symptoms and what are the root causes?

Once the seeds of failure have been defined, what are the solutions required to mitigate the impact of these factors in future?

Human equity continuum

Completing the value chain model is a simple but highly effective way of seeing how the total complex system of employee–customer interaction can be shaped for consistency.

CASE STUDY
IBM

When Lou Gerstner took over IBM in 1993 with a mission to reinstate it as a leading solutions company, his first act was to get his senior team in touch with the customer. He saw that in IBM the customer came second. He realized that they could no longer run the company 'like the Roman Empire confident in their hegemony, certain those barbarians massing at the border were no real threat' (Gerstner, 2002).

He started the process of customer immersion with 'Operation Bear Hug', requiring each of the 50 top executives to make a 'Bear Hug' visit to at least five of their major customers over a three-month period. Each executive had to submit a two-page report detailing the problems they had found. Gerstner read every single report and when the executives realized he meant business, it significantly improved his executives' customer orientation. They in turn followed the same approach with their reporting line and ultimately it permeated the company. IBM was on the path to customer centricity (Duarte, 2015).

KEY TAKEAWAYS

1 There are no easy routes to success, no silver bullet, no one thing that guarantees success – it is, as the maxim goes, 99 per cent perspiration and 1 per cent inspiration.

2 The first 30 days is about really sweating the details on customers' lives, their changing needs, new technologies and internal capabilities. It requires a willingness to engage with long-ignored issues and to view them with honesty through a customer lens.

3 It requires getting to grips with culture, with the employee experience and the link between employee and customer.

4 The voice of the customer and the voice of the employee need to be loud and penetrating, not just present.

References

Duarte, N. (2015) To win people over, speak to their wants and needs. https://hbr.org/2015/05/to-win-people-over-speak-to-their-wants-and-needs

Gerstner, L. V. (2002) *Who Says Elephants Can't Dance?* 1st ed. New York: HarperCollins.

Scott-Morgan, P. (1994) *The Unwritten Rules of the Game: Master Them, Shatter Them, and Break Through the Barriers to Organizational Change.* 1st ed. New York: McGraw-Hill.

Trevail, C. (2017) How SunTrust Bank is creating a purpose-driven customer movement. www.linkedin.com/pulse/how-suntrust-bank-creating-purpose-driven-customer-movement-trevail/

11

The second 30 days

In this second 30-day sprint we are concerned with capability. Do we have the right capabilities to take advantage of our enhanced customer and environmental understanding? If not, how do we get on track to build that capability to best effect?

We have observed company after company focusing on personalization technologies and empathy training for staff because they are 'of the moment' and fashionable at a point in time. Now companies are investing in AI and machine learning while critical core processes continue to diminish the customer relationship.

There is some truth in the adage 'fix the basics first'. It doesn't mean higher-order investments cannot be made concurrently, just do not invest in these at the expense of more important lower-order improvements, and if you are able to invest, do not expect improved NPS or CSAT results until the customer experiences the effect of improvements to core process.

Table 11.1 lists the considerations around how customer journeys can be supported by improved capabilities.

Within this process, there are three significant areas for examination: the technology that can accelerate the impact of capability development; the journeys that customers undertake to achieve life goals and with the company; and prioritization – how projects, and especially portfolios of projects, are managed collectively.

TABLE 11.1   Second 30 days considerations

Inputs	Considerations	Outputs
Six Pillar technology scan	What are the new/emerging technologies that have the power to transform our business?	Candidate technologies for further evaluation Potential long-term implications for enterprise systems architecture
Journey atlas	What customer journeys do we manage as a business? Are these product journeys or customer life journeys?	Clear understanding of enterprise-wide customer journeys
Six Pillar hierarchy Six Pillar prioritization template	Using the volumetric analysis and the Six Pillar journey analysis, which journeys are the most broken and experienced by the most customers?	Prioritized journeys for improvement Critical capabilities analysis
Critical capabilities analysis	What are the hallmark projects, those that will ensure success, no matter how challenging they are?	Projects that require senior leadership oversight
Leadership team agenda	How do we govern implementation and delivery of the hallmark projects?	Leadership team reporting schedule
Portfolio management techniques aligned to maturity modelling	How do we manage version control across all customer journey projects?	Internal centre of excellence
Draft roadmap	What is our big-picture roadmap?	Organization-wide roadmap
Current financial business case methodology	How do we manage the economics of change? Where and how will money be saved so it can be reinvested?	Refined financial business case methodology

Technology scan

The technology scan should look at the array of new technologies and isolate where they might bring commercial benefit, either through enhancing the experience or reducing cost. AI, digital, augmented reality, blockchain – the list is an extensive one, but firms need to understand the role these technologies can play in improving life for both customers and employees. The following case studies show that companies can let technology advantage slip through their fingers or they can harness it to great effect.

In the 1960s and 1970s Xerox Corporation had one of the world's most advanced technology laboratories in the world, based in Palo Alto, California. It employed some of the world's leading scientists, who made gigantic breakthroughs in developing the technologies we now use every day. Xerox was responsible for creating windows and icons, the fundamental interface medium of every computer and mobile device available today. It developed ethernet and networking technologies, digital scanning and laser printing. It was, however, uniquely unable to bring these technologies to commercial fruition: instead they powered other companies such as Apple, Microsoft and Hewlett Packard (Mui, 2012). This provides an object lesson in pursuing technology for its own sake.

Many firms today have design labs, but these are more focused on real, present-day customer problems that can be solved by creative use of advanced technologies. USAA Labs is an example of such customer involvement. It offers customers opportunities to join product-test panels or focus groups, or to confront 'challenges' where members can submit solution ideas on specific topics such as 'how USAA can better communicate, interact or assist members who are working to pay off debts'. There is also a results section where customers can see the impact they have had on products and services (USAA, 2017).

Sephora innovation labs work with customers to create new and often innovative ways of interacting (DeNisco Rayome, 2018). For example, Sephora Virtual Artist is an AI feature that uses facial recognition technology to allow customers to virtually try on makeup products. The software also acts as a booking service for reservations at the Sephora Beauty Studio, and serves as a digital purse for holding a shopper's past purchases information and Beauty 'insider card' (denoting membership of the Sephora customer loyalty programme) as they browse through the aisles. The app can then either send customers to purchase the products online or tell them where they can be found in a store. Sephora has replicated the offline in-store experience online, reacting to increased digital usage among its customers.

Customer journey atlas

With the advent of customer journeys, the genie is out of the bottle. It is unlikely that organizations will ever go back to a functional approach. Helping customers along their journeys is here to stay.

Few businesses, however, have a complete view of all the customer journeys that a customer might have made with them. Fewer still see these journeys in the context of the customer's life rather than just product journeys. The journey atlas is the high-level mapped collection of these journeys viewed from the perspective of the customer's life. Given this view, the business can offer innovation and solutions to the customer, forming a relationship rather than just encouraging consumption.

Consequently, organizations need to make managing in a journey environment a core competence. Unfortunately journey designs often stay on the flip charts or brown paper they were designed on. Journeys will change as needs change – managing journey designs will always be a work in progress so organizations need to equip their businesses to manage ongoing journey improvement successfully.

Leading organizations are forming a Customer Journey Management Centre of Excellence. There are some key elements to this:

- There needs to be a standardized journey design methodology rather than a cottage industry. Well-intentioned teams making it up as they go along is not a recipe for long-term success.

- There needs to be an organizational Centre of Journey Management Excellence charged with keeping the methodology up to data and relevant to the task at hand.

- People need to be formally trained and certified in using the methodology.

- There needs to be a central repository of journey designs that is version controlled, has new design release schedules and is kept current.

Prioritization

There are few executives who do not complain of initiative overload or change fatigue. A phrase a colleague of ours uses is that 'executives are too busy firing arrows to speak to the machine gun salesman'. In this world everything is urgent, there is no time to think, every decision is reactive. Proactive management is hard. Worse still, raging against the machine is seen as a sign of weakness. Such an environment breeds misplaced bravado and a destructive can-do attitude that can have personal costs as well as ending in failure across multiple projects.

So why do executives find it hard to prioritize? One of the reasons is that every project is urgent to someone. There is no absolute against which urgency can be calibrated. Earlier in this book we referred to our work with a major bank which had over 400 live, large-scale initiatives under way, every one of which was labelled urgent. The reality was that actually only 11 of the 400 made any serious improvement for the customer. We labelled these 'hallmark' projects, important enough for the leadership team to check in on their progress every two weeks. Over 100 projects were stopped and the resources freed up to ensure top-quality delivery of the customer-facing projects.

We observe that identifying capability and sequencing are the two areas where companies lose momentum. We believe these areas stall because other parts of the organization are not yet ready to benefit from or integrate the changes. This is more complex than critical path analysis, which tends to be intra-project – this is inter-project.

Portfolio management tends to focus on the hard systems, the technological capabilities, but rarely includes the soft systems, the people-related initiatives, such as culture development, customer behaviours and decision making. Our model of success sees the total system, hard and soft factors, as interdependent. Consequently, it requires oversight of the entire change portfolio. Maturity modelling is helpful here. It enables projects to be sequenced into achieving a desired organizational state, at a particular point in time, not just working to an individual project completion calendar.

When working with a major investment bank we developed a project portfolio management approach which drove activity towards achieving a view of the entire organization's capability at a point in time across six key dimensions: purpose, vision and strategy; customer; employee; organization; technology; and channels. This became an organization-wide maturity statement; it defines at a specific point what the organization as a whole would be capable of. For example:

- All employees will understand what our purpose means for them as individuals and customer-oriented behaviours are evident across the business.
- We are beginning to see demonstrable examples of us living our purpose at key touchpoints in the customer journey. Our people will be comfortable using the brand behaviours with customers.

- Our agile action teams will have delivered their first complete set of sprints and we have moved to a test-and-learn environment.
- We have released the omnichannel interaction technology and customers are getting comfortable with using it.
- We have moved to a customer journey matrix-based organization design and it is a stable platform for moving to full journey management.
- Our leadership meetings are now customer based and decisions across the organization are being fuelled by the voice of the customer programme.

The watchwords here are integration and co-ordination, with clarity on the destination at each major stage in the organization's development. Only then can the full benefits of transformation be achieved.

KEY TAKEAWAYS

1 In a world of rapidly advancing technology, keeping abreast of potential new customer use applications is not a trivial task.

2 For many organizations it requires a specialist lab function, a team of technically gifted people who can not only track new tech but convert it rapidly into customer-useful applications.

3 It is more than just innovation for its own sake; it is how it solves customer problems, how it improves customer journeys and how it makes life simpler and more rewarding for employees.

4 Customer journey management is becoming a critical organizational competence.

References

DeNisco Rayome, A. (2018) How Sephora is leveraging AR and AI to transform retail and help customers buy cosmetics. www.techrepublic.com/article/how-sephora-is-leveraging-ar-and-ai-to-transform-retail-and-help-customers-buy-cosmetics/

Mui, C. (2012) The lesson that market leaders are failing to learn from Xerox PARC. www.forbes.com/sites/chunkamui/2012/08/01/the-lesson-that-market-leaders-are-failing-to-learn-from-xerox-parc/?sh=3a54a87b6829

USAA (2017) Introducing USAA Labs: member-driven innovation. https://communities.usaa.com/t5/Money-Matters/Introducing-USAA-Labs-Member-driven-innovation/ba-p/114187

12

The final 30 days

We are now concerned with establishing the processes by which change will be managed and momentum created. In many ways these processes will provide the antidote to the ways of the past. They establish the environment within which the desired change can take place in a controlled, cohesive and consistent way. In this chapter we look at what is required to create a compelling case for change, to overcome the natural organizational inertia and to signal that change is not optional.

Table 12.1 outlines the considerations that executives need to make when attempting to free up the organization to make it more flexible when it comes to changing ingrained processes and procedures. In particular, we draw on the concepts of agile and servant leadership, discussed more fully in earlier chapters.

- **Innovation:** We are firm believers that innovation arises from a deep understanding of a customer's problems and a broad-based understanding of the possible solutions. We subscribe to the innovation approach of 'jobs to be done', which is particularly useful in customer experience innovation: it leads to a deeper understanding of the problems that a customer is dealing with. As such it is a useful mechanism for surfacing customer issues that the organization can help with.

- **Agile at scale:** New agile methodologies are a radical alternative to command-and-control-style management. In creating empowered cross-functional teams they release energy to the frontline and provide a means of dramatically reducing time to market. Agile at scale expands the methodology from the IT world into mainstream organizations design. Agile brings a set of well-considered techniques that enable a rapid implementation of a cross-functional team-based approach while ensuring this is not followed by chaos.

TABLE 12.1   Final 30 days considerations

Inputs	Considerations	Outputs
Innovation methodologies, e.g. 'jobs to be done'	How do we drive experience innovations?	Innovation strategy
Current experience and knowledge of agile	What are the agile cross-functional teams that will take forward the priorities?	Agreed way forward with agile
Draft framework	How will we measure success? What is the measurement framework?	Agreed measures of success
Line-of-sight approach	How do we link all our people to the customer?	Commission a line-of-sight exercise
Current communications process and shortcomings. Does it communicate or create understanding?	What will be our employee communication process, which ensures understanding and a desire to act?	Implement an 'understanding process' Ensure that the communications process is agreed and understood
Ideas from previous considerations	What are our Trojan mice? The totems and symbols needed to change and reinforce mindsets?	Agreed 'mice' to implement
Leaders' pledges and commitment	Leadership alignment – are we all committed to the new purpose, employee experience and customer experience? How we will guide implementation?	10 commandments – cabinet responsibility

- **Line of sight:** Various studies have shown that when employees have clear line of sight to the company's strategy and purpose, they are more engaged and energized. Jan Carlson summed it up: 'If you are not serving customers your job is to serve someone who is' (Hyken, 2018). Employees need to have line of sight between their role, their unique contribution and how that ultimately affects the customer.

- **Leadership alignment:** Ultimately these 90 days have been about reaching leadership alignment: creating the space to air and resolve issues and getting everyone on the same page. Together, you will have created a common understanding of the task at hand and the parameters within which it will be taken forward. Leaders now need to make a firm commitment to that way forward.

Middle management psychological recruitment

No matter how carefully thought through the strategy, ultimately successful change is dependent upon middle managers. They are the shock absorbers, the interface between strategy and implementation – without their ability to mobilize often invisible networks, the strategy is likely to remain just that, a well-thought-through articulation of a future direction but of no value unless it is enacted.

Middle managers tend to get a bad press. In one organization they were described as the marzipan layer because everything was sweetened as it was passed upwards. In another organization they were described as the permafrost layer because nothing passed through it. Middle managers are also the community likely to be the recipients of ongoing and continual instructions. Change fatigue is a feature of many middle management groups: 'Here comes another one.'

If they are to be motivated and engaged then they must be part of this process – nothing builds commitment like ownership. They need to feel not just involved but instrumental to its success. In our leading organizations it is empowerment that drives ownership and focus. The direction is 20 per cent of a change programme, but 80 per cent is how it is implemented, and middle managers need to participate in the first and own the second.

Trojan mice

The process of creating understanding can be accelerated by 'Trojan mice', small, well-focused changes which are introduced inconspicuously, are small enough to be accepted and understood by all but have powerful change properties and symbolism embedded within them.

In Chapter 10 we talked about Lou Gerstner's way of getting senior IBM executives to focus on the customer. The act was a simple one: 'Go and speak to five customers and report back.' But it had embedded within it a profound change dynamic. We call these Trojan mice. A seemingly simple ask that at first glance goes under the radar but leads to major change.

We were first alerted to the power of Trojan mice when working with a major bank. An entirely new executive team was keen to restore 'humanity to banking' and to focus on service, not sales. Staff had previously been driven hard on sales and this had led to some poor customer behaviours: customers had become targets rather than people with needs.

At the outset of this process we were sitting in a staff rest room, above a branch. An agent came into the room and said, 'I have one credit card and three personal loans, who wants them?' Customers had been dehumanized to the level of their potential to buy specific products. It was symbolic of an organization which had in effect painted targets on its customers' backs. It led to a culture whereby staff saw customers only in terms of their immediate value and made no attempt to nurture a mutually beneficial relationship over the long term.

The new executive team believed that if customers were exposed to an outstanding experience with their needs at the centre, then sales would follow, customers would buy, without the need for coercion. For this to happen, they had to 'break' the sales-focused mentality. They unleashed a Trojan mouse – one simple step that led to a rapid change in culture.

They banned all sales management information, indeed all sales numbers. Previously branches had competed against each other and sought to perform well in league tables. Now they had no idea of what they or anyone else had sold. The explanation was simple: treat the customers well and they will buy, we don't have to sell. All staff instantly understood why. The decision left a vacuum which each branch sought to fill with more customer-oriented behaviours. They were encouraged to apply their own thinking to making life great for the customer. In that year the company rose 140 places in its country's customer experience league table, posted a 60 per cent increase in shareholder value and became a leading bank for customer experience.

We witnessed a further example when listening to the engineering director of an airline address his 4,500-strong engineering and maintenance team. The airline had habitually responded to a non-serious fault mid-flight, where there was no engineering base at the destination, by turning the aircraft round and returning it to base where it could be repaired more easily. The company had become aware that the practice was unnecessarily scaring passengers, who would naturally believe that the fault must be serious; they might experience hours of worry, as well as a massive interruption to their travel arrangements.

From the platform, the director decreed that this practice would cease 'from now'. He never wanted to have passengers worried again. In future the plane would continue to its destination and an engineering repair crew would fly out on a replacement aircraft. A simple change to operating procedures wrapped a powerful change dynamic around a clear message: the customer comes first.

Post-90 days consolidation

This is where the work of the previous 90 days is put into action. It is often difficult for an organization to digest massive change in one go. It takes time for the organization to catch up with the executive team. Executives will come back from this exercise inspired and committed to driving change, but their people haven't been on the same journey. The lag in understanding can cause a negative reaction and often resistance to a change programme.

Executives need to bring their people on the journey they have been on, enabling others to internalize what it means for them. This is a process of building shared understanding, something considerably more than communication. The danger of executives returning like Moses from the Mount, pronouncing 'This is what we are going to do and why', has long gone. 'Tell and sell' drives outright resistance, tacit compliance without commitment or, worst of all, silent sabotage. Involvement across the whole organization is crucial. The 90-day programme establishes the platform, the shaping mechanism that keeps the business moving in the right direction. It will guide behaviour and mindset. But now we need to engage the whole organization: two-way communication becomes the glue that holds it all together.

At IBM, Lou Gerstner didn't just bear hug customers, he also bear hugged employees. Daily he travelled to company sites and hosted gatherings to share information, debate ideas and address concerns. Holding 90-minute unscripted sessions he sometimes addressed as many as 20,000 employees at one time. He listened hard, reserved judgement and attempted to remain objective, while all the time guiding and refining the change activity (Hunsaker, 2010).

The Trojan mice need to be monitored and refined. That requires regular feedback from employees and ongoing inquiry into how the change programme is bedding in. We know that change activities can have unintended consequences: it is important that leaders keep in touch with what is happening across the organization. The job isn't done once the strategy is defined – that, to misquote Churchill, is not even the end of the beginning.

Ongoing governance

Managing the implementation of the CX strategy and maintaining connectivity and cohesion across activities are crucial. Effective governance is key to this. The outputs of the 90 days need to be carefully translated for implementation. This requires a governance structure.

Governance for customer experience is not just about oversight. These structures will also establish processes that force customer experience considerations into the mix when making day-to-day business decisions. In many companies, governance is centred on a customer committee comprising the 8–10 executives most involved with experience delivery. At the very least, this should include HR (CPO), IT (CIO), marketing and brand (CMO), operations (COO) and customer (CCO). Together, this team is responsible for the delivery of internal and external experiences across the enterprise. They are the custodians of the 90 days' outputs and the team that is keeping things on track.

This does not replace the leadership role, which is to model and inspire changed behaviour. Once, when we were sharing a stage with a leading CEO, he was asked by a member of the audience, 'Who in your organization is responsible for the customer?' He responded, 'You are looking at him.'

The governance committee's cross-functional composition lies at the heart of cohesion and integration. The scope for such a committee should encompass the following:

1 **Customer experience strategy:** This team is responsible for implementing the organization's purpose. It does this by the way in which it segments its customers; the creation and maintenance of the target experience; maintaining the link between the employee experience and the customer experience. These actions, if implemented, ensure a customer-centric culture.

2 **Prioritization and sequencing:** This entails managing the capability for dynamically rebalancing and resequencing activities to the betterment of the whole. Often, once launched, initiatives can develop a life of their own and the result is that some pull ahead of others, some fall by the wayside and the end point moves. Keeping a view of the connectivity across initiatives, the dependencies and the interactions is crucial.

3 **Roles and responsibilities:** In a dynamic environment, with teams forming and reforming, it is vital to manage and communicate who is responsible for what at any given time.

4 **Monitoring and controlling:** Provide a structure for customer experience measurement, including the metrics to track and monitor performance so that examples of excellence are identified and fed into the prioritization and sequencing activities.

5 **Ensuring adherence to design criteria:** Organizations need guidelines to ensure a consistent experience. These might be simple rules, the Six Pillars or design standards. Ensuring these guidelines are being adhered to is part of achieving long-term consistency.

6 **Decision-making frameworks:** Monitor the organization's decision-making processes to ensure the customer insight is actively present as decisions are made. Map customer and employee insight to both KPIs and customer satisfaction metrics.

7 **Managing the understanding:** Analyse employee feedback to ensure that the key messages are not just getting across but are being acted upon.

8 **Commercial outcomes:** Ultimately each initiative has a return on investment and a business case that justifies its position in the portfolio of change. Rarely do organizations circle back and check whether this has been achieved and, if not, why not. This is hard organizational learning, often sidestepped to avoid blame and shame. These fears should be laid to rest in a successful organization: if the reasons for failure are not confronted and dealt with, excellence cannot be anticipated.

CASE STUDY
CX governance

FedEx

FedEx has a customer experience steering committee that meets monthly, chaired by Fred Smith, the company's founder, chairman, president and CEO. The committee reviews customer experience improvement projects and in a process that's described as 'very disciplined' makes decisions about where to move forward (CX Insights, 2017).

Adobe

Adobe has a customer advocacy council that includes cross-functional senior leaders from all the critical areas that impact the customer experience, for example product development, customer support, finance, marketing and business process management. The council meets regularly to review the latest customer insights and metrics. This lets them size, scope and prioritize issues that they believe will make the biggest improvement to the customer experience and have the biggest commercial impact for the firm (CX Insights, 2017).

Adobe's customer advocacy council doesn't work on its own. It partners with another cross-functional group at Adobe, the business process improvement council, which sponsors customer experience improvement initiatives and allocates people to work on them.

Canada Post

Canada Post requires all funding requests from any department to answer 10 customer-focused questions in the business case. This ensures that all leaders think not just about how their projects will affect the bottom line but how they will impact the customer experience.

KEY TAKEAWAYS

1 Overcoming organizational inertia and innovation weariness can become major hurdles for change programmes.

2 Psychologically re-recruiting middle management is essential to success. Middle managers are the organization's shock absorber, the layer that converts strategy into execution – they need help and support.

3 Trojan mice, carefully selected changes that seem small but carry a powerful message, are invaluable in helping middle managers get the message across.

4 Change requires careful governance – a change committee/team aligned with the process and with a clear line of sight across the organization is essential for success.

Conclusion

We have been uniquely privileged to have spent so much of our lives working alongside great organizations. It has enabled us to define the Six Pillars of Experience as proven strategies for driving advocacy, loyalty and ultimately growth.

Our research has given us a deep insight as to what works and what doesn't. It has allowed us to see that there is a clear pathway to success.

Like many things in business life, change is a process: it can be defined and detailed as to what needs to happen when. Yes, we have seen many companies 'make it up as they go along'. There is a corporate machismo that seems to eschew the deep thinking about customers and the organizational response, almost as if the detailed work of IT or governance or project management is where the real work is done.

We argue throughout this book that the real work is understanding customers and meeting their needs, finding new needs and making their lives easier and more fulfilled. We have described in detail the Six Pillars, knowing from experience that they characterize what makes organizations great. For excellence in consistent customer experience they provide a framework upon which companies can hang their ideas and insights; they provide a direct link to best practice; and they ensure that at every interaction the things that are important to customers are given prominence.

But even the Six Pillars are not the whole story. The unique ways in which organizations think, the considerations they make and the capabilities they develop all combine to create excellence in diverse ways.

The many case studies we have used in this book show that excellence is not selective; it is not confined to a certain type of organization or sector – it is a way of being an organization that ensures excellence is built from the inside out and that relationships are then built from the outside in.

It is with some optimism that we have outlined the steps organizations should take to achieve success. We see signs of greatness in most organizations, but to paraphrase futurist and author of leading science fiction novels William Gibson, 'it just isn't connected yet'. We hope that sharing the Six Pillars and the 90-day pathway will lead you, your employees and your customers to new connections and new successes.

References

CX Insights (2017) Significance of governance in customer experience management. https://medium.com/@CXInsights/significance-of-governance-in-customer-experience-management-679c2b4bbe7a

Hunsaker, L. (2010) Customer centric listening. www.mycustomer.com/community/blogs/clearaction/customer-centric-listening

Hyken, S. (2018) Before you can be customer centric, you must be employee centric. www.vonage.co.uk/resources/articles/before-you-can-be-customer-centric-you-must-be-employee-centric/

INDEX

Page numbers in *italic* indicate figures or tables.

CPSIA information can be obtained
at www.ICGtesting.com
Printed in the USA
JSHW021342310721
17438JS00008B/294